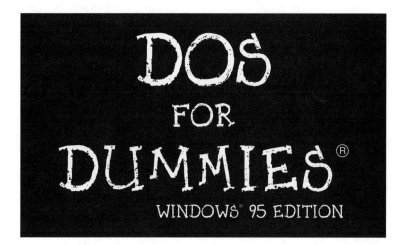

DOS
FOR
DUMMIES®
WINDOWS® 95 EDITION

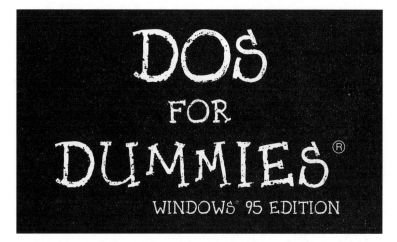

by Dan Gookin

IDG Books Worldwide, Inc.
An International Data Group Company

Foster City, CA ♦ Chicago, IL ♦ Indianapolis, IN ♦ Braintree, MA ♦ Southlake, TX

DOS For Dummies®, Windows® 95 Edition

Published by
IDG Books Worldwide, Inc.
An International Data Group Company
919 E. Hillsdale Blvd.
Suite 400
Foster City, CA 94404

Library of Congress Catalog Card No.: 95-82355

ISBN: 1-56884-646-0

Printed in the United States of America

10 9 8 7 6 5 4 3

1B/SR/QT/ZW/IN

Distributed in the United States by IDG Books Worldwide, Inc.

Distributed by Macmillan Canada for Canada; by Computer and Technical Books for the Caribbean Basin; by Contemporanea de Ediciones for Venezuela; by Distribuidora Cuspide for Argentina; by CITEC for Brazil; by Ediciones ZETA S.C.R. Ltda. for Peru; by Editorial Limusa SA for Mexico; by Transworld Publishers Limited in the United Kingdom and Europe; by Al-Maiman Publishers & Distributors for Saudi Arabia; by Simron Pty. Ltd. for South Africa; by IDG Communications (HK) Ltd. for Hong Kong; by Toppan Company Ltd. for Japan; by Addison Wesley Publishing Company for Korea; by Longman Singapore Publishers Ltd. for Singapore, Malaysia, Thailand, and Indonesia; by Unalis Corporation for Taiwan; by WS Computer Publishing Company, Inc. for the Philippines; by WoodsLane Pty. Ltd. for Australia; by WoodsLane Enterprises Ltd. for New Zealand.

For general information on IDG Books Worldwide's books in the U.S., please call our Consumer Customer Service department at 800-762-2974. For reseller information, including discounts and premium sales, please call our Reseller Customer Service department at 800-434-3422.

For information on where to purchase IDG Books Worldwide's books outside the U.S., contact IDG Books Worldwide at 415-655-3021 or fax 415-655-3295.

For information on translations, contact Marc Jeffrey Mikulich, Director, Foreign & Subsidiary Rights, at IDG Books Worldwide, 415-655-3018 or fax 415-655-3295.

For sales inquiries and special prices for bulk quantities, write to the address above or call IDG Books Worldwide at 415-655-3200.

For information on using IDG Books Worldwide's books in the classroom, or ordering examination copies, contact the Education Office at 800-434-2086 or fax 817-251-8174.

For authorization to photocopy items for corporate, personal, or educational use, please contact Copyright Clearance Center, 222 Rosewood Drive, Danvers, MA 01923, or fax 508-750-4470.

 is a trademark under exclusive license to IDG Books Worldwide, Inc., from International Data Group, Inc.

About the Author

Dan Gookin

Dan Gookin got started with computers back in the post slide-rule age of computing: 1982. His first intention was to buy a computer to replace his aged and constantly breaking typewriter. Working as slave labor in a restaurant, however, Gookin was unable to afford the full "word processor" setup and settled on a computer that had a monitor, keyboard, and little else. Soon his writing career was underway with several submissions to (and lots of rejections from) fiction magazines.

The big break came in 1984 when he began writing about computers. Applying his flair for fiction with a self-taught knowledge of computers, Gookin was able to demystify the subject and explain technology in a relaxed and understandable voice. He even dared to add humor, which eventually won him a column in a local computer magazine.

Eventually Gookin's talents came to roost as he became a ghost writer at a computer book publishing house. That was followed by an editing position at a cheesy San Diego computer magazine, at which time he also regularly participated on a radio talk show about computers. In addition, Gookin kept writing books about computers, some of which became minor bestsellers.

In 1990, Gookin came to IDG Books with a book proposal. From that initial meeting unfolded an idea for an outrageous book: a long overdue and original idea for the computer book for the rest of us. What became *DOS For Dummies* blossomed into an international bestseller with hundreds of thousands of copies in print and many foreign translations.

Today, Gookin still considers himself a writer and computer "guru" whose job it is to remind everyone that computers are not to be taken too seriously. His approach to computers is light and humorous yet very informative. He knows that the complex beasts are important and can help people become productive and successful. Yet Gookin mixes his knowledge of computers with a unique, dry sense of humor that keeps everyone informed — and awake. His favorite quote is, "Computers are a notoriously dull subject, but that doesn't mean I have to write about them that way."

Gookin's titles for IDG Books include *Real Life Windows; Buy That Computer!;* the best-selling *DOS For Dummies,* 1st and 2nd Editions; *PCs For Dummies; Word For Windows For Dummies;* and the *Illustrated Computer Dictionary For Dummies.* All told, he's written over 35 books on computers. Gookin holds a degree in Communications from the University of California, San Diego, and currently lives with his three wives and four boys in the as-yet-untamed state of Idaho.

ABOUT IDG BOOKS WORLDWIDE

Welcome to the world of IDG Books Worldwide.

IDG Books Worldwide, Inc., is a subsidiary of International Data Group, the world's largest publisher of computer-related information and the leading global provider of information services on information technology. IDG was founded more than 25 years ago and now employs more than 7,700 people worldwide. IDG publishes more than 250 computer publications in 67 countries (see listing below). More than 70 million people read one or more IDG publications each month.

Launched in 1990, IDG Books Worldwide is today the #1 publisher of best-selling computer books in the United States. We are proud to have received 8 awards from the Computer Press Association in recognition of editorial excellence and three from Computer Currents' First Annual Readers' Choice Awards, and our best-selling ...For Dummies® series has more than 19 million copies in print with translations in 28 languages. IDG Books Worldwide, through a joint venture with IDG's Hi-Tech Beijing, became the first U.S. publisher to publish a computer book in the People's Republic of China. In record time, IDG Books Worldwide has become the first choice for millions of readers around the world who want to learn how to better manage their businesses.

Our mission is simple: Every one of our books is designed to bring extra value and skill-building instructions to the reader. Our books are written by experts who understand and care about our readers. The knowledge base of our editorial staff comes from years of experience in publishing, education, and journalism — experience which we use to produce books for the '90s. In short, we care about books, so we attract the best people. We devote special attention to details such as audience, interior design, use of icons, and illustrations. And because we use an efficient process of authoring, editing, and desktop publishing our books electronically, we can spend more time ensuring superior content and spend less time on the technicalities of making books.

You can count on our commitment to deliver high-quality books at competitive prices on topics you want to read about. At IDG Books Worldwide, we continue in the IDG tradition of delivering quality for more than 25 years. You'll find no better book on a subject than one from IDG Books Worldwide.

John J. Kilcullen
President and CEO
IDG Books Worldwide, Inc.

IDG Books Worldwide, Inc., is a subsidiary of International Data Group, the world's largest publisher of computer-related information and the leading global provider of information services on information technology. International Data Group publishes over 250 computer publications in 67 countries. Seventy million people read one or more International Data Group publications each month. International Data Group's publications include: **ARGENTINA:** Computerworld Argentina, GamePro, Infoworld, PC World Argentina; **AUSTRALIA:** Australian Macworld, Client/Server Journal, Computer Living, Computerworld, Digital News, Network World, PC World, Publishing Essentials, Reseller; **AUSTRIA:** Computerwelt, PC TEST; **BELARUS:** PC World Belarus; **BELGIUM:** Data News; **BRAZIL:** Annuário de Informática, Computerworld Brazil, Connections, Super Game Power, Macworld, PC World Brazil, Publish Brazil, SUPERGAME; **BULGARIA:** Computerworld Bulgaria, Networkworld/Bulgaria, PC & MacWorld Bulgaria; **CANADA:** CIO Canada, ComputerWorld Canada, InfoCanada, Network World Canada, Reseller World; **CHILE:** Computerworld Chile, GamePro, PC World Chile; **COLUMBIA:** Computerworld Colombia, GamePro, PC World Colombia; **COSTA RICA:** PC World Costa Rica/Nicaragua; **THE CZECH AND SLOVAK REPUBLICS:** Computerworld Czechoslovakia, Elektronika Czechoslovakia, PC World Czechoslovakia; **DENMARK:** Communications World, Computerworld Danmark, Macworld Danmark, PC World Danmark, PC World Danmark Supplements, TECH World; **DOMINICAN REPUBLIC:** PC World Republica Dominicana; **ECUADOR:** PC World Ecuador, GamePro; **EGYPT:** Computerworld Middle East, PC World Middle East; **EL SALVADOR:** PC World Centro America; **FINLAND:** MikroPC, Tietoverkko, Tietoviikko; **FRANCE:** Distributique, Golden, Info PC, Le Guide du Monde Informatique, Le Monde Informatique, Reseaux & Telecoms; **GERMANY:** Computer Business, Computerwoche, Computerwoche Extra, Computerwoche Focus, Electronic Entertainment, GamePro, I/M Information Management, Macwelt, PC Welt; **GREECE:** GamePro, Macworld & Publish; **GUATEMALA:** PC World Centro America; **HONDURAS:** PC World Centro America; **HONG KONG:** Computerworld Hong Kong, PCWorld Hong Kong, Publish in Asia; **HUNGARY:** ABCD CD-ROM, Computerworld Szamitastechnika, PC & Mac World Hungary, PC-X Magazine; **INDIA:** Computerworld India, PC World India, Publish in Asia; **INDONESIA:** InfoKomputer PC World, Komputek Computerworld, Publish in Asia; **IRELAND:** ComputerScope, PC Live!; **ISRAEL:** PC World 32 BIT, People & Computers; **ITALY:** Computerworld Italia, Computerworld Italia Special Editions, Lotus Italia, Macworld Italia, Networking Italia, PC Shopping, PC World Italia, PC World/Walt Disney; **JAPAN:** Macworld Japan, Nikkei Personal Computing, SunWorld Japan, Windows World Japan; **KENYA:** East African Computer News; **KOREA:** Hi-Tech Information/Computerworld, Macworld Korea, PC World Korea, Super Game; **MACEDONIA:** PC World Macedonia; **MALAYSIA:** Computerworld Malaysia, PC World Malaysia, Publish in Asia; **MEXICO:** Computerworld Mexico, GamePro, Macworld, PC World Mexico; **MYANMAR:** PC World Myanmar; **NETHERLANDS:** Computable, Computer! Totaal, LAN Magazine, Macworld, Net Magazine; **NEW ZEALAND:** Computer Buyer, Computerworld New Zealand, MTB, Network World, PC World New Zealand; **NICARAGUA:** PC World Costa Rica/Nicaragua; **NIGERIA:** PC World Africa; **NORWAY:** Computerworld Norge, Computerworld Privat, CW Rapport Klient/Tjener, CW Rapport Nettverk & Telecom, CW Rapport Offentlig Sektor, IDG's KURSGUIDE, Macworld Norge, Multimedia World, PC World Ekspress, PC World Nettverk, PC World Norge, PC World's Produktguide, Windows Spesial; **PAKISTAN:** Computerworld Pakistan, PC World Pakistan; **PANAMA:** GamePro, PC World Panama; **PARAGUAY:** PC World Paraguay; **P. R. OF CHINA:** China Computerworld, China Infoworld, Computer & Communication, Electronic Product World, Electronics Today, Game Camp, PC World China, Popular Computer Week, Software World, Telecom Product World; **PERU:** Computerworld Peru, GamePro, PC World Profesional Peru, PC World Peru; **POLAND:** Computerworld Poland, Computerworld Special Report, Macworld, Networld, PC World Komputer; **PHILIPPINES:** Computerworld Philippines, PC Digest, Publish in Asia; **PORTUGAL:** Cerebro/PC World, Correio Informático/Computerworld, Mac•In/PC•In Portugal; **PUERTO RICO:** PC World Puerto Rico; **ROMANIA:** Computerworld Romania, PC World Romania, Telecom Romania; **RUSSIA:** Computerworld Rossiya, Network World Russia, PC World Russia; **SINGAPORE:** Computerworld Singapore, PC World Singapore, Publish in Asia; **SLOVENIA:** MONITOR; **SOUTH AFRICA:** Computing S.A., Network World S.A., Software World; **SPAIN:** Computerworld España, COMUNICACIONES WORLD, Dealer World, Macworld España, PC World España; **SWEDEN:** CAP&Design, Computer Sweden, Corporate Computing, MacWorld, Maxi Data, MikroDatorn, Nätverk & Kommunikation, PC/Aktiv, PC World, Windows World; **SWITZERLAND:** Computerworld Schweiz, Macworld Schweiz, PCtip; **TAIWAN:** Computerworld Taiwan, Macworld Taiwan, PC World Taiwan, Publish Taiwan, Windows World; **THAILAND:** Thai Computerworld, Publish in Asia; **TURKEY:** Computerworld Monitor, MACWORLD Turkiye, PC WORLD Turkiye; **UKRAINE:** Computerworld Kiev, Computers & Software Magazine, PC World Ukraine; **UNITED KINGDOM:** Acorn User, Amiga Action, Amiga Computing, Amiga, Appletalk, CD Powerplay, CD-ROM Now, Computing, Connexion, GamePro, Lotus Magazine, Macaction, Macworld, Open Computing, Parents and Computers, PC Home, PC Works, The WEB; **UNITED STATES:** Cable in the Classroom, CD Review, CIO Magazine, Computerworld, Computerworld Client/Server Journal, Digital Video Magazine, DOS World, Electronic, InfoWorld, I-Way, Macworld, Maximize, MULTIMEDIA WORLD, Network World, PC World, PUBLISH, SWATPro Magazine, Video Event, WebMaster; **URUGUAY:** PC World Uruguay; **VENEZUELA:** Computerworld Venezuela, GamePro, PC World Venezuela; and **VIETNAM:** PC World Vietnam   10/17/95

Acknowledgments

The progenitors: Michael McCarthy, Jeremy Judson, Bill Gladstone, Matt Wagner.

Chief motivator: John Kilcullen.

Fine souls at IDG: Milissa Koloski, Diane "woman of" Steele, Bill "Chico" Helling, Mary "the bee" Bednarek, Brandon Nordin, Polly Papsadore, Corbin Collins, Susan Diane Smith, Barbara Potter, Tricia Reynolds, Beth Jenkins, Drew Moore, Cindy Phipps, Tony Augsburger, Valery Bourke, and many others who contribute to this book's success in ways I'm totally clueless about.

Former IDG souls who also deserve credit: David Solomon, Janna Custer, Megg Bonar, Sandy Blackthorn, Tracy Barr.

Special pal of *DOS For Dummies*: David Israel, who consistently remarks in all the press interviews that I "wrote a great book." Thanks!

Without whom: Sandy and the boys: Jordan, Simon, Jonah, Jeremiah.

Special thanks: This book's legions of fans.

No particular thanks: Microsoft. Actually, I really should thank Microsoft. If it wasn't for their 15+ years of bumbling manuals and confusing operating systems, I'd be managing a restaurant in San Diego right now.

Publisher would like to give special thanks to: Patrick J. McGovern, without whom this book would not have been possible.

Credits

**Senior Vice President
and Publisher**
Milissa L. Koloski

Associate Publisher
Diane Graves Steele

Brand Manager
Judith A. Taylor

Editorial Managers
Kristin A. Cocks
Mary Corder

Product Development Manager
Mary Bednarek

Editorial Executive Assistant
Richard Graves

Editorial Assistants
Constance Carlisle
Chris Collins
Kevin Spencer

Production Director
Beth Jenkins

Production Assistant
Jacalyn L. Pennywell

**Supervisor of
Project Coordination**
Cindy L. Phipps

Supervisor of Page Layout
Kathie S. Schnorr

**Supervisor of Graphics and
Design**
Shelley Lea

Reprint/Blueline Coordination
Tony Augsburger
Patricia R. Reynolds
Todd Klemme
Theresa Sánchez-Baker

Media/Archive Coordination
Leslie Popplewell
Melissa Stauffer
Jason Marcuson

Project Editor
Bill Helling

Editor
Susan Diane Smith

Technical Reviewer
Jim McCarter

Project Coordinator
J. Tyler Connor

Project Coordination Assistant
Regina Snyder

Graphics Coordination
Gina Scott
Angela F. Hunckler
Carla Radzikinas

Production Page Layout
E. Shawn Aylsworth
Brett Black
Elizabeth Cárdenas-Nelson
Kerri Cornell
Maridee Ennis
Jill Lyttle
Jane Martin
Kate Snell
Michael Sullivan

Proofreaders
Joel K. Draper
Christine Meloy Beck
Gwenette Gaddis
Dwight Ramsey
Carl Saff
Robert Springer

Indexer
Sherry Massey

Cover Design
Kavish + Kavish

Contents at a Glance

Cartoons at a Glance

By Rich Tennant

Table of Contents

· ·

Introduction

● ●

*W*elcome to *DOS For Dummies, Windows 95 Edition,* a book that explores a subject many feared too insignificant to tread: The remnants of DOS that live in Windows. Believe it or not, DOS is still alive. And you may have some DOS software, stuff you're forced to use now under Windows — which means not only must you deal with DOS, but you must also contend with those things that supposedly make Windows fun and useful. So it's still a torture chamber, but at least it's painted in bright, cheery colors.

This book carries on the traditions of the original, multi-million copy bestseller, *DOS For Dummies*. It's still assumed that you're a smart person, but a DOS dummy. You have absolutely no intention of ever becoming a DOS wizard, nor do you really care that much for Windows. You don't want to learn anything. You don't want to be bored by technical details or background fodder. All you need to know is that single answer to one tiny question, and then you can close the book and be on with your life. This is the book you're looking for.

About This Book

This book isn't meant to be read from front to back. It's more like a reference. Each chapter is divided into sections, each of which has self-contained information about doing something in the DOS imprisoned within Windows. Typical sections include:

- ✔ Firing up a DOS prompt
- ✔ Using long filenames with your DOS commands
- ✔ Adding your program to the Windows Start thing
- ✔ Deleting a group of files
- ✔ "I want to make my DOS program run in the text screen when it starts"
- ✔ Finding a lost file
- ✔ "Where am I?"

You don't have to remember anything in this book. Nothing is worth memorizing. You'll never "learn" anything here. The information here is what you need to know to get by, and nothing more. And if any new terms or technical descriptions are offered, you'll be alerted and told to ignore them.

How to Use This Book

This book works like a reference: You start by looking up either in the table of contents or the index the topic that concerns you. That step will refer you to a specific section in the book. In that section, you'll read about doing whatever it is you want to do. Some special terms may be defined, but usually you'll be directed elsewhere if you want to learn about the terms.

If you're supposed to type something in, it will appear in the text as follows:

```
C> TYPE IN THIS STUFF
```

Always press Enter after you're told to type something in. In case you're baffled, a description of what you're typing usually follows (with explanations of the more difficult stuff).

Windows menu commands are shown like this:

```
Choose File⇨Exit
```

This means to select the File menu and choose the Exit command from the menu. You can use your computer's mouse, or you can press the underlined letter in the command: Alt+F to activate the menu, and then X.

Key combinations you may have to type in are shown like this:

Alt+F

This means to press and hold the Alt key, type an F, and then release the Alt key. It works just like pressing Shift+M on the keyboard produces the upper case M letter.

If you need more information, you'll be directed to that chapter and section. And if anything goes wrong, you'll be told what to do and how to remedy the situation.

At no time does this book direct you back to the Windows manual — primarily because this manual doesn't exist! Instead, I recommend you pick up a good book on Windows. And if you need more basic DOS knowledge, refer to the original *DOS For Dummies*, or its companion, *More DOS For Dummies*.

What You're Not to Read

Several sections offer extra information and background explanations. (I just couldn't resist — after writing 35-odd books on using computers, I can't compel myself *not* to do this.) Those sections are clearly marked and you can quickly skip over them, as you please. Reading them will only increase your knowledge of DOS — and that's definitely not what this book is all about.

Foolish Assumptions

Here are some assumptions this book makes: You have a PC and you use Windows 95 as its operating system. You should be familiar with your computer's mouse and know how to *point*, *click*, *double-click*, *select,* and *drag*. Again, your favorite book on Windows 95 should detail these actions for you if you need help.

Furthermore, I'm going to assume that someone else set up your computer and may have even given you a few brief lessons. It's nice to have someone close by (or on the phone) who can help. But you know how unbalanced they can become when you ask too many questions (and don't have enough M&Ms or Doritos handy).

How This Book Is Organized

This book has six major parts, each of which is divided into two or more chapters. Inside each chapter are individual sections that pertain, for the most part, to the chapter subject. Aside from that level of organization, the book is really modular. You can start reading at any section. However, thanks to tradition, I've outlined the entire book below:

Part I: The Absolute Basics

This part of the book contains general background information on starting Windows and getting into DOS. It's the primary stuff, the things you'll be doing most of the time or have questions about.

Part II: DOS Life in the Windows 95 Gulag

Since Windows is now in charge, this part of the book goes into a few of those Windows things that control DOS's life. Chapters discuss how DOS fits into a window and how DOS has fits in a window. Also covered is copying information between DOS windows, along with a brief lecture on editing DOS text files.

Part III: The Non-Nerd's Guide to Disks and Files

This part of the book contains information about using disk and file commands, as well as general information on working with disks and files.

Part IV: Yikes! (or Help Me Out of This One!)

Good news: Computers don't blow up in your face like they do on 1960s TV shows. Bad news: They still do horrible things that will leave your mouth agape and your soul yearning. The chapters here will soothe your savage nerves.

Part V: The Part of Tens

This part of the book contains several chapters that are lists of ten-somethings: Ten common beginner mistakes; ten things you should avoid; ten things to throw at the computer. You get the idea.

Part VI: Windows 95 DOS Command Reference for Real People

DOS is nothing more than a mean computer program, plus about 50 or so unusual commands and cryptic utterances. They're all listed here in various categories, with descriptions directly relating to how useful or useless the command is.

Icons Used in This Book

 This alerts you to nerdy technical discussions you may want to skip (or read — for that nerd in all of us).

 Any shortcuts or new insights on a topic are marked with this icon.

 A friendly reminder to do something.

 A friendly reminder *not* to do something.

 Some Windows 95 specific thing you may or may not care to know about.

Where to Go from Here

Now you're ready to use this book. Look over the table of contents and find something that interests you. Just about everything you can do with DOS is listed here. But primarily you'll be spending your time in what Chairman Mao called "the great struggle with the computer." Do so. Toil, toil, toil. But when you hit a speed bump, look it up here. You'll have the answer and be back to work in a jiffy. Or half a jiffy if you're a quick reader.

Good luck!

Part I
The Absolute Basics

The 5th Wave   By Rich Tennant

"ALRIGHT, STEADY EVERYONE. MARGO, GO OVER TO TOM'S PC
AND PRESS 'ESCAPE',...VERY CAREFULLY."

In this part...

Don't you hate those books that have long-winded, stuffy introductions? The wannabe aristocratic author goes on and on about his or her qualifications, rattles off the names of the 400 or so people who helped with this or that, and mentions his or her relatives and loved ones, the entire computer industry, the lone soul who really wrote the book, and so on. These books are usually long on hot air, short on facts, and big on margins. But all you want to do is get to work (and could care less about the author's loftiness).

Well, this book is different.

Chapter 1

Getting Into DOS

• •

• •

O wherefore art thou, DOS? Shoved off into a corner, DOS takes a back seat to the flashier Windows. Microsoft didn't light up the Empire State Building when they announced MS-DOS 6.22, did they? No way! DOS is a lovable embarrassment — like Uncle Cedric who rinses his teeth in the water glass after dinner, even in the finer dining establishments.

Well, the truth is that DOS lives. DOS still has tons of software available for it and, I'll be the first to admit, there's lots of things you can do in DOS that are just plain faster than doing them in Windows (see Chapter 20 for the full list).

Everything Starts with Windows (Now)

Since Windows is in charge, you'll notice some things don't start out the way they used to. And if you're new to DOS, you'll notice that it's given a rather minor walk-on, non-singing role in this new graphical opera. Windows takes center stage and sings all the big numbers. (It even plays the piano in one.)

Turn the darn thing on

If your computer isn't already up and running, you'll need to turn it on. This is done by flipping it's Big Red Switch, which often is neither big nor red. Even so, somewhere on your computer, right on the front or around on the side, will be a power switch. You flip that switch or push that button to turn on your computer. There's nothing more to it.

✔ Nerds often refer to "turning on a computer" as *powering up*. Sheesh.

✔ Turn on the monitor before you turn on your computer (though there's really nothing sacred about the order here). I'm mentioning this because the monitor has its own power switch and it must be turned on before you can see anything on the screen. I mean, like, *duh!*

✔ If you have any other *peripheral* devices — printers, modems, external beige or tan boxes with cables and blinking lights — you can turn them on as well.

✔ I usually don't turn on any peripherals unless I plan on using them. So, for the most part, the printer sleeps until I need it. When I go to print something, though, I turn it on — often times *before* I need to print, occasionally after.

Look! Up on the screen!

Is it a burp? Is it a pain? No! It's . . . Windows 95! Welcome to the gulag.

Even though you see Windows 95, your PC may still flash some text your way, some copyright notices and whatnot . . . . then comes the final blast from the PC's all-text past:

```
Starting Windows 95...
```

You're doomed! DOS is gone, hello Windows.

Starting the computer with the Big Red Switch is the mechanical part. What you're starting is the computer hardware, which is really nothing but a lot of heavy, cold, and calculating electronic junk that the cat likes to sleep on. Eventually, your computer's software actually brings the computer to life, allowing it to do something. With Windows 95 you see the "Windows in the clouds" scene, which is only meant to entertain you while Windows seemingly takes several weeks to get out of bed.

Eventually, Windows splashes its way onto the screen (see Figure 1-1). Hooray for Microsoft! They finally killed off DOS. But not really, since DOS is merely hidden off, tucked away like a secret all-day sucker your kid stashed under the couch; wipe off the lint and, heck, it's still good.

Figure 1-1:
Now, wait a minute. This isn't DOS!

✔ Sometimes you may see some text when the computer starts, some startup stuff and information that scrolls by like the start of a *Star Wars* movie but without any consequential background information or plot.

✔ There's a reluctant pause after the Starting Windows 95 message as the computer thinks, "Not this again." This message and Windows itself does not appear if you're using an older version of DOS.

✔ The nuances of computer hardware and software, as well as more detailed information on turning your computer on and off, are covered in the delightful tome *PCs For Dummies*, by myself, from IDG Books Worldwide.

Roadblocks on the highway to Windows nirvana

If you're using Windows on a network, it will want you to "log in" before you start getting any work done. This is because no computer should start right off and allow you to be productive — no way! You must piddle around first. Go ahead and type in your log name (like the timber people do) and a password. Keep in mind that you can also just press the Esc key to forgo the ordeal and get on with your work.

Another stumbling block may be the cheeky Welcome to Windows dialog box. Saints begorra! It's Tip O'Day, that jolly leprechaun ready to impart his congenial wit and warmth. Have another pint of Guinness, m' lad. Click the Close button to get that dialog box outta here. You can also click the mouse in the box by Show this Welcome Screen next time you start Windows to never be bothered by Tip again.

Firing up a DOS Prompt

DOS is now called the MS-DOS Prompt "program." No respect. To find it, follow these steps in Windows 95:

1. Click the Start button using your mouse.

The Start button can usually be found in the lower left corner of the screen, on the left end of the Taskbar. Or you can be a man and press the Ctrl+Esc key combination. Up pops the menu.

2. Click on the <u>P</u>rograms menu item.

Programs has a triangle by its name, meaning that another submenu lurks just hither to the right.

If you want to be a man again, just press the P key instead of using your mouse. Heck, *throw that mouse away!*

The Programs menu appears, which will look something like Figure 1-2. Additional sub-menus appear at the top of the menu. Programs appear at the bottom, in alphabetical order (more or less).

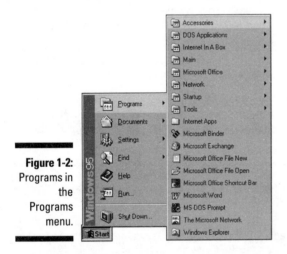

Figure 1-2:
Programs in
the
Programs
menu.

3. Locate the MS-DOS Prompt **item.**

The list of programs is alphabetical, so MS-DOS appears in the M's section, with the little MS-DOS icon floating next to it. There. You've found DOS.

4. Click on the MS-DOS Prompt **item.**

You can point the mouse and click its left button (the normal button you always press), or if you enjoy pressing the ↓ arrow key, you can wood-pecker it until the MS-DOS Prompt item appears highlighted, then press the Enter key.

5. DOS splashes all over the screen, sorta.

Soon you'll see a DOS prompt and something that looks like the screen _used to_ look before Windows 95, but everything's in a window and it's all yucky and gross-looking. Congratulations, it's a mere DOS "box" living uncomfortably inside Windows. Figure 1-3 shows how uncomfortable DOS looks.

```
Microsoft(R) Windows 95
     (C)Copyright Microsoft Corp 1981-1995.

C:\WINDOWS>
```

Figure 1-3:
This is no way to run a famous operating system.

You can do anything in the DOS prompt window that you used to do at the DOS prompt itself (save for turning the computer off). The following bullets tell you some interesting things that may or may not cheer you up:

- ✔ What can you _do_ at the DOS prompt? Anything you did before, plus some things you _still_ can't do in Windows. The remainder of this part of the book goes into the basic DOS details.

- ✔ DOS prompt keyboard shortcut: Ctrl+Esc, P, M, M, . . . (keep pressing the M key until MS-DOS Prompt is highlighted), Enter.

- ✔ By the way, a "real man" computer user can be either a male or female of the species. This fact was relayed to me by Hillary Clinton after the recent Beijing Women's Rights conference.

- ✔ The DOS window has its own button bar, as well as an assortment of typically Windows gadgets and gizmos. Chapter 4 tells you all about it.

- ✔ Also see Chapter 4 for information on changing the font that Windows uses to display DOS text. Yeah, it can look pretty ugly, but some decent fonts and sizes are available.

- ✔ Like everything else in Windows, DOS programs have their own _properties_ — special settings used to control how the program behaves. This subject is covered in Chapter 7.

- ✔ If you miss your CONFIG.SYS and AUTOEXEC.BAT files, also look up Chapter 7, which discusses where they went and how to get back to them.

- ✔ When you're done with DOS you need to *quit* it, as you would quit any other program. This rule applies to DOS programs as well. See the section "Quitting Your DOS Prompt," later in this chapter, for the finely detailed instructions.

And when you long for those old, full text screen days . . .

You don't have to see DOS graphically as a window on the screen. To look at the old, familiar text screen, press the Alt+Enter key combination: Press and hold the Alt key then tap the Enter key. Thwoop! The graphical DOS window goes full screen text. Press Alt+Enter again to switch back.

This trick works with any DOS program in Windows.

If you forget how to switch back, just type WIN at the DOS prompt. That displays a list of three tips for using DOS in Windows. (Of course, if you forget to type WIN, you're hopeless.)

Don't forget that you've switched to full screen mode and haven't instead traveled back in time to a pre-Windows 95 era. Get in the habit of typing the EXIT command when you're done using DOS, as described in the section "Quitting Your DOS Prompt," later in this chapter.

- ✔ This trick may not work with some DOS graphics programs and games, which like to run full-screen. In those cases, you can switch to graphical window mode, but Windows won't run the program since the results would be slower than you'd expect. Just press Alt+Enter to switch back to full screen whenever that happens.

Oops! Firing up yet another DOS prompt

You're not limited to running just one DOS program at a time. If you want a second DOS prompt (for example, if you're from Venus and have three arms and six eyeballs), you just fire up another DOS prompt. Here are the instructions as written in a typically cryptic Windows manual:

From the Start menu choose Programs⇨MS-DOS Prompt and, lo, you have another DOS prompt window on the screen.

How many times can you do this? Dozens! Litter the screen with DOS prompt windows! Eventually, Windows will tell you its going crazy (i.e., it's out of memory). But you can really go gonzo if you like.

Now *why* you would want more than one DOS window is a puzzle I'll leave for you to finish. And if you do try this, I'd read a little bit of Chapter 10 on multitasking so you can easily switch between your many DOS windows.

Here's a nerdy way to start another DOS window (and don't tell anyone you read it in *this* book):

```
C> START COMMAND
```

Type the word START, a space, then COMMAND. Press the Enter key. Another DOS window magically appears on the screen. Presto, neat-o.

Finding your favorite DOS programs

Whether or not your DOS programs appear on Windows Start thing menu depends on how well you set up Windows before you upgraded. If you were a DOS user suffering under Windows and kept all your DOS programs in their own little "group," then they'll be on their own little menu, as shown in Figure 1-4.

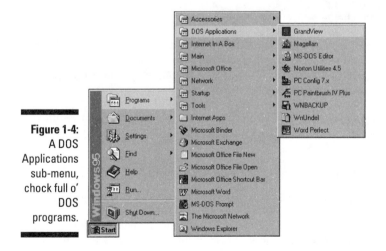

Figure 1-4:
A DOS
Applications
sub-menu,
chock full o'
DOS
programs.

✔ If you have a DOS Applications-type of menu (Figure 1-4), you can start your DOS programs from there just as you started the MS-DOS Prompt program.

✔ If you don't have a DOS Applications-type of menu, don't worry about it. Just start a DOS window as described in the previous section and run your DOS programs as you used to in your former life. For example, to run the good-old WordPerfect (version 5.1), you fire up a DOS window and type WP at the prompt:

```
C> WP
```

Press the Enter key and WordPerfect comes up in the DOS window, maybe a little bit anxious, but still there for you to work with.

✔ OK, if it bothers you, Chapter 5 tells you how to create a DOS Applications-type of sub-menu on Windows' Start thing.

✔ There's an outside chance Windows 95 found some of your DOS programs and set them up in a DOS Programs menu for you when it was installed. (Then again, there's a chance you may win the *Power Ball* someday, but don't count on it.) If not, you can always create your own group, though this is a task I'd advise a Windows guru or someone else you can easily bribe to do for you.

Quitting Your DOS Prompt

Before Windows 95, you couldn't quit DOS. It was impossible! But since DOS now sits in the first railroad car (where all the smoke gets in — oh, and there are mice), you have a choice. Doing away with mighty DOS is now on a par with quitting the lame Calculator program in Windows.

The first, best way to quit a DOS prompt window is to type the EXIT command at the DOS prompt:

```
C> EXIT
```

Type **EXIT** and press the Enter key. The DOS window goes away.

The second way, like the lame Calculator program, is to click the mouse on the X button in the DOS prompt window's upper right corner (see Figure 1-3). Like any other Windows program this one closes the DOS "window."

The X button may not always work. In fact, it *only* works if you see a DOS prompt on the screen. If you're running a DOS program, then Windows won't let you quit that way. A nasty error message is displayed if you even attempt to quit (see Figure 1-5).

Figure 1-5:
This means
"Don't use
the X button
to close this
window."

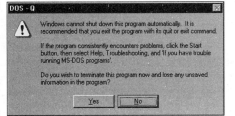

Click the No button in the warning box to make it go away. Then quit your DOS program properly and, if you need to, type the EXIT command at the next DOS prompt to close the DOS window.

- ✔ If you run a DOS program straight from the Start thing's menu, you need to quit that program to close the window; the X button never works in that case.

- ✔ You'll need to type the EXIT command or click the X close button for each and every DOS window you have open on the screen. There are, however, advantages to running several programs at once. Chapter 6 discusses this somewhat.

- ✔ Some DOS programs stop when they're done but do not close their window on the screen. For them, you need to manually close the window by clicking on the X button. Chapter 7 tells you how to train such a DOS program into automatically closing when it's done.

- ✔ If you desperately need to quit a DOS program window and none of these tricks work, skip up to Chapter 14.

Starting the Computer in DOS Mode

It's entirely possible to forego that Windows 95 nonsense and fire up your PC in DOS, the way God intended. What you get isn't exactly "DOS 7"; though it secretly is DOS 7, Microsoft calls it Windows 95 version 4.00. At least, that's what the screen says. Anyway, enough beating around the graphical bush.

But first, here are two by-the-ways:

- ✓ If you start your computer in DOS mode, you obviously don't need to use the Windows 95 Shutdown command to turn off your computer. Instead, know that it's "safe" to turn off your PC any time you see a DOS prompt on the screen. Never turn off the computer to quit a program; always quit the program first, and then go to the DOS prompt and turn off the computer there.

- ✓ This book assumes you're using DOS under Windows 95 and not starting your computer in the DOS mode. Even so, all the DOS commands described here work the same either way.

The polite way you're supposed to do it

When you first turn on your computer (or after a reset), you see the following message displayed on the screen:

```
Starting Windows 95...
```

At that point in time, press the F8 key on your keyboard. This halts Windows 95 from loading and presents you with a screen full-o-options, as shown in Figure 1-6.

```
Microsoft Windows 95 Startup Menu
========================================

1. Normal
2. Logged (\BOOTLOG.TXT)
3. Safe mode
4. Safe mode with network support
5. Step-by-step confirmation
6. Command prompt only
7. Safe mode command prompt only

Enter a choice: 1




F5=Safe mode   Shift+F5=Command prompt   Shift+F8=Step-by-Step confirmation [N]
```

Figure 1-6:
The actual
Windows 95
startup
menu.

From the menu, choose option 6, `Command prompt only`. Press the 6 key, then the Enter key.

Windows 95 continues to start up and you may even see the graphical "Here's Windows 95!" screen displayed. Whatever. Eventually, you'll see a familiar, happy DOS prompt:

```
C>
```

✔ Using a DOS prompt to control your computer is covered in the next two chapters, so keep reading if you're confused and soon you won't be.

✔ Other items may appear in the startup menu. If there's an item that allows you to start a "previous" version of DOS, select it to start your computer the way you did before you upgraded to Windows 95. (It's usually option 8.)

✔ Not that you'd really care or anything, but if you want to run Windows 95, just type the WIN command at a DOS prompt:

```
C> WIN
```

Type **WIN** and press the Enter key. DOS then starts Windows, just as it should.

✔ See the message that says Shift+F5=Command prompt at the bottom of the Startup menu (Figure 1-6)? Ignore! Ignore! Ignore! It doesn't do what you think it does.

The way to do it "out the door"

If you forget to press the F8 key when Windows 95 first starts, don't sweat it. You can always quit Windows and start the DOS prompt — just like Windows used to quit to DOS in the olden days. This is cinchy:

1. **Choose the Sh̲ut Down command from Windows Start menu.**

   From the keyboard you can press Ctrl+Esc, U.

   The Shut Down Windows dialog box appears, as shown in Figure 1-7.

2. **Choose the third item in the shutdown dialog box:** Restart the computer in MS-DOS mode?

   Click the mouse in the hole by that item or press Alt+M.

3. **Click Y̲es.**

   That tells Windows 95 to go away, and soon the computer lovingly presents you with a DOS prompt, where you can get all your *real* work done.

Figure 1-7:
Here is how you can restart the PC in DOS mode.

Shut Down Windows ☒

Are you sure you want to:

○ S̲hut down the computer?
○ R̲estart the computer?
● Restart the computer in M̲S-DOS mode?
○ C̲lose all programs and log on as a different user?

[Y̲es]   [N̲o]   [H̲elp]

The sneaky way you can do it all the time

This is a somewhat nerdy thing for me to reveal, and I have two reasons for that: First, I just learned how to use a soldering iron, which is frightening in and of itself. Second, there may, someday, actually be an MS-DOS version 7 from Microsoft, which makes this somewhat nerdy thing to do unnecessary. So, as you can tell, you may actually be wasting serious time obeying these steps that make your computer boot into Windows 95's DOS mode all the time instead of the normal graphical mode:

1. **Fire up a DOS prompt.**

   See the section "Firing up a DOS prompt" earlier in this chapter for the details.

2. **Type in the following DOS command:**

   ```
   C> attrib -r -h -s c:\msdos.sys
   ```

   At the DOS prompt, type attrib, a space, then minus R, a space, minus H, a space, minus S, a space, then the filename C, colon, backslash, msdos, period, sys. Review your typing and press the Enter key, forcing DOS to obey you.

   If you make a mistake and see some dreadful error message, re-type the command again. Two common goofs: Forgetting some spaces and using a forward slash instead of the required backslash in the filename.

3. **Now type in this DOS command:**

   ```
   C> echo bootgui=0 >> c:\msdos.sys
   ```

   Type echo, a space, then bootgui, an equal sign and a zero — not a capital letter O. Then type a space, two greater-than signs, a space and the filename (again) C, colon, backslash, msdos, period, sys. Review your work and press the Enter key.

4. **And finally type in this DOS command:**

   ```
   C> attrib +r +h +S c:\msdos.sys
   ```

   This is just like the command in step 2, though you're putting in plus signs instead of minus signs. Review the detailed text-like instructions in step 2 for the typing intricacies. Press the Enter key when you're sure you got it right.

5. **Okay, you're done.**

   Quit the DOS prompt by typing in the EXIT command:

   ```
   C> EXIT
   ```

   Type the word **EXIT** and then press the Enter key. DOS withers away.

You can keep on working if you like, or just shutdown the computer as described in your favorite Windows book. Then, next time you turn your PC on, you'll see it fire up into MS-DOS prompt mode without you pressing any key or straining your elbows.

The ultra-nerdy explanation of what's going on (very optional reading)

The MSDOS.SYS file is a text file that contains various settings for Windows 95 to start. It's boring, though you can "read" it with the following DOS command:

```
type c:\msdos.sys
```

(Big deal.) What you need to do is stick a BootGUI=0 command in there at the end. This overrides any early BootGUI=1 commands, which is what tells Windows 95 to start in graphical mode. When BootGUI=0 is present (as the last thing), Windows gives up the ghost, and you have DOS on the screen when you start the computer. Ta-da!

The ATTRIB command is necessary to strip the *read-only, hidden,* and *system* file attributes from the MSDOS.SYS file. That way you can edit the file. (Without it you get all sorts of errors.) The ECHO command with the >> characters appends the text BootGUI=0 to the end of the file. (This is covered in my book, *MORE DOS For Dummies,* available from IDG Books Worldwide.)

The final ATTRIB command is necessary to re-apply the read-only, hidden, and system attributes to the MSDOS.SYS file. Without them, your computer will nag and nag when you try to reset.

Chapter 2

The PC Hokey-Pokey (or That's What It's All About)

*T*his chapter contains a zippy summary of some basic computer stuff and everyday things you can do on your beloved PC using the DOS prompt enslaved in Windows 95. These items don't collectively fit into any specific category. These are things you may be doing a lot or topics you have questions about. As with the rest of the book, everything here is cross-referenced.

Refer to the section "Firing up a DOS Prompt" in Chapter 1 for more information on running a DOS prompt window in Windows 95.

Running a Program

You get work done on a computer by running a program. If you're lucky, somebody's set up your computer so it automatically runs the program you need. Turn on the PC and *zap!*, there's your program. For example, quite a few Windows 95 computers are set up to automatically run the Microsoft Office collection of programs.

The only time you've got a problem is when something goes wrong and the program *crashes* or it doesn't turn on like it's supposed to. (Or while you were at lunch, Petey from the mailroom came in and played games, leaving you with a blank screen to puzzle over.)

If you're on your own and nothing seems to happen automatically, you need to start a program yourself. There are a number of ways to do this, depending on how your PC is set up.

Starting a DOS program from the Start thing menu

DOS programs live on the Start thing's menu just like any other program in Windows. To start the program, click on the Start button, then click on the word Programs to display that menu. Then look for your program on the Programs menu or in various sub-menus.

For example, the MS-DOS Prompt program — the DOS "window" — can be found on the main Programs menu. You may also find WordPerfect or Lotus 1-2-3 there as well. If so, click on the program name with the mouse. Figure 2-1 shows WordPerfect living at the bottom of the Programs sub-menu.

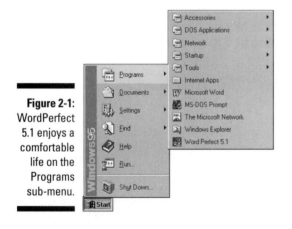

Figure 2-1:
WordPerfect
5.1 enjoys a
comfortable
life on the
Programs
sub-menu.

If your program can't be found in the Programs menu, look in the various sub-menus, those menus with little triangles by them. On my system, all the DOS programs are kept in the DOS Applications sub-menu, though a few other programs are lurking elsewhere. (I put the game DOOM in with Windows' games, which are in the Accessories⇨Games sub-sub-sub-menu.

- ✔ Your DOS programs might be located in the Start thing's menu, along with various Windows programs.

- ✔ To start your program, click on the Start button, then click on the Programs menu and start a-huntin'.

- ✔ Keyboard shortcut department: Press Ctrl+Esc to pop-up the Start thing, then press P to see the Programs menu. You can use the arrow keys to move around through the various menus; press the Enter key to start your program. Press the Esc key to "back up" a menu.

- ✔ Oh well, if your program isn't on the menu, you can always start it in a DOS prompt window, as described in the next section.

Starting a DOS program in a DOS prompt window

If you opt to start your program the way things were done in the good old days, you need to know one very important thing: the program's name. Then you type that name at the command prompt.

For example, WordPerfect is named WP. To *run* WordPerfect in your DOS prompt window, type **WP** at the *DOS prompt* and then press the Enter key:

```
C> WP
```

Making any program start automatically when Windows starts (if you really want to know)

It's nice to have Windows automatically start your favorite programs every time it starts itself. It's that type of convenience that the computer makers promise in the ads. Alas, it's up to you to tell Windows which programs to automatically start first, though they can be either Windows or DOS programs.

The trick is to put the programs into the special Startup sub-menu located off the Start thing's Programs menu. This is a technically bothersome affair, which is why I recommend you have a Windows guru do it for you. Just tell them which programs to stick in the Startup sub-menu and they'll do the rest. Hopefully. If not, bribe them with some pretzels and Jolt cola.

Table 2-1 lists the names of several popular DOS programs and what you type at the DOS prompt to run them. Note that you don't need to type what's listed in the parentheses; those lines are extra instructions or information about the program.

✔ What? No DOS prompt? See Chapter 1.

✔ If your favorite DOS program isn't on the list in Table 2-1, you either have to read the manual to find out what name you type or ask someone who knows. When you find out what name you type, add it to the list in Table 2-1 (that's what the blank lines are for).

✔ If your computer has been set up to run some sort of menu system, try typing **MENU** at the DOS prompt to run it.

✔ Several of the programs in Table 2-1 enable you to type additional information after the program's name: WordPerfect enables you to type the name of the document you're editing; dBASE can be followed by the name of a database program to run. If you do this, remember to place a space between the program's name and any other information that follows.

✔ Yes, Quattro Pro and Quicken both have the same name, Q.

✔ Other terms for *running* a program include *loading* a program, *launching* a program, and *starting* a program.

Table 2-1	Popular DOS & Windows program names
Program	**Name to Type/Instructions**
Backup	BACKUP (may have to change directories first)
Calculator	CALC
Clock	CLOCK
Control Panel	CONTROL
dBASE	DBASE
Excel	EXCEL (may have to change directories first)
Explorer	EXPLORER
Freecell	FREECELL
GrandView	GV
Harvard Graphics	HG
LapLink	LL
Lotus 1-2-3	123
Magellan	MG

Program	Name to Type/Instructions
Mail	MSMAIL
Media player	MPLAYER
MultiMate	WP
Notepad	NOTEPAD
Paint	MSPAINT (may have to change directories first)
PC Tools	PCSHELL
ProComm Plus	PCPLUS
Prodigy	PRODIGY
Q&A	QA
Quattro Pro	Q
Quicken	Q
SideKick	SK
Solitaire	SOL
Terminal	TERMINAL
Ventura Publisher	VP
Windows	WIN
Word	WORD (The non-Windows Word — Word for MS-DOS)
Word for Windows	WINWORD (may have to change directories first)
WordPad	WORDPAD (may have to change directories first; can type in WRITE if you upgraded from an older version of Windows)
WordPerfect	WP
WordStar	WS

Commanding Windows programs from the DOS prompt

Sure, DOS may be just another Windows "program" now, but that doesn't mean you can bend Windows' arm behind its back and force it to do things for you.

To run any Windows program from the DOS prompt, just type its name. For example, the silly Calculator program is named CALC. To run it, type that command at the DOS prompt and press the Enter key:

```
C> CALC
```

The Calculator program will start, its window eclipsing the DOS prompt window.

- ✔ Unlike running a DOS program, when you run a Windows program the DOS prompt doesn't go away; it's still there, ready for you to type in another command if you like.

- ✔ Refer to Chapter 6 for information on switching between any Windows program you start and your DOS prompt window. Yes, you can run *both* at the same time. Amazing stuff.

- ✔ See Table 2-1 for the names of a few popular Windows programs.

- ✔ Also see the section on the START command nestled in a sidebar below.

- ✔ You may need to *change directories* before you can run some Windows programs, such as WordPad or Paint. See the section titled "Changing Directories (or Folders)" later in this chapter for some brief info.

TECHNICAL STUFF

Trivial asides on the START command you don't need to read

One of the new DOS-in-Windows commands I find kind of funny is the START command. It seems redundant since DOS starts anything you type at the prompt anyway. But the beauty of the START command is that it lets you run Windows programs (or other DOS programs) in four special modes. To wit:

```
C> START /M CALC
```

The preceding command starts the Windows calculator program *minimized* — as a button on the taskbar, not a window. To start a program *maximized* to fill the entire screen, use the following version of the START command:

```
C> START /MAX WORDPAD
```

The command starts the WordPad word processor full-screen.

Two other switches are available with the START command: /W tells Windows to run the other program and then return to the DOS window when the other program is done. And /R just runs the program normally (*restored*), which means you never need to use it at all.

Please check out the section in Chapter 5, "About the Darn Command Formats," for more information on a DOS command's /-slash options. Also see Chapter 23 for a full list of the six new commands that come with the DOS that lives under Windows 95's harsh reign.

Background information worth skipping

Programs are also known as applications, though the term *application* is more general: WordPerfect is a word processing application. The program is WordPerfect, and its file is named WP.EXE. You type the name of the file at the DOS prompt. DOS then loads that program into memory and executes the instructions.

Under DOS, all program files are named with either a .COM, .EXE, or a .BAT ending (called a filename extension). Don't bother typing in that part of the name at the DOS prompt — and you don't have to type the period that sepa-rates .COM, .EXE, or .BAT from the file's name. Refer to the discussion under "Significant Filenames" in Chapter 12 for more information (worth skipping).

The DIR Command

The most popular DOS command is DIR, which displays on the screen a list of files on disk. This is how you can find which programs and data files are located on a disk. DIR is especially helpful if you're missing something; it will help you locate that document or spreadsheet you were recently working on.

To see a list of files, type **DIR** at the DOS prompt and press Enter:

```
C> DIR
```

If the list is too long, you can type the following DIR command:

```
C> DIR /P
```

The /P makes the listing pause after each screenful of files. (Remember, "Wait for the P.")

To see a list of filenames only, type the following DIR command:

```
C> DIR /W
```

The /W means wide, and it gives you a five-column short-name-only list. (The longer, Windows 95 filenames don't appear in the output.)

If you want to see the files on a floppy drive, follow the DIR command with the letter of the floppy drive:

```
C> DIR A:
```

Here, DIR is followed by A:, indicating that it should list files on any disk in that drive. (There should be a disk in the drive before you use that command.) If you want to find out which files are on drive B, for example, substitute B: for A:.

✔ You can use the DIR command to find files by name, as well as locate files in other *subdirectories* on disk. Refer to Chapter 11 for information on subdirectories.

✔ The output of the DIR command shows a list of files on your disk. The list has six columns: the file's name, the file's extension (part of the name), the file's size (in bytes or characters), the date the file was created or last modified, the time of the last modification, and finally the file's longer Windows 95 name.

✔ For additional information on hunting down lost files, refer to "Name That File!" in Chapter 12. (You can find even more information on the DIR command in Chapter 12.)

✔ To view the files on disk in Windows you use either the My Computer or Explorer programs. In fact, DOS's DIR command displays files on disk the same way both of those Windows programs do in their "Details" mode. Even so, you can use the DIR command to display only a select group of files, whereas My Computer or the Explorer always show you everything. See Chapter 20 for more information on what DOS can do better than Windows.

Tech tidbits to skip

The DIR command's output may throw you. When you want to name a specific file, you glue both the file's name and extension together with a period. For example, the following is how a file may look in the DIR command's display:

```
LETTER    DOC   2,560   04-19-97   2:49p
```

However, the name of the file is really:

```
LETTER.DOC
```

The DIR command spaces out the name and extension to line everything up into columns. If you don't want to see files listed in this format, try the following DIR command:

```
C>DIR /B
```

And if the names fly by too fast for you to see, try the following instead:

```
C>DIR /B/P
```

Even more tech tidbits to skip

Windows 95 supports l-o-n-g filenames, but DOS's DIR command treats them like ugly second cousins (and justly so). These longer filenames appear at the butt end of the DIR command's list. For example, you might see:

```
LETTER~1 DOC   2,560   04-19-97   2:49p Letter to Mom.doc
```

The file's name in Windows is LETTER TO MOM.DOC, complete with all the spaces. In DOS, the filename is LETTER~1.DOC.

Confused? Yes, this is definitely worth considering selling the PC and taking up knitting as your second hobby. But before you take such a drastic step, consult with Chapter 12 for some consoling words of advice.

 Confusing or not, my advice is to use the first, ugly filename at the DOS prompt. Sure, it's painful to type LETTER~1.DOC, especially since they put that ~ (tilde) key in a really awkward spot. But doing that small amount of typing is a certain thing whereas messing with longer filenames (covered in Chapter 12) is truly horrible.

Looking at Files

There are two types of files on a PC: *English* and *Greek*. You can use the TYPE command to display any file's contents. You'll be able to read the ones in English (or *ASCII* — see "Fancy jargon section" later in this chapter). The files in Greek — actually in secret computer code, but it might just as well be Greek — are program files or data files or any other stuff you cannot read.

To look at a file, you must know its name. (If you don't know the name, you can use the DIR command; refer to the preceding section.) You type the file's name after the TYPE command and a space:

```
C> TYPE FILENAME.EXT
```

Press Enter to see the contents of the file, which in the preceding example would be FILENAME.EXT. To see the contents of the LETTER.DOC file, for example, you would enter the following command:

```
C> TYPE LETTER.DOC
```

The file is then displayed on the screen.

✔ A really simple way to view and edit text files is to use the DOS Editor. Skip merrily up to Chapter 8.

✔ If you get a `File not found` error message and you're certain that the file exists, you probably mistyped its name. Reenter the command and check your typing. Or you can use the DIR command to verify that the file exists.

✔ In Windows, locate the file's icon and right-click the mouse on it (click the mouse's right button). From the pop-up shortcut menu that appears, choose the Quick View command. That action displays the file's contents, describes the file's contents, or simply tells you that Windows has no clue as to what's in the file.

✔ Text files usually end with .TXT in their filename. The .DOC ending is also popular, though .DOC doesn't necessarily mean it's a text file. Some common text filenames are READ.ME or README or sometimes README.TXT.

✔ If the file still can't be found, refer to "Finding a Lost File" in Chapter 12.

✔ You won't be able to see all files, even though your application may display them perfectly. These "Greek" files typically contain special codes and functions for the computer, stuff that the program will eat and then spit back at you as non-Greek information. Unfortunately, the TYPE command just isn't that smart.

Fancy jargon section

Files you can see are referred to as *ASCII* files. These files contain only regular alphabetical stuff, not computer code, and they're typically formatted in a manner that makes them easily displayed by the TYPE command. ASCII is the name of the coding scheme, and what it stands for is not important, but pronouncing it *ASK-ee* is. (Don't call it *ASK-two*, or you'll be pelted with small rocks.)

An easier yet more advanced way

If the file scrolls by too quickly, you can use the following version of the TYPE command:

```
C> TYPE LETTER.DOC | MORE
```

That's a TYPE command, the name of the file you want to type, a space, and the *bar* character, followed by another space and the word MORE. This command causes the file, LETTER.DOC in the preceding example, to be displayed one screen at a time. Press the spacebar to see the next screen.

The secret to this command is the MORE filter, which is just a special program that reads text and then shows it back to you one screen at a time. The prompt — MORE — is displayed at the bottom of the screen, prompting you to press any key for more text. Another format is:

```
C> MORE < LETTER.DOC
```

This command has the same effect as the longer version: The file LETTER.DOC will be displayed one screen at a time. Is that command cryptic looking, or what?

Changing Disks

Steps: Removing a 5 ¹/₄-inch floppy disk from a drive

Step 1. Make sure that the drive light is not on. You should never remove a disk from the drive when the light is on.

Step 2. Open the drive's latch. The disk may spring out a bit, enabling you to grab it. If the disk doesn't pop out, pinch it and remove it from the drive (just as you would snatch a stubborn piece of toast from the maws of an electric toaster — and don't use a fork either).

Step 3. Put the disk into its paper sleeve. Disks should always be kept in these sleeves when they're not in a drive. If you have a disk caddy or storage locker, put the disk (in its sleeve) there.

Steps: Removing a 3 ¹/₂-inch floppy disk from a drive

Step 1. Make sure that the drive light is not on. You should never remove a disk from the drive when the light is on.

Step 2. Push the button below or to the side of the drive. The disk will spring out from the drive (like the computer is sticking its tongue out at you). Pinch it and slide the disk out all the way.

Step 3. Put the disk into its proper storage place. Unlike 5 ¹/₄-inch disks, you don't have to keep the rugged 3 ¹/₂-inch jobbies in a sleeve.

Steps: Inserting a 5 $1/4$-inch floppy disk into a drive

Step 1. Make sure that a disk is not already in the drive. If there is a disk in the drive, remove it.

Step 2. Make sure that the disk drive's door or latch is open.

Step 3. Insert the disk, label side up and toward you. Slide it in all the way.

Step 4. Close the drive door or latch.

Steps: Inserting a 3 $1/2$-inch floppy disk into a drive

Step 1. Make sure that a disk is not already in the drive. If there is a disk in the drive, eject it — ptooey!

Step 2. Insert the disk, label side up and toward you. (It only goes in one way.) Slide it in all the way. At some point, the drive will "grab" it and take it in the rest of the way.

- ✔ Access the floppy drive only after you've inserted a disk. If you do otherwise, you'll get an error. Refer to Chapter 16 for dealing with that kind of error.

- ✔ Never change a disk while you're using it. For example, wait until you've completely saved a file before removing the disk.

- ✔ If the drive door latch doesn't close, the disk isn't inserted properly. Try again.

- ✔ Keep your 5$1/4$-inch disk drive doors open when there isn't a disk in the drive.

- ✔ Never force a disk into a drive. If it doesn't fit, you're either putting the disk in wrong, a disk is already in the drive, or what you're sticking the disk into isn't a disk drive. (Many times disks get wedged into the space between two drives; don't be embarrassed, even the "pros" do it. In fact, a former editor-in-chief of mine confessed to me in an unguarded moment that he did it and had to practically disassemble his computer to get the disk out!)

- ✔ OK, because sticking a disk between two drives is an issue, take one of those tiny, sticky write-protect tabs that came with your disks and tape one or more over the space between your floppy drives — or just about any other slot on the front of the computer into which you might someday slip a disk.

- ✔ For more information on disks, refer to Chapter 10.

Changing Drives

Your computer, even with blessed Windows 95 installed, can only pay attention to one disk at a time. To switch its attention from one drive to another, type that drive's letter followed by a colon. Press Enter to *log to* that drive. (Whichever drive the computer is currently using is referred to as the *logged drive; using* equals *logged* in computerspeak.)

For example, to change from drive A to drive C, type:

```
A> C:
```

To change from drive C to drive B, type:

```
C> B:
```

A colon always follows a drive letter in DOS. (Windows, too.)

- ✔ Drive A is always the first floppy drive; drive C is always the first hard drive. A second floppy drive is drive B. Any additional drives in the system are lettered from D on up through Z.

- ✔ On most systems, the DOS prompt indicates which drive you're currently using, or logged to. If it doesn't, refer to "Prompt Styles of the Rich and Famous" in Chapter 3.

- ✔ Don't change to a floppy drive unless there is a disk in that drive. Refer to the preceding section.

- ✔ If you see the message `Drive not found`, that drive doesn't exist on the system. If you know this to be untrue, refer to Chapter 16.

- ✔ You can change to CD-ROM drives, Magneto-optical drives, even drives on other computers (if you're using a network) using the same commands: drive letter, colon, press the Enter key. See? Isn't DOS easier than Windows?

Technical background and other drivel

Using a drive is the same as being logged to it. Any time you're using your PC, you're logged to one drive or another. This situation is usually reflected in the DOS prompt.

The *drive designator* is how you tell DOS to log to another drive. It's basically nothing more than the drive letter followed by a colon (not a semicolon). Otherwise, the drive letter by itself could be mistaken for a filename or the name of a program or DOS command. So you must specify a colon whenever you're referring to a disk drive.

Even if you don't have a drive B, you can log to it by typing **B:** and pressing Enter. On single-floppy drive systems, drive B is a *phantom* drive. DOS will prompt you to *switch disks* when you change from drive A to drive B and back again. (It's an ugly text screen message — try it to see!) This message is helpful when you are working with more than one floppy disk, but generally speaking it can be a real pain in the elbows. (Maybe someday Andrew Lloyd Webber will write an opera about the Phantom B Drive. Then again, maybe not.)

Changing Directories (or Folders)

Changing drives is no big deal. You can see drive A (or drive B if you have it). And you know that drive C is inside the box somewhere, humming away. But changing directories, or using another one of Windows' *folders,* is another matter. That's done using the CD command, but it also involves a bit of techy-speak because the whole idea of directories (or *subdirectories*) isn't as entrenched in reality as the concept of your A and C drives. Therefore, all the changing directory information is handily stuffed into the following technical section.

- ✔ Windows calls them *folders,* DOS calls them directories. Same thing. In fact, you'll even see *directory* used in Windows' own "help" file.
- ✔ This book uses the term *directory* since DOS's commands refer to them as such (DIR for directory, CD for Change Directory, and so on.)

Real boring technical details — but read it anyway because you'll get lost if you don't

Your PC's disks can be divided up into individual work areas, called *directories.* Each disk has one main directory, the *root directory.* The root directory's symbol is the single backslash (\). All other directories on disk are subdirectories of (under) the root directory.

Directories can have directories of their own, which can have even more directories. That is how a *pathname* is created. If your instructions tell you that your files are to be found in the \WORK\DOCS directory, that means that the directory DOCS is a subdirectory of WORK, which is a subdirectory of the root directory. Note how the backslash is used to separate items:

```
\              The root
\WORK          The WORK directory under the root
\WORK\DOCS     The DOCS directory under the WORK directory
               under the root
```

This subject is painfully elaborated on later in this book, primarily all over Chapter 11.

Using the CD command

To change to another directory on a disk, you use the CD command followed by the name of the directory:

```
C> CD \WP51\LETTERS
```

In this example, the CD command changes directories to the \WP51\LETTERS subdirectory. Note the space between CD and the directory's pathname.

To change to the root directory of any disk, use the following command:

```
C> CD \
```

- ✔ Directories and subdirectories are work areas on a disk.

- ✔ Windows calls them *folders*. Same deal.

- ✔ For more information on the root directory, refer to the discussion under "The Root Directory" in Chapter 11; for information on pathnames, refer to "What Is a Pathname?," also in Chapter 11.

- ✔ A longer version of the CD command is CHDIR. Both do the same thing. I use CD because it's quicker to type.

- ✔ Directory names contain backslashes (\). This is not the same character as the forward slash (/). The slash (/) character is below the question mark symbol on your keyboard. The backslash is on a key usually positioned somewhere above the Enter key.

- ✔ The name of the directory typed after the CD command never ends with a backslash, though it may contain several backslashes. Note that not all directory names you type will start with a backslash. (It depends on *where you are* on the disk, which is elaborated on in "Finding the Current Directory" and "The Tree Structure," both in Chapter 11.)

- ✔ If you see an `Invalid directory` type of error, you may not be entering the correct directory name. Refer to your sources (software manuals, books, etc.) for the correct pathname. Plan ahead: Ask them for the full pathname and type that in after the CD command.

Changing Diapers

Steps: Changing soiled diapers on a wee li'l baby

Step 1. Open and unfold the new diaper. Lay baby wearing used diaper on top of new diaper.

Step 2. Unfasten used diaper. If it's a boy baby, open just a little bit at first because air tends to make Junior want to go right then and there.

Step 3. Gather baby's feet and lift. Remove the dirty diaper, wad it up, and — if it was his or her turn to do this — toss it at your spouse.

Step 4. Clean baby.

Step 5. Gently lower baby onto the new diaper.

Step 6. Fasten diaper on baby. Say something cute, such as "Oogie booga do boo." Baby will smile and prepare to soil diaper again.

For more information be sure to check out IDG Books Worldwide's *Parenting For Dummies* (really), which my wife wrote and seriously elaborated on the preceding.

Chapter 3
Life at the DOS Prompt

• •

In This Chapter

▶ Understanding DOS names and versions

▶ Using the DOS prompt

▶ Entering DOS commands

▶ Dealing with two common DOS error messages

▶ Reading manuals and books on entering DOS commands

▶ Using the nifty F3 shortcut key

▶ Canceling a DOS command

▶ Changing the DOS prompt

• •

*P*erhaps one of the most disgusting ways to work with a computer is to type secret codes at a hieroglyphic prompt. But let's be realistic. What's the end result of trying to make something too easy? It becomes *boring*. The DOS prompt may be cryptic, but it's definitely interesting. (OK, and physical torture can be interesting, but that doesn't mean you or I would volunteer for it.)

This chapter contains information about using the DOS prompt. These are mostly tips, though some of the items here will give you valuable shortcuts and make using the prompt — obscure as it is — a bit easier.

Remember, since this is Windows, you must first make a DOS prompt appear on the screen before you start your work. See Chapter 1 for various strategies to make this so.

Names and Versions

What this book calls *DOS* started out as a computer program created by Microsoft. Its version was called *MS-DOS,* short for Microsoft Disk Operating System. The version Microsoft sold to IBM was called *PC DOS,* short for Personal Computer Disk Operating System. Microsoft sold other versions as well.

Various computer hardware manufacturers label DOS using their own names: Compaq DOS, Tandy DOS, Wambooli DOS, and so on. It was all DOS, but that's changed now that Windows 95 has come around.

Your DOS version, no matter what, is now MS-DOS, since Microsoft makes Windows 95 for everyone. The only way you can find a Tandy DOS or PC DOS is to use that as your PC's operating system instead of Windows 95.

Before things became uniform, the VER command was used to see which specific version of DOS you were using:

```
C> VER
```

Press Enter and DOS displays its name and version number. In the case of Windows 95, you'll always see something like the following:

```
Windows 95. [Version 4.00.950]
```

> ✔ Aside from being perhaps the simplest and most stupid DOS command, VER can be used to determine which version of DOS is installed on a computer. If you wind up using an alien computer, type **VER** to see which make and model of DOS is installed. That may explain why some DOS commands function weirdly, or why some commands aren't available.

The Prompt, or "What Do You Want?"

The DOS prompt is how DOS tells you it's ready for your input, for you to type something, enter information, or just idly sit back and swear at the computer. In this book, the following prompt is used as an example:

```
C>
```

The prompt on your system may look like this:

```
C:\>
```

Or — yikes! — like this:

```
C:\WINDOWS>
```

> ✔ Sometimes the DOS prompt will be called the *command prompt*. Same thing. On the Windows Start menu you'll see it called *MS-DOS prompt*.

> ✔ The letter in the prompt tells you which disk drive you're currently using (or *logged to*). Refer to the discussion under "Changing Drives" in Chapter 2.

Unimportant and useless background info

The term *OEM* is used to describe an enterprise that puts together a computer. IBM, Tandy, Dell, Gateway 2000, Micron, Compaq — these are all OEMs, or Original Equipment Manufacturers. Each of them may license its own version of DOS from Microsoft and then repackage and sell that DOS under its own label. Of course, they now license Windows 95, so you'll never see any of the fancier OEM versions of DOS that existed in the old days. Oh well.

Even so, you may someday stumble upon an unknown computer and discover that it has some weird, OEM version of DOS on it. If you're curious (and you wouldn't be reading this section otherwise), the OEM versions of DOS usually add programs specific to their machines, including their own custom version of the Basic programming language. If you have PC DOS or Compaq DOS, note that the version of Basic supplied only works on IBM or Compaq computers.

Sometimes you'll see sub-minor versions of the OEM DOS. For example, the first version of Tandy DOS for the first Tandy 1000 computer was 2.11.34. That's the second major version of DOS, the 11th minor version, plus 34 tweaks by Tandy. The current version of MS-DOS in Windows 95 is called 4.00.950. That actually means it's the fourth version of Windows, first (zeroth) release, sub-minor version 950. Whatever.

Usually, a minor release of DOS (or any software for that matter) warrants the printing of a new manual. To get around this expense, and usually for only very slight modifications, you'll see a tiny minor release, such as DOS 4.01 — or maybe version 4.00.951 in the next version of Windows 95. This kind of release number indicates only minor *bugs* have been fixed or subtle features changed.

- ✔ The greater-than sign (>) is the all-purpose computer prompt. It means "What do you want?"

- ✔ Other variations of the droll DOS prompt exist. Some contain the name of the current directory, some may show the date and time, and some may look like Bart Simpson. (Refer to "Finding the Current Directory" in Chapter 11 for information on the current directory; refer to the FOX television network for Bart Simpson.)

- ✔ You can change your system prompt using the PROMPT command. Refer to "Prompt Styles of the Rich and Famous" later in this chapter.

Prompt Error Messages

Two common error messages are produced at the prompt: file not found and bad command or file name. File not found means that the file you've specified doesn't exist. Don't panic; you may have just typed it in wrong. Check your typing. If that fails, refer to "Finding a Lost File" in Chapter 12.

`Bad command or file name` is similar to file not found, though in this case the message is really *program not found*. You may have mistyped the name of a program, added a space, or forgotten something. Refer to "Where Is My Program?" in Chapter 14 for additional information on solving this problem.

✔ The `file not found` error message is usually followed by the name of the file not found. For example, if you mistyped the filename BLECH you might see something like the following error message:

```
File not found — belch
```

✔ Individual programs produce their own unique error messages for `file not found`. The messages vary in syntax, but they all mean the same thing.

✔ Other error messages are possible at the prompt, some of which will really burn your buns. Refer to Chapter 16.

Typing at the Prompt

You use the prompt by typing after it. All the text you enter at the keyboard appears on the screen next to the prompt. Of course, what you type are DOS commands, the names of programs, or general insults to the computer.

The information you enter at the DOS prompt is the command line, which is an assortment of words, cryptic and English, that direct the computer to do something. Sending that information to DOS is done by pressing the Enter key. Only by pressing Enter is the information sent, which gives you an opportunity to back up and erase or to change your mind and press Ctrl+C or the Escape (Esc) key to cancel.

✔ As you type, the underline cursor on the screen moves forward. The cursor marks the spot on the screen where all text appears.

✔ If you make a mistake typing at the DOS prompt, press the Backspace key to back up and erase.

✔ If you want to discard the entire command line, press Esc. On some computers, the backslash (\) is displayed and the cursor moves down to the next line on the screen. You can start over from there. (Other computers may just erase the line and let you start over.)

✔ I don't need to mention that the DOS prompt is unfriendly. In fact, DOS is arrogant and only understands certain things. When it doesn't understand something, it spits back an error message (refer to the preceding section).

✔ On the bright side, there's really nothing heinous you can do at the DOS prompt. Most of the deadly things you can do involve typing in specific commands and then answering Y (for yes). If you accidentally stumble into one of those situations, type N (for no). Otherwise, there's little you can do at the DOS prompt that will damage your PC.

Beware of Spaces!

There are three bad tendencies beginners have when using the DOS prompt: They don't type in any spaces, they do type in spaces, or they type in periods.

Always keep this in mind: The DOS prompt is not a word processor. You don't need to type formal English; punctuation, capitalization, and spelling are often overlooked. So never end a command with a period. In fact, periods are only used when naming files that have a second part or extension.

Spaces are another sticky point. You must stick a space (and only one space) between two separate items. For example:

```
C> CD \FRIDGE\LEFTOVER
```

Here the CD command is followed by a space. You must put a space after CD or any DOS command.

```
C> WP CHAP02.DOC
```

Here the program *WP* is run. It's followed by a space and the name of a file.

Just as you shouldn't type in too few spaces, don't type in too many spaces, either. In the preceding example, there is no space in the file named CHAP02.DOC. If you're a touch typist, you may have a tendency to type a space after the period. Don't. Always type in a command exactly as you see it listed in a book, magazine, or computer manual.

✔ Some books and magazines may use a funny typeface to indicate *the stuff you type in*. This may make it look like extra spaces are typed in a command, typically around the backslash (\) character. Watch out for this potential pitfall!

✔ A few DOS commands may end in a period, but only when that period is part of a filename. For example:

```
C> DIR *.
```

The preceding DIR command lists all files that don't have a second part or filename extension. The *. is a legitimate part of the command. This is about the only instance in which a DOS command ends with a period.

▶ If you forget to type a space at the proper place, you'll probably get a `bad command or file name` error message.

Beware of User Manuals and English Punctuation!

Manuals and instruction books often tell you what to type at the DOS prompt. But there is no established convention for doing this.

This book uses the following method:

```
C> VER
```

The DOS prompt is shown followed by the text you enter in a different typeface than the rest of the text in the book. The prompt is always going to be C> in this book, though it may appear in some other way on your screen.

Some manuals follow what you type with the word *Enter,* sometimes in a bubble or in some other happy typeface. That means to press the Enter key after you type the command; don't type in the word *Enter* on the command line.

Some manuals list what you type on a line by itself, without the prompt:

```
VER
```

Some manuals include the command in the text — which is where this can get tricky. For example, they may say

```
Enter the VER command.
```

Here VER is in uppercase, meaning you type it at the DOS prompt. Sometimes it may appear in lowercase, italics, or boldface. The worst is when they put the command in quotes:

```
Type the "DIR *.*" command.
```

In that example, you can gather that you type the DIR command, followed by a space, an asterisk, a period, and another asterisk. You would not type in the double quotes surrounding the command. In this book, the command would be specified as follows:

```
C> DIR *.*
```

So far so good. But when English punctuation rears its ugly head, you may see one of the following:

```
Type the command "DIR *.*".
Type the command "DIR *.*."
```

The first example is grammatically incorrect: The period is on the outside of the double quote. Of course, the period ends the sentence — it's not part of the command you should type in. The second example is what most computer book editors do to DOS commands. No, the period is not part of the command, but a period on the inside of a quote is grammatically correct in that circumstance.

If you type in the period as part of the DOS command, you'll see one of DOS's inflammatory error messages.

✔ DOS commands and program names can be entered in uppercase or lowercase. Most manuals and books, including this one, use uppercase.

✔ No DOS command ends in a period. There are exceptions, but the point here is that if you see a command ending in a period in a manual or computer book, it's probably a part of English grammar and not something you need to type.

✔ DOS commands contain spaces. Spaces follow the name of the command, separating filenames and any other options typed after the commands.

✔ The DIR command outputs filenames with spaces separating the name and the extension. When you type a filename at the DOS prompt, a dot separates the name and extension. Do not use spaces.

✔ It is possible to use long, Windows 95 filenames in DOS, in which case they *do* have spaces in them. That can of worms is discussed in Chapter 12. Refer there for the special deals you need to pull to get a space in a filename.

✔ No user manual is 100 percent correct. If you type in the command exactly as it's listed and the computer still produces an error, try it again with a space or without a period.

The Handy F3 Key

The F3 key provides a handy shortcut whenever you need to retype a DOS command. For example, to list files on the disk in drive A, you type the following command:

```
C> DIR A:
```

If the file you wanted isn't on that disk, remove it and replace it with another disk. Then, instead of retyping the same command, press F3. You'll see the same command displayed:

```
C> DIR A:
```

 Press Enter and the command is executed a second time.

If this doesn't work, you may have a *keyboard macro* enhancement program operating. In that case, try pressing the up-arrow cursor key instead.

"My DOS Prompt Beeps at Me!"

If you try to type something at the DOS prompt and Windows just beeps at you (or honks or hoots or generally ignores your keystrokes), then you must tell Windows to pay attention: Click the mouse once on the MS-DOS Prompt window to make it *active* again.

- ✔ What's happened is that you (or Windows) has switched away to another window on the screen. By clicking on your MS-DOS Prompt window, you switch Windows' attention back to where you're looking.

- ✔ Yes, this doesn't happen at all when you run DOS full-screen. Press the Alt+Enter key combination to run DOS full-screen. See Chapter 1 for more information.

- ✔ The ability of Windows to run more than one program at a time is called *multitasking* (because *runningseveralprogramsatonceing* looks too German). See Chapter 6 for more information on this phenomenon, er, thing.

Canceling a DOS Command

The universal cancel key in DOS is Control+C or Ctrl+C. Pressing this key combination halts most DOS commands. In some cases, it may even halt a DOS operation in progress.

To press Ctrl+C, hold down the Ctrl (Control) key and type **C**. Release the Ctrl key. You'll see ^C displayed on the screen and then another DOS prompt.

> ✔ The Ctrl+Break key combination works identically to Ctrl+C. Note that the Break key is usually a shared key; you may find the word *Break* on the front of the key instead of the top.
>
> ✔ Always try Ctrl+Break first. You never want to reset — or worse, turn off — your computer to get yourself out of a jam.
>
> ✔ Applications programs use their own cancel key, which is usually the Esc key. (There are exceptions, however. WordPerfect, for example, uses the F1 or F3 key.)
>
> ✔ The caret or hat symbol (^) is used to denote *control*. So when you see ^C it means Control+C or the Ctrl+C keystroke. Likewise, ^H means Control+H, ^G means Control+G, and so on. Some of these keys have significant meaning, which there's no need to get into here.

Prompt Styles of the Rich and Famous

The DOS prompt is a flexible thing. It can really look like anything you imagine, contain interesting and useful information, and so on. The secret is to use the PROMPT command.

Other books offer you a tutorial on the PROMPT command and how it works. Rather than bother with that, here are some popular prompts you can create. Just type in the command as listed and you'll have your own excellent DOS prompt.

The standard, boring prompt:

```
C>
```

To create the standard prompt, which contains the current drive letter and a greater-than symbol, type in the following command:

```
C> PROMPT
```

Yawn. Nothing new.

The most common DOS prompt shows the current drive, directory, and the greater-than sign. Type in the following command:

```
C> PROMPT $P$G
```

This creates the typical MS-DOS-in-Windows prompt:

```
C:\WINDOWS>
```

To create the date and time prompt, type in this command:

```
C:\> PROMPT $D$_$T$_$P$G
```

This prompt contains the current date, time, and then the drive and directory information found in the example below. Note that the date and time information is current only while the new prompt is first displayed; it's not constantly updated on your screen.

```
Wed 7-31-1996
12:34:25.63
C:\DOS>
```

To make your favorite prompt permanent, you need to place the PROMPT command into DOS's AUTOEXEC.BAT file. This is covered in Chapter 7.

Additional, worthless information

The prompt can contain any text you like. Simply specify that text after the PROMPT command:

```
C:\> PROMPT Enter command:
```

Or the ever popular:

```
C:\> PROMPT What is thy bidding?
```

You cannot directly specify the following characters in a PROMPT command: less than (<), greater than (>), and the pipe (I). Instead, use the following: $L for less than (<); $G for greater than (>); and $B for the pipe (I).

Because the dollar sign ($) is used as a special prefix, you'll need to specify two of them ($$) if you want $ as part of your prompt. That's OK; when money's involved, greed is good.

Part II

DOS Life in the Windows 95 Gulag

"IT WAS AT THIS POINT THAT THERE APPEARED TO BE SOME SORT OF MASS INSANITY."

In this part...

In Greek mythology, Zeus and his Olympian gods took over when they decided to do in all their ancestors, the Titans. This proved two things: That most people could really care less about ancient Greek mythology and that children, even of gods, seem to be eternally ungrateful to their parents. DOS gets the same kind of disrespect from Windows.

Once upon a time, Windows relied upon DOS for everything. Heck, Windows was a *DOS shell*. A mere tool to make DOS easier to use. Bah! Now things have switched around. DOS now relies upon Windows. You must first toil there before you can see a C prompt, see? Of course, most folks like it that way. Still, if you're a DOS user, that gives you more stuff to get used to, which is what this section goes into. And, on the up and up, at least there's no ancient Greek chow-on-the-children themes involved with any of this. Egads, no!

Chapter 4

Going Graphical

*P*ut DOS in a window and what do you get? Why, a gaggle of graphical gadgets, you bet. Bothersome things, gizmos, and do-dads. Buttons and sliders and menus — egads! Things to fiddle with and play, to tweak and adjust. But Windows is in charge now. So getting used to these things we must.

DOS Does Windows

DOS and its DOS applications now live in a graphical window on Windows' screen. It almost looks like your old DOS screen, though a lot of windows float around on the outside of things.

✔ If you don't want to run your DOS programs in a wee li'l window, chicken out and switch them over to text mode. Chapter 1 describes how to do this in the section "And when you long for those old, full text screen days . . ." (though I can sum it up here by telling you: Alt+Enter).

✔ You should also check out Chapter 7 for information on making any of your DOS programs start in the text screen.

✔ If you don't chicken out, you can use a few fancy Windows gizmos to help control the way your DOS window looks. The following sections mull over the possibilities.

✔ By the way, these tricks apply to all DOS programs run in Windows, not just the MS-DOS Shell window.

"I want to make my DOS window bigger"

For me, all it takes is one doughnut and I can't fit into my pants. In Windows, you make things bigger by clicking on a window's maximize button. You'll find this booger conveniently located in the upper-right corner of the window. Click once to make your DOS window a larger size.

- ✔ Clicking the maximize button does not switch you to text mode. Press the Alt+Enter key combo for that trick.

- ✔ Also, clicking the maximize button may change your DOS font to something huge. See the section "Fonts and Stuff" later in this chapter.

- ✔ Unlike Windows applications, your DOS window can be maximized only to a certain size, usually dependent upon your PC's screen resolution, available fonts, and the computer's disposition.

- ✔ M&Ms make me fat, too.

"I want to make my DOS window back the way it was"

To "undo" a maximized window, click on the restore button. This bloops the window down to the size and position it lived in before being maximized.

Note that the restore button appears only when a window has been maximized, as described in the preceding section. Don't freak if you don't see it.

"I want to minimize my DOS window"

To shrink your DOS window down, transforming it into a button on Windows' taskbar, click on the minimize button — which could arguably be said looks like a button on the taskbar (though I'm not going to argue). This is known in Windowspiel as *minimizing* or "getting the heck out of the way."

- ✔ Your DOS program may or may not continue to run "in the background" while it lives as a button on the taskbar. See Chapter 6 to be certain.

- ✔ Why minimize? To get something out of the way. Too many windows on the screen can lead to clutter. Some Windows users like to minimize their programs instead of closing them outright, just to keep them handy.

- ✔ No, you can't minimize your children.

- ✔ To get your window back, just click on its taskbar button. Figure 4-1 shows what a DOS window may look like living as a button on the taskbar. After you click the button, the window returns to the exact size and position it lived in before you so cruelly minimized it.

Figure 4-1:
A minimized
MS-DOS
Prompt
window.

"I want to move my DOS window"

Your DOS window can float anywhere on Windows' screen. To move the DOS window about, point the mouse at the title bar, which is the upper part of the window. (The program's icon and name are on the left side, and three buttons are on the right; see Figure 4-2.) Press the mouse button and *drag* the window to a new position, moving the mouse. Release the mouse button when you've found a new home for the window.

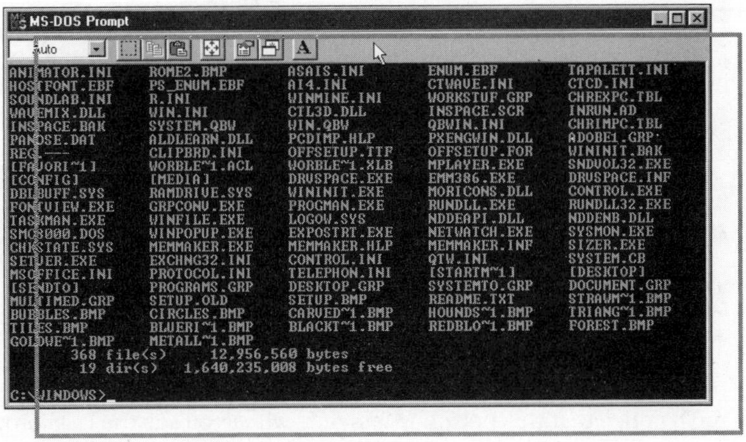

Figure 4-2:
Dragging a
DOS
window
around the
screen.

✔ No, this won't leave any skid marks.

✔ Refer to your favorite Windows book for information on dragging something with the mouse.

"I want to change the size of my DOS window"

Changing the size of your DOS window is tricky because it only comes in certain sizes. Those sizes depend on which size and type of font you're using, but that's another story with a lousy plot and stilted dialog that I won't go into right now.

To change the size of your DOS window, point the mouse at one of the window's corners. I use the lower-right corner since I'm lower-right handed. The mouse pointer changes to a diagonally pointing arrow. Drag the mouse in one direction or another to change the window's size. Release the mouse button when you're happy.

For example, to make the window larger, point the mouse at the lower-right corner and drag the mouse down and to the right. To make the window smaller, drag the mouse up and to the left.

✔ You can grab any edge of the window to change its size. If you grab a corner you can change the window's size in two directions at once.

✔ You may notice the window's fuzzy outline changes in rather jerky steps to specific sizes. Those are the sizes the DOS window is limited to, based on the DOS fonts available (which is covered later in this chapter).

✔ Sometimes a too-small window size means Windows has to put scrollbars on the window so you can see all of it. Gadzooks! If you notice scrollbars on your DOS window, change the size again. No one wants to use DOS with scrollbars. Yech!

✔ Alas, the scrollbars don't let you "back scroll" through your DOS session. That would have been a nice touch, but Microsoft's programmers were probably too busy ironing the bugs out of Windows' e-mail program to bother with it.

"I want to close my DOS window and I forgot the EXIT command"

 Click the X close button.

You'll notice that this button works only when you see the DOS prompt in the window or when a program has quit running and just kinda sits there kinda stupid.

If you try to use the window's X close button at the wrong time, such as when you're in the middle of WordPerfect or 1-2-3, Windows displays a horrid error message, as shown in Figure 4-3. This means DOS is being safe (what a change!). You should quit your DOS program first and then close the window; click the No button or press the Enter key to close the warning dialog box.

Quit your DOS program properly. If the DOS window doesn't close at that time, you can click the X close button to make it go away.

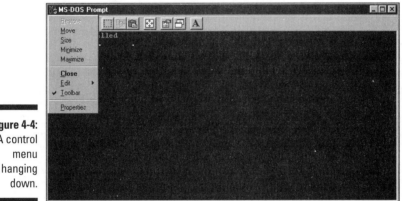

Figure 4-3:
Better quit
the DOS
program
first.

"Some dorky manual tells me to access the 'control menu'"

The control menu is hidden under every window's advertisement icon, located in the window's upper-left corner. You can click on this icon once with the mouse, or press the almost-intuitive Alt+Spacebar key combo to see the menu, as shown in Figure 4-4.

Figure 4-4:
A control
menu
hanging
down.

Each of the items in the control menu allows you to do one of the things described in the previous sections: Restore, Move, Size (as in resize), Mini-mize, Maximize, and Close. The other items in the menu are discussed later in this chapter.

Press the Esc key to make the control menu go away if you don't need it.

If you access the Move or Size items in the control menu, Windows expects you want to move or resize the DOS program window using the arrow keys on your keyboard. What a joke! Use the mouse as described in the proper sections earlier in this chapter.

Belly-up to the DOS toolbar

Another Windowsy item you'll see on your DOS window is the DOS program toolbar. It's a collection of buttons that won't help you one iota with any of your DOS software. It does, however, help you finagle some Windows dojobbies that control how your DOS program works.

The first item sitting at the toolbar is the font size selection drop-down list thing. See the section titled "Fonts and Stuff" later in this chapter for more information on using this thing. Most of the time, it should say *Auto,* meaning DOS would rather be out driving a car than living in Windows.

The second item sitting at the DOS toolbar is the trio of Mark, Copy, and Paste buttons. These are used to share text between your DOS program's window and other DOS and Windows programs. The sordid subject is covered in Chapter 6.

The "I don't know which way I'm going" button is really the "switch to full-screen mode" button. Same thing as pressing the Alt+Enter key combo. Same thing.

Properties button, just like in Monopoly. Actually, this button lets you change a few of the nerdier aspects of how a DOS program runs under Windows. Heinous stuff. Covered in Chapter 7.

Mysterious *Background* button. What does it do? Better turn to Chapter 6. That information is too vital to the success of the rebellion for it to be listed here.

Big A, little a, what begins with A? Nothing this button is associated with. It's the font button. Shoulda been F. See "Fonts and Stuff" later in this chapter.

"But I can't see the toolbar" or "I don't want to see the toolbar!"

If you just can't stand the idea of the toolbar on a DOS window, heed these steps:

1. **Click the mouse on the control menu.**

   It drops down, making a twonk noise if your PC is equipped with a sound card and you've doodled with Windows to make a twonk noise every time you drop down a menu.

2. **Choose the <u>T</u>oolbar item.**

   It has a check by it. Choosing this item removes the check and removes the ugly toolbar from your sight.

If you want to be a Power User, forgo the mouse. Nay, toss it aside! Press Alt+Spacebar, T. This adds or removes the toolbar, depending on how often you go through that key combination.

TECHNICAL STUFF

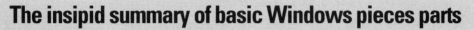

The insipid summary of basic Windows pieces parts

Maximize button; click to make your DOS window bigger.

Restore button; click to return your DOS window to its previous size before you maximized it.

Minimize button; click to transform your DOS window into a button on the taskbar.

Close button; click to close a lazy DOS window (but it won't close a running DOS program).

Control menu icon; click to access some stuff you don't really need to access anyway.

Fonts and Stuff

Windows has so many beautiful and exotic fonts available. Oh, you can play all day and come up with some really wacky, if not annoying, documents. Unfortunately (or fortunately) DOS can't use Windows' fonts. Not one.

Instead of fancy fonts, DOS and its applications are resigned to using a few select fonts, the size of which directly affects the size of the DOS window on the screen. So this section covers not only fonts, but window sizes as well. (A value-added bonus.)

These font selections have no effect on DOS programs you run full screen. Those programs will continue to use the cruddy DOS font you're used to.

You Auto pick this font

The best way to choose a font for your DOS window is to select the *Auto* font. That way Windows automatically (get it — auto?) chooses a font based on the size of the DOS program's window. Change the window's size and Windows automatically picks a new font. Neat-o.

To select the *Auto* font, choose the word Auto from the drop-down list that appears on the DOS program's toolbar; click the mouse on the down-arrow by the drop-down list and pluck Auto — the first item — from the list by clicking on it with the mouse.

Wasting time with the Fonts panel in the Properties dialog box

If you want to mess with fonts in a DOS window (and I'm assuming you have gallons of time on your hands for this), you can mess with them directly in the Fonts panel, which can be found in any DOS program's Properties dialog box.

The shortcut way to get to the Font's panel is to click on the Font button (the A) on your DOS program's toolbar. This displays the Fonts panel as shown in Figure 4-5.

If you can't see the toolbar, then press Alt+Spacebar, P and keep pressing the Ctrl+Tab key combination until the Fonts panel is in front.

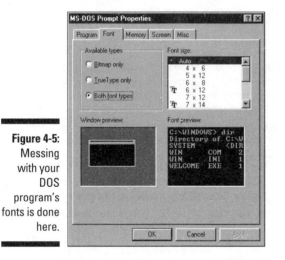

Figure 4-5:
Messing
with your
DOS
program's
fonts is done
here.

The Fonts panel has four areas:

✔ In the Available types area, make sure the Both font types item is selected (it has a dot by it). That gives you the best options for your DOS fonts.

✔ The Font size area is where you pick your fonts, which is covered later.

✔ The bottom two areas (Window preview and Font preview) are preview windows, which show you how big the DOS program window will be on your screen and the size and shape of the fonts you select.

To choose a new font, click on a size in the Font size area of the dialog box. They're listed from smallest to largest. Here are some other interesting (or not) tidbits:

✔ The numbers indicate the width and height of the font in pixels, *pixel* being Latin for "little dot on the screen."

✔ A double T by a font means its a TrueType font, which is Microsoft's fancy you-can-stretch-it-any-old-way font. These fonts tend to look thinner and uglier than the other fonts, like bony fingers on a corpse.

✔ Use the scrollbar to scroll through the list of fonts. The smallest one I see is 4 x 6; the largest is 12 x 22. Your sizes will vary, depending on whether you have the same computer as I do.

✔ If you click on a font, the preview windows in the dialog box change to show you how and where the DOS window will float on the screen and how the text in that window will look. Feel free to mess with this all you like; nothing is set until you click the OK button.

✔ I have this huge monitor I just paid several visits to the chiropractor for, so my DOS windows appear rather small. If you have a normal, non-back-pain-inducing monitor, the DOS windows appear larger on the screen.

When you're done messing around, click the OK button to lock in the changes. Or, if you're unhappy and wish you really wouldn't have wasted so much time, click the Cancel button.

Clicking the Apply button changes the DOS window on the screen without locking in any changes. That step allows you to see what you're gonna get in "real life." If you like it, click OK. If not, click Cancel.

Chapter Bonus: Changing the Number of Lines per Screen

DOS always had the ability to show you more than the typical and, I might add, paltry, 25-lines-per screen. For today's massively overstuffed-with-files hard drives, 25 lines just aren't enough. So, using various chants and by incanting just the right spell, you could order DOS to show you 43 or even 50 lines per screen. An amazing feat, but awkward to pull off.

Well, thank goodness for Windows 95. Now you can instantly switch to a larger DOS window in a snap. Follow these bonus steps:

1. **Bring up the DOS window's Properties dialog box.**

   If you see the toolbar, click on the Properties button. If you don't see the toolbar, press Alt+Spacebar, P.

2. **Click the mouse on the Screen panel.**

   Point the mouse at the word Screen and click the mouse's button. Using the keyboard, press the Ctrl+Tab key combination until the Screen panel is "in front." What you see should look something like Figure 4-6.

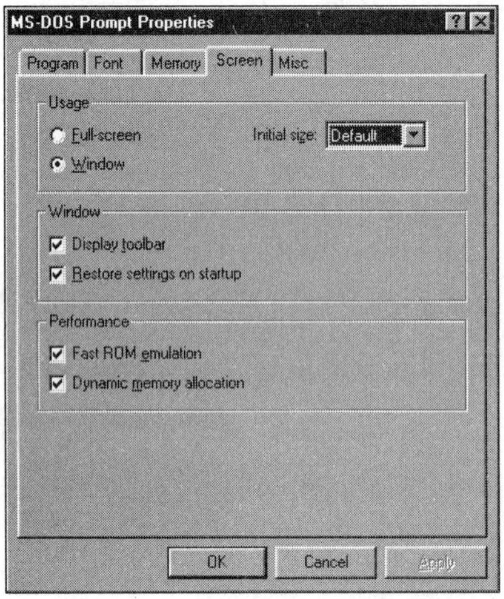

Figure 4-6:
The Screen
panel in a
DOS
program's
Properties
dialog box.

3. **Ignore everything in that panel except for the** Initial size **thing.**

   The Initial size thing is located on the right side of the top area (the Usage area) on the panel.

4. **Choose a new number of screen lines from the drop-down list thing.**

   Click the mouse on the down-pointing arrow, or press the Alt+↓ key combination. This drops down a little list showing you three screen sizes: 25, 43, and 50 lines. (That's lines going *up and down;* the number of columns across stays at 80.) The Default item means, well, gosh, I have no idea.

   If you want to see more lines per screen, choose 43 or 50 from the list. Use your mouse or the ↑ and ↓ arrow keys. Press Enter to lock in your choice if you're using the keyboard.

5. **Click** OK.

   Or press the Enter key.

Now here's the rub: Nothing happens. Drat! It didn't work! Actually, you need to "wake up" Windows to let DOS know it has a new number of lines per screen. The quickest way to do this is to resize the window as described earlier in this chapter (see "I want to change the size of my DOS window").

Another way to wake up the DOS window is to close it and then restart it. You may still need to resize the window, since Windows is stupid and still won't realize you have more lines per screen.

You'll soon notice that your DOS applications may recognize the new screen size. A few biggies do, such as WordPerfect (as shown in Figure 4-7). Of course, the text gets mighty small — unless you paid your chiropractor a lot for a large monitor as did I.

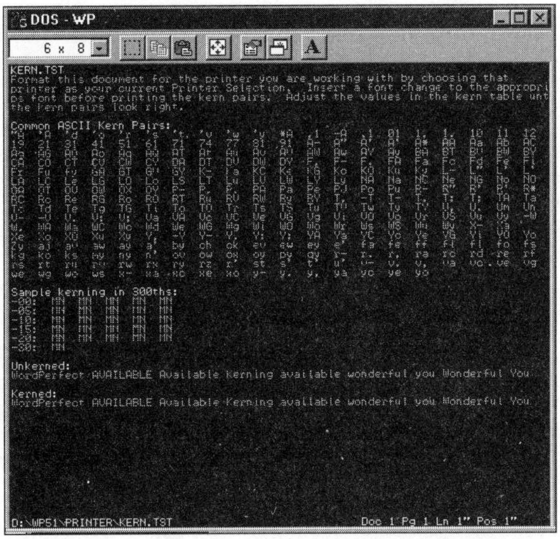

Figure 4-7: A DOS window with 50 lines per screen.

"WELL, RIGHT OFF, THE RESPONSE TIME SEEMS A BIT SLOW."

Chapter 5

Basic Software Setup

● ●

In This Chapter

▶ Locating DOS software

▶ Installing software (generally speaking)

▶ Adding a DOS program to the Start menu

▶ Operating a new program and performing basic functions

▶ Learning a new program (the best way)

▶ Reading a command format

● ●

Setting up software hasn't changed much since DOS was thrust into Windows. Hopefully, you'll never have to install any software on your PC. Someone else, someone who loves to do such things, will install the software for you. To install a program, you have to learn steps that are required only once. So making someone else do it for you can be a blessing — doubly so since Windows and DOS have different plans of attack when it comes to software installation.

This chapter is about using software for the first time. It also includes information on selecting and installing a program, which can be pretty involved. There is also a strategy covered here on learning and using software for the first time — not that you'd want to become an expert or anything.

From Whence Shall My DOS Software Come?

DOS software still lives, thrives, and dwells — though don't expect many popular software stores to stock it. You'll still find DOS games, plus some second-tier DOS applications (mailing lists, educational stuff, home finance, and so on). But looking for major applications like word processors, spreadsheets, and databases will get tougher and tougher.

Companies like Lotus, Novell (WordPerfect), and Borland still sell and support DOS software. To find some of the stuff, you may have to phone them up directly; the software store can do this for you, but you may have to take down the numbers and do it yourself.

As DOS software gets scarce, another option is to look for companies that sell remainder software. I got a big catalog in the mail the other day packed with all sorts of good old DOS software the big boys used to sell. Cheap, too.

And, by all means, hang on to your old DOS software. I was using WordPerfect 5.1 the other day and it *screams* — a much faster word processor than anything Windows has to offer, even running in a tiny window on Windows 95.

Installation

When you find a new piece of DOS software, you need to install it. *Installation* means copying the program you've just bought from floppy disks or a CD-ROM to your computer's hard drive. It also means, more typically, configuring or setting up the program to work with your particular PC, printer, and the rest of that stuff. That is why installation is best left up to your local computer guru. If not, you can follow the outline given here.

Remember that this process isn't the same way Windows programs are installed. They use a special part of the Control Panel to set themselves up. In DOS, every computer program installs itself differently. Because of this fact, the following material is covered in a broad sense. But it gives you a general idea of the task you're about to undertake.

Read me first!

Computer manuals and those national sweepstakes with you-know-who's picture on the envelope both have something in common: You have lots of little pieces of paper and instructions for the interesting things you must do. But computer manuals are easier to deal with. Seriously. You don't need to hunt through everything, fill out various forms, or paste Uncle Ed's picture in the TV set. Just look for a sheet of paper somewhere that says *Read me first!* Read it, and you're on your way.

Start your DOS window

Because you're adding a DOS program to Windows, you have to start by running the MS-DOS Prompt program. This step is one I'll bet *all* the programs leave out, because most of this stuff doesn't assume DOS is now a slave to Windows.

Refer to the instructions in Chapter 1, "Firing Up a DOS Prompt," for more information on starting your DOS window.

The installation program

You install a program by sticking Disk 1 into your PC's first floppy drive (drive A) and then running the installation program. If the disk doesn't fit into drive A, stick the disk into drive B and substitute B for A in the following instructions.

The name of most DOS installation programs is usually *install*, though *setup* is also popular. There are two steps here. The first is *logging to drive A*. This is covered in the section "Changing Drives" in Chapter 2. Basically, after sticking Disk 1 into floppy drive A (and closing the drive door latch for a 5¹/₄-inch disk), you type in the following:

```
C> A:
```

Typing A and a colon logs you to drive A. Press Enter.

Next, you enter the name of the installation program. This name is probably listed in the manual, on the disk label, or on the *Read me first!* sheet of paper, or that paper will tell you where to find these instructions. Be wary! Even though installing the program is the first thing you'll ever do with it, it's rarely the first chapter in the manual. (I've always wondered why that's the case.)

For example, if the name of the installation program is INSTALL, you type

```
A> INSTALL
```

Press Enter.

Sometimes the installation program is called SETUP. If so, you type this:

```
A> SETUP
```

Press Enter here, too.

Don't forget to *read the information on the screen!* It's important, especially for an installation program. In fact, many "experts" usually screw up software installation by not reading the screens. Follow the instructions closely.

The location

The first thing the installation program asks you is, "Where do you want to put me?" Dumb question. You want to put the program in your computer.

The application needs its own workspace on your hard drive. This is referred to as a *subdirectory*. Only advanced users may have some special scheme or plan in this instance. You should accept whatever suggestion the installation program makes — it's probably a good one.

Configuring a computer application

Configuration is the stupidest part of setting up a computer application. This is where the program asks you information about your own computer: "What kind of printer do you have? What kind of display or monitor is attached? How much memory do you have? Do you have a mouse?" These questions are ridiculous! After all, the computer program is asking you those questions, and it's already inside the computer where it can look around more easily than you can.

Still, you may have to tell the computer what it has (which, again, is like asking other people how old you are at your next birthday party). These questions can be difficult. If you don't know the answers, grab someone who does. Otherwise, guess. The *default* or *automatic selection* options tell the program to guess on its own, so if they're available, select them.

An important item to select is a *printer driver,* which is a fancy way of telling the application which printer you have manacled to your PC. Look for your printer's name and model number listed. If it's not there, select *Dumb* or *Line* printer. (This printer issue is one of the major reasons people upgrade to Windows, since Windows handles all the printing, not your software.)

The READ.ME file

Finally, there are last-minute instructions or information offered in a special file on disk. It's given the name *README, READ.ME, README.TXT,* or *README.DOC.* Good installation programs ask you if you want to view this file. Say yes. Look through the file for any information that applies to your situation.

A utility is usually offered with a program to provide automatic viewing of the READ.ME file. If not, you can view it using the following DOS command:

```
C> MORE < READ.ME
```

That's the MORE command, a space, a less-than sign (<), another space, and the name of the READ.ME file. If the file is named just README, type it in without a period in the middle.

📌 For information on pathnames and directories, refer to Chapter 11.

📌 For information on using the TYPE command for viewing files, refer to "Looking at Files" in Chapter 2.

📌 A great way to view a README file is using the DOS Editor or Windows's Notepad, which is covered in Chapter 8.

The post-installation reset warning!

Some DOS software will install itself, and then attempt to reset your computer. This action is wholly improper in Windows 95. When the software attempts it, your DOS window will merely close itself; Windows will not reset.

If the program asks you to reset the computer, merely close your DOS window, and then open it again to run the program.

There may be an off-chance the program will not run properly right away. If that's the case, and you get some sort of "missing file" or "bad driver" error message, you must restart Windows. Here's how:

1. **Choose Sh<u>u</u>t Down from the Start thing's menu.**

   Point your mouse at the Start button and click once; then choose the Sh<u>u</u>t Down item — which is the bottom one on the menu. Using the keyboard (always quicker), press Ctrl+Esc, U.

   The Shut Down Windows dialog box appears.

2. **Choose** `Restart the computer?`

   Click your mouse in the hole by `Restart the computer?` or press Alt+R. This tells Windows to restart as opposed to shut down entirely (the first item up for bids).

3. **Click Yes.**

   Or press Alt+Y. This restarts the computer.

   If you have any unsaved Windows business, you'll be asked to save it before Windows quits. If you have any unfinished DOS business, the whole operation will stop; properly close your DOS windows (see Chapter 1), and then do these steps over again.

Adding Your Program to the Windows Start Thing

Windows is utterly oblivious when you add a new DOS program. While the program can be run from any DOS prompt window, you won't find it on the Windows Start thing menu. You'll have to put it there manually yourself, probably by following these instructions:

1. **Bring up the Taskbar Properties dialog box.**

   Click the Start button to pop-up its menu, and then choose Settings ⇨Taskbar. From the keyboard, you can press Alt+Esc, S, T.

2. **Click on the Start Menu Programs tab to bring that panel forward.**

   Click on the tab with the mouse, or press the Ctrl+Tab key combination so that the dialog box looks similar to Figure 5-1. You add programs to the Start thing's menu by choosing the Add button in this dialog box.

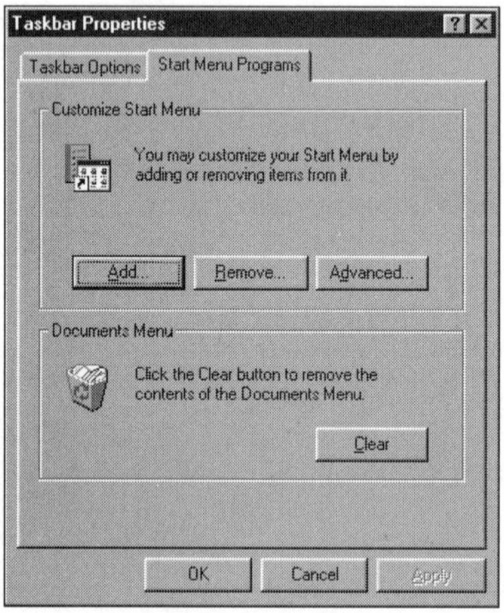

Figure 5-1: The Start Menu Programs panel in the Taskbar Properties dialog box.

3. **Click the mouse on the Add button.**

   Or press Alt+A. The Create Shortcut dialog box appears (see Figure 5-2), which is the first of several steps you need to go through to add your DOS program to the menu.

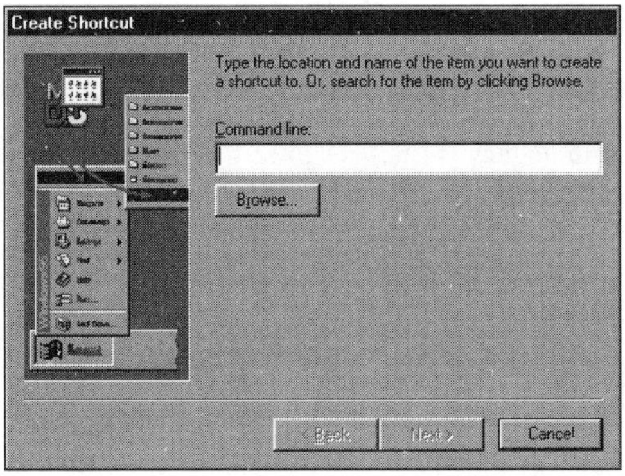

Figure 5-2:
Type your
DOS
program
command
into this box.

4. **Type the command used to start your DOS program.**

   The command goes into the box labeled Command line. For example, if
   you type WP to start WordPerfect at the DOS prompt, type **WP** into the
   box. If you type Q to start Quicken, type **Q** into the box.

   Don't press the Enter key!

5. **Click the mouse on the** Next> **button.**

   The Select Program Folder dialog box appears, looking similar to the one
   shown in Figure 5-3. Now you tell Windows where to stick your program in
   the Start thing's menu.

   If you have a DOS Applications sub-menu, locate that folder and click on it
   once with the mouse. Otherwise, click on the folder name in which you
   want your DOS program to appear.

   If you can't make up your mind, click on the Programs folder (which
   should be highlighted already in the dialog box, as shown in Figure 5-3).

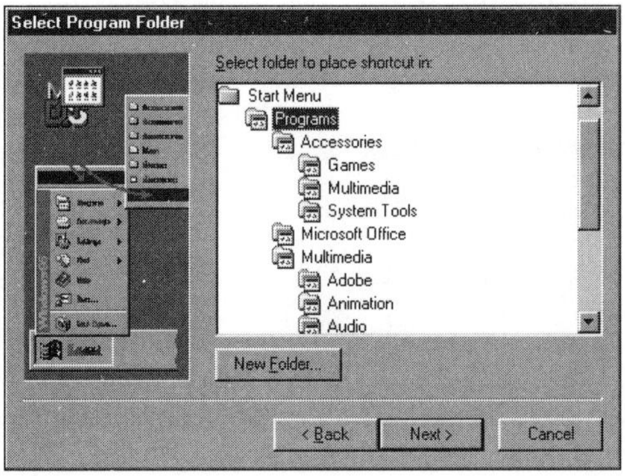

Figure 5-3:
The Select
Program
Folder
dialog box.

Making your own DOS Applications sub-menu

If you don't have a DOS Applications sub-menu, you can make one in the Select Program Folder dialog box. Here are the steps:

1. Click on the New Folder button, or press Alt+F.

A new folder (actually a sub-menu) appears in the list, most likely given the dopey name `Program Group (1)`.

2. Type `DOS Applications`.

This is the new name for that sub-menu, which Windows will create in the Start thing's menu for you.

3. Press the Enter key.

This locks in the new name, and it also selects that folder/sub-menu as the folder you'll be putting your new program into.

Continue with step 6, assigning a name to your DOS program in the menu.

---

6. Click the `Next>` **button.**

The Select a Title for the Program dialog box appears.

Don't be confused, since the next screen looks like the first screen. It's not. This is where you give a name to the *menu item,* not the program.

7. Type a name for your program, a name that will appear in the Start thing's menu.

So if you typed in `Q` for Quicken, you can type `Quicken` in this box. That name will appear in the menu. Likewise, if your program name is `WP`, feel free to type `WordPerfect 5.1` (or whatever) here.

Don't press the Enter key!

8. Click the `Next>` **button.**

The Select an Icon dialog box appears, as in Figure 5-4. This is where you can pick a token icon for your DOS program. Not that it matters, but it is kinda fun.

Figure 5-4:
Pluck an icon for your DOS program from this bunch.

To pick an icon, point the mouse at it and click. You can also use the arrow keys to hunt through the assortment.

Use the scrollbar to see more icons, though they're all pretty unimaginative.

By the way, you can change your DOS program's icon if you like. Some details are offered in Chapter 7. A sidebar is even there on creating your own icon (though it's not as easy as it sounds).

9. **Click the** `Finish` **button.**

You're done. Now your program lives as a menu item on the Start thing's menu, and you can start it from there just as you can any other program in DOS, er, Windows.

10. **Click the** `Cancel` **button in the Taskbar Properties dialog box.**

This step closes that thing, which should have closed automatically anyway, getting it out of the way. Now you're *really* done.

Using Your New Software

To use the new program, type its name at the DOS prompt. A list of popular program names is provided in Chapter 2. If your program isn't on the list, type the name mentioned in the manual. (If nothing happens, refer to the section "Where Is My Program?" in Chapter 14.)

You complete this step just to make sure that the program works as advertised. If something doesn't work, don't be too quick to blame yourself. Programs have bugs. Keep in mind that the features of a new program aren't immediately obvious.

If anything out of the ordinary happens, do the following: Check with your computer supervisor or local computer guru. Check with the software developer (the help number should be listed somewhere in the manual or in the material that came with it). Finally, you can check with your dealer. Dealers try to be helpful, but for them to know the details of every piece of software they sell would be impossible. They can, however, replace defective disks for you.

Learning Your Software

Using software to get work done is why, unfortunately, we need computers. But using software involves learning its quirks. That takes time. So my first suggestion for learning any new software is to give yourself plenty of time.

Sadly, in today's rush-rush way of doing everything, time isn't that easy to come by. It's a big pain when the boss sends you down to the software store expecting you to come back and create something wonderful before the end of the day. In the real world, that's just not possible (not even if you're an "expert").

Most software comes with a workbook or a tutorial for you to follow. This is a series of self-guided lessons on how to use the product. It also tells you about the program's basic features and how they work.

I highly recommend going through the tutorials. Follow the directions on the screen. If you notice anything interesting, write it down in the tutorial booklet and flag that page.

Some tutorials are really dumb, granted. Don't hesitate to bail out of one if you're bored or confused. You can also take classes on using software, though they may bore you as well. Most people do, however, understand the program much better after the tutorial.

After doing the tutorial, play with the software. Make something. Try saving something to disk. Try printing. Then quit. Those are the basic few steps you should take when using any software program. Get to know it and then expand your knowledge from there as required.

If you feel bold, you can take a look at the manual. Who am I fooling? Computer manuals are awful. Sometimes they help, especially if the manual is a reference, enabling you to quickly thumb to what you want, read it, and then get right back out (like this book). But never read the manual all the way through.

> ✔ Some businesses may have their own training classes that show you the basics of using the in-house software. Take copious notes. Keep a little book for yourself with instructions for how to do what. Take notes whenever someone shows you something. Don't try to learn anything, just note what's done so you won't have to make a call should the situation arise again.

About the Darn Command Formats

Whenever you see a DOS command listed in a book or manual, you'll often see its *command format*. This is perhaps the most cryptic part about using DOS. The command format tells you what to type, what's optional, what's either/or-ish, and what everything does. If street signs were like this, every car in the world would be driving around those circle things in England right now.

The command format has three parts, though they're not separate:

- ✔ Requirements
- ✔ Options
- ✔ Switches

The *requirements* are items that you must type at the command line. Take the FORMAT command. Here is what its command format may look like:

```
FORMAT drive:
```

FORMAT is the name of the command. It's required. *Drive* (and a colon) is also required, but it's in italics. This means that you must type something there — something that means "drive" — but what you type is up to you. Here, *drive* means to put a drive letter (and a colon) there. This would be explained in the command's description: *Drive* is required and indicates a disk drive letter. For *drive* you would substitute A: or B:.

The following command contains an *option:*

```
VOL [drive:]
```

The VOL command is required. But anytime you see square brackets, it means that what comes between them is optional. In the preceding example, *drive* (and a colon) appears in brackets, meaning that a drive letter (and a colon) is optional after the VOL command. Again, this would be explained in the definition that follows the command format. It will also explain what happens if you don't specify the option.

Note that you do not specify the brackets when you type the command at the DOS prompt. Brackets are only a visual clue in the command format. Here's an example:

```
VOL B:
```

Here the volume label of the disk in drive B will be displayed. B: is the optional [*drive*:] part of the command, as specified in the preceding example (and without the brackets).

Here is a command format for the DEL command, which deletes files:

```
DEL filename [/P]
```

Here DEL and *filename* are both required. *Filename* indicates the name of the file you want to delete, which can be any file on your disk. The /P (slash-P) is a *switch,* and it's optional, appearing in brackets. What /P does and why you would want to list it would be listed in the instructions.

All switches start with either a slash or a dash, and most of them are optional. The typical switch is a single letter, and it can be either upper- or lowercase. Some switches are more than one letter, and some have options. Here's an example:

```
[/D=drive:]
```

That whole whatchamacallit is optional. The switch (/D) is followed by an equal sign and *drive,* which indicates that you must specify a disk drive letter (and a colon) in that spot. So /D is optional, but if you use it you have to fill in a disk drive letter.

Finally, there are optional either/or situations. These are options where you must specify either one switch or the other. This is written as follows:

```
[ON|OFF]
```

In this example, the item is optional because it's in brackets. If you specify it, you must either use ON or OFF, not both. The vertical bar or pipe character (|) tells you to pick one or the other if you want this option.

✔ These command formats are used in the official DOS manual, as well as in DOS's online "help." For more information about the online help, refer to Chapter 15.

✔ When a command requires a filename, it's often written in the following format:

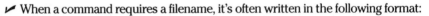

```
[drive:][path]filename
```

The filename part is required, but specifying a drive letter (the drive-colon) or a path or both is optional. The drive allows you to specify on which drive the file lives; the path is used to identify the file's subdirectory. More information about paths can be found in Chapter 11.

Chapter 6

Yechy Windows Stuff: Multitasking, Copying, and Pasting

• •

In This Chapter

▶ Switching between windows on the screen

▶ Using the Alt+Tab key combo to switch windows

▶ Organizing windows

▶ Ordering a DOS program to run "in the background"

▶ Copying text or graphics from a DOS window

▶ Pasting text into a DOS window

• •

*I*t may shock you to know that you can open up more than one DOS window at a time. Personally, I was stunned. It took several swigs of Mocha Java Spazzo to revive me. After all, several DOS windows at once would be forbidden in the old days. But under Windows, it's no big deal. It's almost like you live in Hawaii where all the windows (and doors) are open year round and no one ever notices or cares.

So imagine: You can have a DOS prompt window sitting there, a window with WordPerfect, a window with Lotus 1-2-3, and — providing your monitor is big enough or you're using teensy, tiny fonts — you can see them all work at once. That's the essence of multitasking, that's the reason why Microsoft is pushing Windows on the world (that, and the craving for another stock split).

Too Many DOS Windows on the Screen!

While having more than one DOS program running at once sounds great, my mother would remind me that too much of anything leads to clutter. And clutter is followed by mess, chaos, and eventually filth. So some cleanup is eventually required. Also, you'll need a way to switch between those windows if you ever expect to get more work done than you did using DOS one program at a time.

- Refer to "Oops! Firing up yet another DOS prompt" in Chapter 1 for information on starting more than one DOS prompt window on the screen.

- This information applies to both Windows and DOS programs — anything that's a window on the screen.

The old point-click-and-switch

If you have more than one window visible on the screen, you can switch between them using your mouse. Just point at the window you want to see "up front" and click the mouse button. That window instantly marches to the front.

A better way to do this, especially when the screen has too many windows or some windows hide behind others, is to use the taskbar. Just locate your window's button on the taskbar and click that button.

In Figure 6-1, three DOS programs are running: WordPerfect, DOS (an MS-DOS prompt window), and Magellan. To switch to the DOS window, you just point the mouse over there and click. But to switch to the almost-hidden WordPerfect window, you should click on its button on the taskbar.

Figure 6-1:
Three DOS
windows
are open
with three
programs in
them.

Nerds will note that DOS prompt windows all appear with the name DOS or MS-DOS Prompt on their taskbar buttons. However, if you've run a program from your DOS prompt window, its name follows DOS on the taskbar button. For example, it might say DOS-Q for a Quicken window when you've run Quicken from the prompt.

Switching between windows with Alt+Tab

One nifty way to switch between several running programs is to use the Alt+Tab key combination. The reason most people don't use this trick is that they must be taught properly:

> Press and hold the Alt key down. Keep it down. Then tap the Tab key once. Keep that Alt key down!

A box appears on the screen, showing you a list of open windows by their icons (see Figure 6-2).

Figure 6-2:
The thing
you see
when you
press
Alt+Tab.

Keep that Alt key down!

As you tap the Tab key, a highlight box moves left to right through the list of icons. Some text in the window tells you the name of the program that matches the icon.

All you need to do is release the Alt key to instantly switch to that window. So, as in the figure, if you want to switch to WordPerfect (the WP icon), you need to press the Tab key — while keeping the Alt key pressed — twice. When the WP icon is in the box, release both keys and you're instantly switched to that program.

✔ You can even switch this way if you're using a DOS program "full screen."

✔ If you find yourself switching back and forth between two windows, just press Alt+Tab — no need to keep the Alt key down. One press of Alt+Tab moves you back to whichever window you were dawdling in before. Then press Alt+Tab again to switch back. Back and forth. Back and forth. Alt+Tab switches Windows' attention like spectators' heads at a tennis match.

Arranging your windows just so

You can see two (or more) windows at one time by ordering Windows to arrange them for you. Here's how:

1. **Make sure the two (or more) windows you want to arrange are open on the screen.**

   Minimize all the other windows by clicking on their minimize buttons. (See Chapter 4 for more information on minimizing windows.)

   The Windows I want to arrange can be any size or in any position on the screen.

2. **Right-click the mouse on the taskbar.**

   Click the mouse on a blank part of the taskbar, not on a taskbar button.

   If there isn't any blank spot to click on, right-click the mouse on the current time, which appears to the far right on the taskbar.

   A right-click is where you click the mouse's right button, not the left one you normally click.

3. **A pop-up menu appears.**

   Lo, it's the taskbar shortcut menu, a copy of which is illustrated in Figure 6-3.

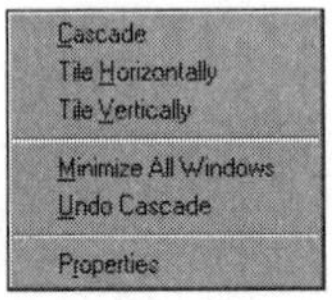

Figure 6-3:
The
taskbar's
shortcut
menu.

> Cascade
> Tile Horizontally
> Tile Vertically
> Minimize All Windows
> Undo Cascade
> Properties

If you right-clicked the mouse on the taskbar's time thing, you'll see an extra item at the top of the menu, `Adjust Date/Time`. Otherwise the menu is the same as the one shown in Figure 6-3.

4. **Choose Tile Horizontally or Tile Vertically from the menu.**

   If you choose Tile Horizontally, your windows are arranged each stacked above the other.

   If you choose Tile Vertically, your windows are arranged next to each other, right to left.

Either one of these actions may change the size and font of your window. Refer to Chapter 4 for more information on changing the font and size of a window (see the section "Fonts and Stuff").

Multitasking Mania

Multitasking is the ability to do more than one thing at a time. This confuses a lot of people. After all, who would want to do more than one thing at a time? It's mentally impossible (though I almost have the gum-chewing-while-walking thing down). And running more than one program at a time? You really need two sets of hands and eyes for that, not to mention an IQ that you could express only in scientific notation.

The secret is that multitasking is a boon to computers. They can do more than one thing at a time. Face it, most of the time when you use a computer you wait. You wait on your modem. You wait for the database to sort. You wait for a graphics program to render a modestly arousing GIF image. You wait, wait, wait, wait.

While you're waiting, the story goes, you could be doing something else. This whole kick got started in the mid- '80s with DOS's *memory resident programs*. So while you were spreadsheeting and someone called on the phone, you could *pop up* a message pad and take notes. Windows takes the concept to (what's supposed to be) a logical end; Windows naturally runs several things at once allowing you to get more and more work done. You work, work, work, work.

Whatever. It's just plain nice to be able to do more than one thing at once. This is especially true if you've been using DOS by itself and haven't yet meddled with the joys of multitasking — of downloading a file while you're sorting a database, while you're writing a nasty letter to the local paper. It can be fun, fun, fun, fun.

✔ Yes, *you* can do only one thing at a time. The computer can do more than one thing, which is the essence of multitasking.

✔ The thing you're doing is referred to as the *foreground task*. This is easy to remember since that window is often in front of all the other windows on the screen, ergo, in the *foreground*.

✔ **ergo** (ur' go) *conj*. **1.** And therefore; it follows that. **2.** The chief bad gorilla in the old *Planet of the Apes* TV series.

✔ All the other programs and windows you're not working on are in the *background*. Yeah, visually, this is also true: Those windows are usually buried beneath the one window in the foreground.

✔ The miracle of multitasking is that background windows contain programs that still run, even when you're not looking at them. Talk about loyalty. . . .

How to keep your DOS program running while you're not there

Your DOS programs and MS-DOS prompt window may or may not continue to toil and spin while you're off doing something else. The way to make sure your program continues to run while you're off paying attention to something else is to click on its Background button.

When the Background button is pressed, the program in your DOS window continues to hum along even when you're paying attention to something else.

When the Background button has not been pressed, the DOS program will "freeze" while you're off doing something else. No information will be lost, and everything will run once again when you switch to that window. But don't expect anything to happen, just like nothing ever happens to characters on a soap opera during the commercials.

✔ If you use your imagination, the image on the Background button kinda sorta looks like two overlapping windows. I suppose the dingbat in the background window is supposed to symbolize that the window contains a program still running. (All that supposition, and I swear I'm completely sober.)

✔ The following section contains a fun tutorial that possibly proves a DOS window can run "in the background."

The Multitasking Mania tutorial

Multitasking is one of those things you must *see* to believe. Oh, I could just resign myself to writing beautifully about it here, but a demo will really show you how it works.

The following tutorial has way too many steps for a *Dummies* book:

1. **Minimize all open windows.**

   Refer to Chapter 4 for information on minimizing. Just shrink everything down, or even quit some stuff you have laying around, like that game I see over there.

2. **Fire up a DOS prompt window.**

   See Chapter 2 for the details.

3. **Start a second DOS prompt window from the first.**

Type the following:

```
C> START COMMAND
```

Type START, a space, then COMMAND. Press the Enter key.

A window appears! Magic.

Now you should have two DOS windows on the screen.

4. Create a DOS batch file, BERSERK.BAT

This batch file contains a *loop,* which is programmer-speak for something that happens over and over again without any purpose — like a well-meaning government program with zero results.

Start creating the batch file by typing the following at the prompt:

```
C> COPY CON BERSERK.BAT
```

Type COPY, a space, CON, a space, BERSERK, period, BAT. Double-check your typing. Press the Enter key.

A blank line appears. Don't panic. You're using the COPY command to create a quick-and-dirty batch file using DOS's secret editor that I don't discuss elsewhere in this book (but information can be found in *MORE DOS For Dummies,* IDG Books Worldwide, if you care to look).

Type the following line:

```
@ECHO OFF
```

That's the @ character (Shift+2), ECHO, a space, OFF. Press Enter.

Type this in next:

```
:LOOP
```

Type a colon, not a semicolon, and the word LOOP. Press the Enter key.

Type the following:

```
ECHO I'm goin' nuts!
```

That's the word ECHO, a space, and the phrase *I'm goin' nuts!* Press Enter, and then type in the next line:

```
GOTO LOOP
```

Type GOTO, a space, then LOOP. Note that GOTO is all one word, not GO TO. Press the Enter key to end that line.

For the final line, press the F6 key on your keyboard. You'll see the following displayed:

```
^Z
```

That's a Control+Z character. For some reason, DOS accepts this character as the end-of-file mark. (Don't ask me why; I don't make this stuff up.)

Press the Enter key and you'll see something like the following:

```
1 file(s) copied
```

There. You've just finished creating the BERSERK.BAT batch file, a program of sorts. If you've never programmed a computer before, congratulations.

5. **Click on the Background button.**

   Click the mouse on the DOS window's Background button. Or just make sure the button looks pressed (not depressed).

6. **Run the batch file.**

   Type the following at the DOS prompt:

```
C> BERSERK
```

   Press the enter key and the BERSERK batch file runs. And runs. And runs. It just runs forever, which is what you want; something running that you can see in a background DOS window.

7. **Switch back to the first DOS window.**

   The quickest way in the universe to do this is to press Alt+Tab. Thwoop, you're back.

   With the first DOS window in the foreground, you should be able to see I'm goin' nuts scroll over and over in the other DOS window, the one in the background (see Figure 6-4). Ta-da! DOS is multitasking.

The BERSERK.BAT batch file, if you care to see it

Here is the entire BERSERK.BAT batch file, if you really want to see the whole thing all at once:

```
@ECHO OFF
```

```
:LOOP
ECHO I'm goin' nuts!
GOTO LOOP
```

Figure 6-4:
Multitasking
two DOS
windows.

✔ Stop the BERSERK.BAT program by pressing the Ctrl+Break key combination: Click the mouse in that window to bring it into the foreground, and then press Ctrl+Break. You'll see the following message:

```
Terminate batch job (Y/N)?
```

The message sounds more serious than it really is: Press the Y key. The batch file is done.

✔ If this demo doesn't appear to work, go back to step 5 and make sure that the Background button is pressed.

✔ Properly close both DOS windows when you're done.

✔ Quit your DOS windows by typing in the EXIT command:

```
C> EXIT
```

✔ The START command is one of the DOS-in-Windows new commands. It's described briefly in Chapter 2 as well as in Chapter 23, which lists a whole lotta DOS commands.

✔ If you click off the Background button, your DOS window will not continue to run in the background. Always make sure this button is pressed if you want your DOS program to run while you're doing something else.

✔ DOS programs can be preset to run in the background, which means you don't have to worry about pressing the button every time you open a window. Chapter 2 tells you how to preset a program to automatically run in the background.

Sharing Your Stuff

How could Windows be superior to DOS? Well, they say that you can easily share information between two programs. Microsoft gives this ability fancy and confusing names, but it's just sharing — like kindergarten. The truth is that it's nothing more than *cut and paste,* or in the case of a DOS window, it's always *copy and paste.*

REMEMBER

✔ You can copy text or graphics from your DOS window. It all depends on whether your DOS program runs in the text or graphics mode.

✔ You can paste only text into a DOS window.

✔ Whatever you copy can be pasted into any Windows program that accepts either text or graphics. Note that some Windows programs don't always accept both types: Paint accepts only graphical images; Notepad accepts only text, for example.

✔ Watch out for some DOS programs that display what looks like text but is really graphics. WordPerfect 6 is like that. Some utilities, such as PC Tools and Norton Utilities, also have graphical modes that look like text.

Copying from a DOS window

Follow these steps to copy something from any DOS window:

1. **Make sure what you want to copy is visible on the screen.**

   Once you start the next step, your DOS window "freezes." You cannot scroll your DOS window up or down to copy a larger piece of text.

2. **Click the Mark button.**

   The window title changes to read Mark - something. That, and the larger cursor you see in the upper-left corner of the window, are your clues that you're in mark-text mode.

   If you don't see the toolbar on your window, press Alt+Spacebar, E, K to enter Mark mode.

3. **Use the mouse to select a portion of your screen.**

   You're going to drag out a large rectangle on your DOS window to select text. Start by pointing at the upper-left corner of the text that you want to mark, and then drag down and to the right. This shows you what's being selected for copying. Figure 6-5 shows a chunk of text marked on the screen.

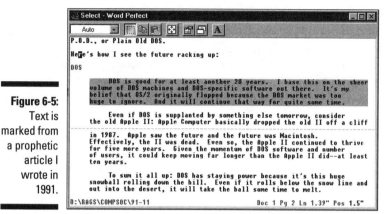

Figure 6-5:
Text is
marked from
a prophetic
article I
wrote in
1991.

- If you make a boo-boo marking the text, click the mouse and start dragging all over again.

- Marking text on a DOS screen is not like selecting text in a word processor. You can work only with a *rectangular* block. You may have to go back a few times to make sure that you get all the text marked in your rectangle.

 4. Click the Copy button.

This is all you can do here; you can't cut, so just click on the Copy button or press Ctrl+C.

The text or graphics you copied is saved in Windows' clipboard storage area for safe keeping. Now any other program that can accept a pasted-in text or graphics image can swallow what you just copied. For example, you can paste text into a word processor, paste graphics into Paint, and so on.

- If you change your mind, just press the Esc key to back out of Mark mode.

- Don't go off somewhere else and forget you're in Mark mode. If you do, your DOS program won't appear to work right when you return. Windows assumes you want to mark something when you're in Mark mode. Press the Esc key to get back to work.

- You cannot copy text from a full-screen, text-mode DOS program. Press Alt+Enter to switch to the graphical mode to do your copying.

Pasting a chunk o' text into a DOS window

Pasting text into a DOS window is cinchy. Just position the cursor where you want the text to appear and click the Paste button on the toolbar. The text is "typed" into the DOS window just as if you were typing it in yourself.

✔ If you can't see the toolbar, choose Alt+Spacebar, E, P to paste in the text.

✔ Don't use Ctrl+V, the Windows shortcut key for pasting stuff, in your DOS programs. It's your DOS program and not Windows that will "read" the Ctrl+V key press, possibly doing something like Voting or Violating or Vacating instead of V-Pasting.

✔ You cannot paste graphics into a DOS window. If you try, Windows displays a message telling you so.

✔ The text you paste can come from anywhere; a DOS program, Windows program, or random thoughts the computer fabricates.

Looking at text in the clipboard

Anything you cut or copy in Windows is saved in the clipboard. That's a special place in memory blah-blah-blah, and there's no need getting into that here.

What's kind of nifty about the clipboard is that you can see whatever's in there by using the special CLIPBRD preview program. You can start this program from the DOS prompt if you like. Type in the following:

```
C> CLIPBRD
```

Type CLIPBRD and press the Enter key. Windows runs the ClipBook Viewer program, similar to the one shown in Figure 6-6.

Figure 6-6:
The ClipBook Viewer shows you what's stored in Windows' clipboard.

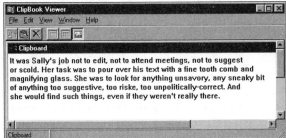

If you don't see the clipboard in the window, choose Window➪1. Clipboard from the menu. (The Local ClipBook is used for networking nonsense that I wouldn't bother touching if I were wearing a moon suit.)

OK. All you can do in the ClipBook Viewer is gawk. Press Alt+F4, the strange but useful key combination that closes any Windows program, to return to your DOS prompt window.

✔ If you upgraded from a previous version of Windows, typing CLIPBRD at the DOS prompt may activate the old Clipboard Viewer. Same diff, though there aren't multiple windows to worry about.

✔ Only one thing can be stored in the clipboard at a time. When you copy text, that text is stored in the clipboard. Copy another swatch of text and you replace whatever was in the clipboard before.

✔ It's a good idea to preview stuff in the clipboard when you're doing dicey work, such as pasting in a *long* bit of text. That way you can be sure what you're pasting in is really what you want.

The 5th Wave By Rich Tennant

"I SUPPOSE THIS ALL HAS SOMETHING TO DO WITH THE NEW MATH."

Chapter 7
Taming DOS Programs

● ●

In This Chapter

▶ Accessing the Properties dialog box

▶ Running your programs full screen when they start

▶ Changing a DOS program's icon

▶ Foiling the screen saver

▶ Editing (or not editing) CONFIG.SYS and AUTOEXEC.BAT

▶ Creating a startup batch file for your DOS window

▶ Running programs in MS-DOS-Only mode

● ●

DOS programs in Windows must behave. They have to. Especially since DOS programs are notorious for being ill-behaved. I'm not implying that DOS programs are nasty or vindictive or in any way evil (forgiving WordPerfect for a moment here). I'm saying DOS programs are rude in that they all think they "own" the whole computer when they run.

Windows tries to appease greedy DOS programs as best it can. Often it succeeds, and you never really need to tame any of your DOS software. In fact, reading this chapter is a very optional thing. But when you grow in the mood for beating down a former prideful DOS program, or if having that extra control gives you a power rush, the following information on a DOS program's Properties dialog box will be of use to you.

Configuring Your DOS Program (the "Properties" Deal)

It seems like everything in Windows has a Properties dialog box attached to it. This box is where you can tweak and muss with just about any part of Windows, sometimes with dreadful consequences.

⊳ Though all DOS programs use the same Properties dialog box, the settings you make affect only the DOS program to which the Properties dialog box is attached.

✔ In the olden days, you controlled DOS programs in Windows with PIF files. Thank goodness they've done away with those.

✔ One whole "panel" in your DOS program's Properties dialog box is devoted to setting fonts. See "Fonts and Stuff" in Chapter 4 for more information.

✔ Most Properties dialog boxes are accessed through a program or icon's shortcut menu: Right-click the mouse on the icon or while pointing at some part of Windows (the desktop or taskbar, for example) and up pops the shortcut menu. The last item in the menu is usually Properties, which brings up a Properties dialog box for eternal fiddling.

Ode to seeing a DOS program's Properties dialog box

Twas in the early morning,

Noshing on cream cheese and lox,

The sudden urge fell on me

To see a DOS program's Properties dialog box.

I wanted to configure,

I felt like messing around.

 So click upon a little button did I,

And the Properties dialog box was found.

And, lo, there sits a DOS icon,

Floating on the Windows desktop.

To see its Properties dialog box I right-click the mouse

And up a shortcut menu doth pop.

Peering at each little item,

I finally spy the one that I need.

Sitting right there on the bottom,

It's the Properties dialog box command, indeed.

✔ To get at the Properties dialog box, click the Properties button on your DOS program's toolbar.

✔ If you can't see the toolbar, press Alt+Spacebar, P.

✔ Make sure you don't confuse the Properties button with the Background button. I always do. But if you're a rabid Windows user, you'll notice that the Properties button on your DOS program's toolbar is identical to other Properties buttons on various Windows programs. Not that that's consoling or anything.

✔ See Chapter 6 for more information about the Background button.

✔ To see the Properties dialog box for any DOS program icon, point the mouse at that icon and click the *right* mouse button. This brings up a shortcut menu for the icon. Choose the last item, P̲roperties, from the menu.

✔ When you access the Properties dialog box from an icon, a new panel appears: General. This panel is common to all Windows programs and contains general information about the program, technical stuff, and trivia. Feel free to ignore.

✔ By the way, you can find DOS program icons floating on the desktop, in a My Computer window or by using the Explorer.

✔ When you're done with the Properties dialog box, click the OK button with the mouse if you want to keep your changes. If you don't like the changes, click the `Cancel` button or press the Esc key to make the Properties dialog box go away.

✔ In some instances, the `Apply` button will be available. Clicking on it allows you to preview your changes, but only when you're allowed to do so (which isn't that often). If you like the changes, remember to click the `OK` button to lock them in; otherwise, click `Cancel`.

✔ Did you leave the iron on?

"I want to make my DOS program run in the text screen when it starts"

Tired of pressing Alt+Enter to switch your DOS windows to text screen? Just whip up that program's Properties dialog box (as discussed in the preceding section) and click the mouse on the Screen tab. You'll see the Screen panel, as shown in Figure 7-1.

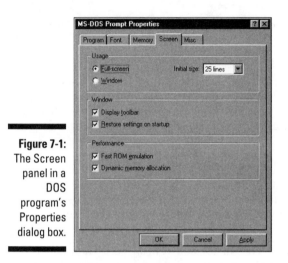

Figure 7-1:
The Screen
panel in a
DOS
program's
Properties
dialog box.

Click the mouse in the hole by Full screen or press Alt+F. This option directs Windows to run your DOS program in the text mode — full screen — just as it would had Windows not grown up to take over the world.

"I want my DOS program's window to close when it's done"

Summon your DOS program's Properties dialog box, and in the Program panel (see Figure 7-2) look near the bottom for the Close on exit box. Click the mouse in that box to put a check mark there, or press Alt+X. That option tells Windows to close the DOS window when your program is done.

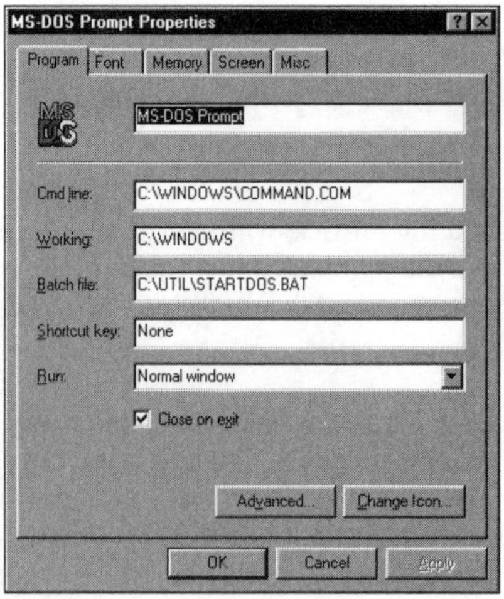

Figure 7-2:
The
Program
panel in the
Properties
dialog box.

✔ Putting a check mark in the box will not automatically close a DOS prompt window. To close it, type the EXIT command at the prompt.

✔ Typically, DOS games may not close when they're done, though I've seen other DOS programs just hang there with a "dead" window when they're done.

✔ Refer to the section "Ode to seeing a DOS program's Properties dialog box" for information on getting to a DOS program's Properties dialog box.

"How do I change my DOS program's icon?"

To put something other than the silly MS-DOS icon on your DOS program, conjure up your program's Properties dialog box. The Program panel should be forward, as in Figure 7-2. If not, click on the Program tab with your mouse.

Click on the Change Icon button, or press Alt+C. The handy but disappointing Change Icon dialog box is displayed, as in Figure 7-3. From here you can pluck out a new icon for your program — but don't expect to find anything wonderful and ideally suited to your program's intent in the list. Here are a coupla suggestions:

Figure 7-3:
The Change
Icon dialog
box.

✔ Use the scrollbar or press the → or Y keys to see the icons in the list.

✔ Yup, all of them are as stupid as the umbrella and thunderstorm you see in the figure. I mean, don't those people who work at Microsoft have any respect for DOS applications?

✔ You can click on the Browse button to open another group of icons if what you see in the list disappoints you. And it will.

✔ If you click the Browse button, look for a file named MORICONS.DLL or maybe MORICONS. (It's in the Windows folder.) This file contains icons more suitable to DOS programs; however, you may only have this file if you upgraded your PC from an older version of Windows.

✔ See your favorite Windows book for more information on using the Browse dialog box.

✔ You can also create your own icons, which is covered in the sidebar, "Building a better icon."

When you've found the icon of your dreams, click the OK button to return to the DOS program's Properties dialog box. You'll see the new icon displayed in the upper-left corner of the Program panel.

Click OK to accept the new icon and close the Properties dialog box. Or, if you're utterly disgusted, click Cancel.

- ✔ Your new icon appears only in Windows. The icon has nothing to do with your DOS program at all.

- ✔ Some DOS programs come with their own icon files: WordPerfect, Magellan, and PC Tools on my computer have them. You can use the Browse button to locate these files, which should be in the same directory (i.e., "folder") as the main program file.

- ✔ The DOS program's icon is used in the Explorer, in My Computer, in the Start menu, and when you paste an icon to the desktop.

- ✔ See "Ode to seeing a DOS program's Properties dialog box" earlier in this chapter for more information on displaying the Properties dialog box.

Building a better icon

The icons that Windows shows you for your DOS programs are so disappointing. But don't think designing your own icon is any better; while those DOS icons may be silly, they sure are good looking. Still, don't let any lack of artistic ability discourage you from rolling your own icon. This effort does require a knowledge of Windows' Paint program, and it is a nerdy thing to do, which is why Mr. Dummyman is sitting up there.

1. **Start the Paint program.**

   It's in the Accessories sub-menu off the Start thing's Programs menu.

2. **In the Paint program, choose Image⇨Attributes or press Ctrl+E.**

   This displays the Attributes dialog box. Type **32** into the Width box. Press the Tab key. Type **32** into the Height box. Press Alt+P to ensure these numbers are measurements in pixels (Pels), not inches. (An icon is 32 x 32 pixels in size.) Click OK.

3. **Draw your icon in the tiny box.**

   You can use the Zoom tool (or press Alt+V, Z, L) to see the image in more detail. Use the paint tools to create your icon. Go ahead! Be creative! (This is the tough part.)

4. **Save your image to disk.**

   Then quit the Paint program.

5. **Follow the suggestions in the section "How do I change my DOS program's icon?" for using the Browse button.**

   In the Browse dialog box, choose All Files from the List files of type drop-down list. Locate your Paint program icon file. (It has the extension .BMP, in case you need to know that.)

6. **When you find the file, click OK in the Browse dialog box, and then click OK in the Change Icon dialog box.**

   Lo, your newly created icon is put to use.

"Windows' screen saver bugs me"

If Windows is set up to blank the screen after a few minutes, you may be unpleasantly annoyed by the fact that its screen saver also blanks out your DOS programs — even when they're running in full-screen mode. Whether this blanking bothers you, or whether you think it's a cool feature you want to keep, it's controlled from the same place.

Beckon your DOS program's Properties dialog box and click the mouse on the Misc tab to bring that panel forward. Look for the item called Allow screen saver in the upper-left corner of that panel. Click in the box by that item to put a check mark there, activating the screen saver. Or if you want the screen saver off, click in the box to remove the check mark.

Click OK to make this setting permanent.

- A check mark = the screen saver is on for your DOS program.
- Refer to your favorite Windows book for information on the screen saver.

"My DOS program uses the Alt+Tab key combination, but Windows steals it away!"

In the Properties dialog box, Misc panel, on the bottom, in MS Sans Serif 8 point font, you'll find a list of seven key combinations that Windows uses for various tasks (see Figure 7-4). I've listed them in Table 7-1, since I haven't made any tables in a while and this book is woefully bereft of tables.

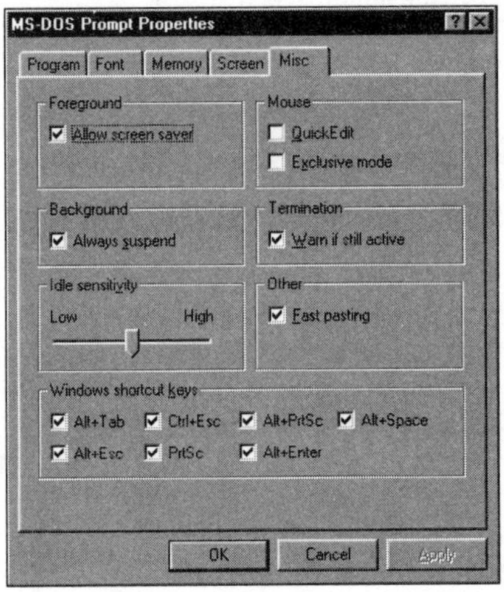

Figure 7-4: The Misc panel in the Properties dialog box.

A problem crops up when your DOS program wants to use one of those key combos. When you press, say, Alt+Tab, Windows takes over and your DOS program never sees the Alt+Tab key pressed. To avoid that problem, you can tell Windows which of the key combos you want it to ignore and, instead, let your DOS program use.

Removing the check mark tells Windows to let your DOS program use the key combination.

Be careful with this command! When you remove a key combination, you also remove a Window command. Remove Alt+Tab, and it's harder to switch (multitask) from a full-screen DOS program. Remove Alt+Space, and you can't access the control menu from the keyboard. You've been warned.

Table 7-1	Windows key combos your DOS program obeys
Key Combo	*Function*
Alt+Tab	Switches from one task, or running program, to another; displays a list of tasks
Alt+Esc	Switches to the next task
Ctrl+Esc	Pops up the Start thing menu
PrtSc	Copies the screen as a bitmap image to the clipboard
Alt+PrtSc	Copies the foreground window as a bitmap image to the clipboard
Alt+Enter	Switches the DOS program between full screen (text) and windowed mode (graphics)
Alt+Space	Pulls down the control menu

"I get my window just right, and then Windows forgets everything next time I open it up"

If you're fussy about your font size, window position, and other esoteric matters, you should tell Windows to remember those things each time it starts up your DOS program's window. To meet that end, muster the DOS program's Properties dialog box and click on the Screen tab to bring that panel forward.

Near the middle of the box you'll find an option titled Restore settings on startup. If a check mark appears in that box, Windows remembers all your font, screen, and other settings each time you open that program's window.

To put a check mark in the box, click the mouse there or press Alt+R. Removing the check mark causes Windows to forget those things.

Some Settings That May Amuse You

For the most part, you really don't need to mess with your DOS program's Properties dialog box. Even so, there are a few things you may find yourself fiddling with (in addition to those already mentioned earlier in this chapter).

Changing a window name

No biggie here, but the first box of text in the Program panel of the Properties dialog box contains the name that Windows slaps onto the top of your DOS program's window. (It says MS-DOS Prompt in Figure 7-2). Anything you type in that box becomes the title of your DOS program's window.

The definition of a "working" directory

You would assume all the computer's directories work, but that has nothing to do with the box in the Program panel of the Properties dialog box (see Figure 7-2). That box contains the name of the directory or folder where your program's data files are.

Normally the directory name is the same as the name found in the box right above, Cmd line (which means Command line, by the way). It doesn't have to be that way. For example, if you're fiddling with 1-2-3 and you keep all your 1-2-3 files in the WORK directory, type **WORK** into that box. That way 1-2-3 starts out using that directory.

The same thing can be done with the DOS prompt window. If you want DOS to start itself at C:\ (the root directory of drive C), type **C:** into the Working box.

The automatic choice for memory

Memory management shouldn't be a problem under Windows. Your DOS programs will steal as much memory as they need and Windows will give it up — provided you have all the automatic settings made in the Properties dialog box's Memory panel.

If you dare to go there, just make sure the word Auto appears anywhere and everywhere. There is really no reason to change that setting, at least none that I've seen in all my long days.

Whatever Happened to CONFIG.SYS and AUTOEXEC.BAT?

Two important DOS startup files are CONFIG.SYS and AUTOEXEC.BAT. They're important to DOS, but Windows could just care less. Only when the occasional program begs you to modify them are they a thorn in your side, and that's pretty rare.

With the dawn of Windows 95, the roles of CONFIG.SYS and AUTOEXEC.BAT have been diminished. The Windows 95 installation program modified these files for you, and you really shouldn't change anything with them. So while they do exist, they aren't for editing — not anymore.

- ✔ But should you mess with your CONFIG.SYS or AUTOEXEC.BAT files? In a word, *no*. Don't change 'em. Don't touch. Don't fuss.

- ✔ If you desperately need to edit CONFIG.SYS or AUTOEXEC.BAT to get your DOS game to run, see the section "The Secret of Running MS-DOS-Only Programs" near the end of this chapter.

- ✔ The rings around Uranus were discovered in 1978.

"But my program tells me to edit my CONFIG.SYS or AUTOEXEC.BAT file!"

Even if your program insists you edit CONFIG.SYS or AUTOEXEC.BAT, it's wrong. Your program probably doesn't know about Windows 95, and it should not mess with those files.

The leading culprits here are some disk-intensive programs that want you to change the FILES= number in CONFIG.SYS. Your manual may see "Make sure you have FILES=50 or higher in your CONFIG.SYS file." Whatever. Such a change should not be necessary under Windows 95.

Another thing to remember: Some new hardware you might install may come with a DOS installation disk. This installation program may modify CONFIG.SYS or AUTOEXEC.BAT. Avoid using it! Instead, use the Add New Hardware wizard in the Control Panel to have Windows update itself; from the Start menu, choose Settings⇨Control Panel, double-click the mouse on the Add New Hardware icon, and obey the wizard.

Creating an AUTOEXEC.BAT-like file for each of your DOS windows

Even though AUTOEXEC.BAT's role is gone, it can still be useful to have a startup batch file to help customize your MS-DOS prompt window. (Gads, I detest calling it an *MS-DOS prompt window!*)

You specify such a batch file in your DOS program's Properties dialog box. In the first panel, Programs, there is a box titled Batch File. Into that box you type the name of the batch file you want to run each time you start that DOS window.

For example, in Figure 7-2, you see the STARTDOS.BAT file in the Batch File box. That batch file runs every time I start a DOS prompt window. (See the following section for the details.) The batch file is saved in the C:\UTIL directory, which is why you see that *pathname* displayed in the box.

If I wanted a specific batch file to run with WordPerfect, I'd open up WordPerfect's Properties dialog box and specify the batch file there.

 ✔ See Chapter 11 for more information on pathnames.

 ✔ The next section contains some brief information on the kind of batch file you might want to specify for your DOS windows. Just move your eyeballs down a hair and start reading.

A sample of one of those startup batch files

The best thing to put in your DOS window's start up batch file are any commands you find yourself typing every time you start your DOS window. Just take those commands and stick them all in a batch file — and have Windows run it for you automatically.

There is only one command I routinely type when I start a DOS window: I run the DOSKEY command, which allows for better editing of the command line.

Here is my STARTDOS.BAT batch file:

```
@ECHO OFF
DOSKEY /INSERT
```

That's it. Two lines.

The first line is `@ECHO OFF`, which is the traditional way all batch files are begun. What that command does is prevent the batch file from spewing mysterious text all over the screen. A nice thing not to have happen.

The second command activates the DOSKEY command line editor and puts it into the INSERT mode.

Those two commands are two lines in a text file I created and saved to disk as STARTDOS.BAT. DOS then runs them every time a DOS window starts, saving me the time and trouble of typing them myself.

- ✔ Another type of startup batch file may run a calendar program, dial up MCI Mail for you, check your appointments, display a menu, or do any of a number of things you may have to manually type in yourself every time you start a DOS window. All you need to do is stick those same commands into a batch file and let the computer do the work.

- ✔ You use a text editor to create a batch file. Just stick all the command lines in the text file, each on a line by itself. Chapter 8 tells you how to create and edit text files.

- ✔ When you save a batch file to disk, you must give it the .BAT file extension. For this reason, it's best to create a batch file using DOS's editor, not a Windows editor. (The Windows editors save all files to disk as text or document files.)

- ✔ Chapter 6 shows a sample batch file, BERSERK.BAT, which you can look at as another example of a DOS batch file. Don't specify BERSERK.BAT as your DOS window's startup batch file, though. (See Chapter 6 and you'll understand why.)

- ✔ A batch file is nothing more than a collection of DOS command lines, one on top of the other. These command lines are "typed" by DOS when you run the batch file.

- ✔ For more information on batch files, refer to *MORE DOS For Dummies,* also from IDG Books Worldwide. If you can find it, a book I wrote a few years back covers batch files in marvelous detail and still applies to DOS-in-Windows today. Look for *Batch Files and Beyond* from Windcrest/McGraw-Hill, ISBN 0-8306-4384-2. (Good luck!)

- ✔ The DOSKEY command is also covered in *MORE DOS For Dummies,* which means you should probably rush out and buy that book right now before the nerdy-looking guy down the block snatches the last copy.

The Secret of Running MS-DOS-Only Programs

Windows has a special "I forgive you, DOS" mode for running some especially stubborn DOS programs. It's called the MS-DOS-Only mode and what it does is essentially shut down Windows and run your DOS program all by itself — just like the olden days.

To run a program in the Only mode, bid thy DOS program's Properties dialog box come hither. In the Program panel, click on the Advanced button. You'll see the Advanced Program Settings dialog box, as shown in Figure 7-5.

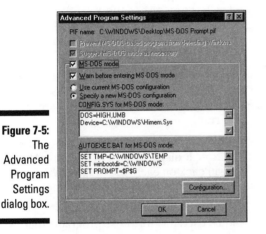

Figure 7-5:
The
Advanced
Program
Settings
dialog box.

The setting you need to make here is MS-DOS mode, as shown in Figure 7-5. Click the mouse in that box, or press Alt+M, to put a check mark there. Also make sure a check is in the box by Warn before entering MS-DOS mode. The other settings you can mess with at your own peril.

Whenever you run an MS-DOS-Only program, Windows shuts down. Your computer is actually reset and started in MS-DOS mode, where your program runs as King RAM Hog of the Computer. Obviously this is ideal for those programs that want Windows way out of the way.

One example of such a program is the UNDELETE program, which you may have on your PC if you upgraded to Windows 95 from a previous version of DOS or Windows. When you type UNDELETE at the DOS prompt, you see the warning dialog box, as shown in Figure 7-6. If you press Enter or click on the Yes button, all of Windows shuts down so that UNDELETE can run.

Figure 7-6:
The warning
displayed
when an
MS-DOS-
Only
program
runs.

UNDELETE (dos)

⚠ This program is set to run in MS-DOS mode and cannot run while other programs are running. All other programs will close if you choose to continue.

Do you want to continue?

[Yes]   No

✔ My advice: Don't bother with DOS's UNDELETE command. See Chapter 9 for more information.

✔ When you check the box by Warn before entering MS-DOS mode, Windows displays a message telling you the program is an MS-DOS-Only program and that Windows will shut down if you continue. It's really a lovely thing to see.

✔ The two boxes at the bottom of the Advanced Program Settings dialog box allow you to build custom CONFIG.SYS and AUTOEXEC.BAT files for your DOS session. Just click the mouse in either box to edit, though you really, *really* need to know what you're doing before attempting this.

✔ Better than editing CONFIG.SYS and AUTOEXEC.BAT in the dialog box, click on the Configuration button. It displays a list of common MS-DOS program wants and needs. You can click on each one to have Windows automatically configure your DOS program without having to mess with CONFIG.SYS or AUTOEXEC.BAT.

✔ The MS-DOS-Only mode should be used just for those programs that cannot, will not, or should not be run with Windows. This category includes some demanding games plus perhaps other software that you may not want to multitask for whatever reason.

✔ Most games — including Doom — run fine in Windows 95 without the MS-DOS-Only mode. You need to run those programs full screen, however. And it helps to have oodles of memory.

Chapter 8

Editing DOS Text Files

* *

In This Chapter

▶ Summoning a Windows editor

▶ Using the DOS Editor

▶ Editing a file already on disk

▶ Printing a file

▶ Quitting the Editor

* *

*O*ne of the most useful tools available with DOS (at least starting with versions 5.0 several years ago) is the Editor, which is called EDIT (because the word "Ed" was trademarked long ago by the Mr. Ed people). This program works like a word processor, enabling you to create and edit text files on disk. Although it lacks the full-blown power of a major word processor, DOS's Editor does contain some nice features and can be used in a variety of situations when a word processor is just too clunky. For example, rumor has it that Elvis answers all his fan mail using the DOS EDIT program.

This chapter covers using the DOS Editor program. As a bonus, I've also tossed in some brief info on using Windows' own editors from the DOS prompt. Why? Because sometimes you just need a graphical editor and, by god, I'm not going to leave it out of this book.

Summoning a Windows Editor

Windows has one text editor and one mini-word processor. The text editor is named Notepad and the mini-word processor is named WordPad.

You can use either Notepad or WordPad to create *text files* on disk. These are files that contain text only — no formatting or page numbers or footnotes or anything impressive. Just text. And while you may ponder why anyone would want a text-only file, the reality is that lots of programs use or require a text-only file. So there.

You can start either Notepad or WordPad from any DOS prompt window by typing in their names. Here's how you would start Notepad:

```
C> NOTEPAD
```

Type NOTEPAD and press the Enter key. The Notepad text editor appears on the screen in its own window.

Here's how you would start WordPad:

```
C> WORDPAD
```

Type WORDPAD and press the Enter key. Like Notepad, the WordPad mini-word processor appears in its own window on the screen. Or maybe not. If you get a Bad command or file name error message, try this instead:

```
C> WRITE
```

Type WRITE and press Enter. Write was the name of Windows old mini-word processor, and typing in its name actually runs WordPad.

- You'll need to refer to your favorite book on Windows for more information on how these text editors work. Even so, instructions for using them are littered throughout the rest of this chapter.

- If you want to use the Notepad to read one of those README.TXT files, you type the following:

```
C> NOTEPAD README.TXT
```

Follow NOTEPAD (or WORDPAD, if you prefer to use it) with a space and the name of the file you want to edit or view.

- When you save a file using WordPad, be sure to save it as a text document. Use the Save as type drop down list in WordPad's Save As dialog box and choose Text Document from the list.

- WordPad actually doesn't like to save files in the text format. It may vex you about this with various dialog boxes. Ensure that you always choose Text Document as the type of file you want to save.

- WordPad doesn't run on most computers because you need to be *logged* to the C:\PROGRAM FILES\ACCESSORIES directory. Instructions on how to log to various directories are offered in Chapter 11.

- You cannot use Notepad or WordPad to create batch files. Those files must be saved with the .BAT extension, and neither program will let you do that. (You can save the file and rename it using DOS, but that's a pain.) It's best to create batch files using DOS's Editor.

Using the DOS Editor

DOS comes with a program called EDIT, which you can use to sanely create or edit *text files* on disk.

EDIT works like a word processor, but it lacks many of the fancier features — like the capability to print interesting fonts, apply fancy formatting, spell check, create graphics, and so on. However, for just writing text — plain ol' English — EDIT is a fine and dandy thing to have. And you'll find yourself using it often in your DOS travels.

> ✔ You may or may not have the EDIT program on your computer. If you've upgraded to Windows 95 from an earlier version of DOS or Windows, you probably have it. But maybe not. The only way to know for sure is to see the next section.

> ✔ A *text file* is a file that contains only text — no fancy information, no Greek or any other unorthodox or unreadable stuff. For example, files you can see by using the TYPE command are text files (see "Looking at files" in Chapter 1).

> ✔ If you were used to the old DOS text editor EDLIN, panic! There is no more EDLIN! The program that upgraded your PC to Windows 95 may have also deleted EDLIN from your computer. Sniff, sniff. Farewell. Au revoir. Good riddance!

Starting the Editor

You start the DOS Editor by typing **EDIT** at the DOS prompt:

```
C> EDIT
```

After pressing Enter, you'll see the Editor's start-up screen, as shown in Figure 8-1. Press the Esc key, and you'll be ready to start typing.

If you want to start the Editor in another window, type the following command:

```
C> START EDIT
```

Type START, a space, EDIT, and press Enter. This opens another DOS window on the screen with a copy of the Editor in it. Why bother? Because you can!

> ✔ When you start the Editor, it gives you the dreadful "blank page," that same mind-numbing concept that has induced writer's block in generations of scriveners. Some things just don't change.

> ✔ Refer to the section "Editing the text" later in this chapter for tutorial typing tips.

✔ If you don't see the DOS Editor, or you get a Bad command or file name error message, it's time to contact someone else for help. Double-check the instructions here first. Also, make sure to tell the person that you've already tried to do it yourself. Even the most surly of computer wizards appreciate effort.

✔ See Chapter 6 on multitasking for information on handling multiple DOS program windows — if you dare.

Figure 8-1:
The DOS
Editor in
action.

Starting the Editor to edit a file

If you know the name of the text file you want to edit, you can follow EDIT with that filename. For example, if you felt a burning desire to edit the text file BLORF.TXT, you would type the following:

```
C> EDIT BLORF.TXT
```

First comes EDIT, a space, and then the name of the text file you want to edit, BLORF.TXT, as shown in the preceding line.

If the file already exists, the Editor will load it from disk, displaying it on the screen ready for editing. If the file doesn't exist, the Editor lets you create it from scratch.

✔ Most text files end with the .TXT extension. I use .TXT when I create or save a text file because that extension lets me know a file is a text file. Windows also relies upon this extension to identify text documents. Refer to Chapter 12 for more information on filename extensions.

✔ If you want to edit a file with a long filename, remember to enclose that filename in double quotes:

```
C> EDIT "I must remember something shorter"
```

The file named I MUST REMEMBER SOMETHING SHORTER is loaded for editing in the editor. (You can also use the file's shorter name, which can be seen with the DIR command.)

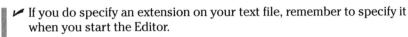

✔ If you do specify an extension on your text file, remember to specify it when you start the Editor.

✔ To quit the Editor, refer to the section "Quitting the Editor," later in this chapter.

✔ Another file to use with the Editor is README.TXT, the "read me" file included with most new software packages. You can easily view such files using the Editor. PgUp, PgDn at your leisure or print the whole ding-dang-doodle.

Editing the text

You use the Editor to either create a new file or edit a text file already on disk. This tutorial shows you how to create a new file on disk. Because you may be dry on ideas, I'm providing a sample file, though you should feel free to type in anything you like (a list of suggestions is nearby).

Start by firing up the Editor to work with a sample file. The one I've created is called ARNOLD.TXT. Here is the DOS command to use for creating ARNOLD.TXT in the Editor:

```
C> EDIT ARNOLD.TXT
```

Type in the EDIT command, followed by a space, and then the name of the file you want to edit, such as ARNOLD.TXT. Press Enter.

If the ARNOLD.TXT file already exists, you'll see it on your screen. Otherwise, you'll have to type in the file's contents. The following is what I typed in for my ARNOLD.TXT file:

```
Hercules
Joe Santo
Conan
Terminator
Kalidor
Dutch
Ben Richards
Ivan Danko
Julius Benedict
Mr. Kimble
Quaid
```

Here are some general Editor typing and editing rules:

✔ Press Enter at the end of each line.

✔ No "word wrap" is available in the Editor (though it is in Notepad and WordPad).

✔ Use the Backspace key to back up and erase if you make a mistake.

✔ You can type long lines if you like, though they'll "scroll" to the right across the screen. Typing more than a screenful of text causes the Editor to scroll down.

✔ Lines of text in the Editor can be up to 255 characters long; the entire text file can be utterly huge — a size so boggling you'd have to be a pretty darn prolific writer to see the `Editor full` error message.

A list of Editor key commands, specifically those that move the cursor around, is shown in Table 8-1. Test these commands out. Press Ctrl+End to move to the end of your text, Ctrl+Home to move to the start, Ctrl+→ to move right a word, and Ctrl+← to move left, and so on. Play, play, play!

Table 8-1	Editor key commands
Key Command	*Function*
↑ (Up arrow)	Move the cursor up one line
↓ (Down arrow)	Move the cursor down one line
← (Left arrow)	Move the cursor left (back) one character
→ (Right arrow)	Move the cursor right (forward) one character
PgUp	Move up to the previous page (screen)
PgDn	Move down to the next page (screen)
Ctrl+←	Move left one word
Ctrl+→	Move right one word
Ctrl+↑	Scroll the screen up one line
Ctrl+↓	Scroll the screen down one line
Delete	Delete current character
Backspace	Delete previous character
Insert	Switch between insert and overwrite editing modes
Ctrl+Home	Beginning of file
Ctrl+End	End of file

✔ WordPad and Notepad use key commands similar to those in Table 8-1.

✔ You can also use your mouse to position the cursor on the screen: Point the mouse where you want the cursor to be and click it once to move the cursor to that very spot.

✔ To save your all-important text file, refer to the section, "Saving your stuff to disk." Remember: Always save before you quit!

Playing with blocks

You can mark text in the Editor and treat that text as a single unit — a block, with which you can have lots of fun. For example, you can copy a block of text, cut and paste it, or just zap it all to kingdom come. There are two ways to mark a block:

1. **Use your mouse to *drag* over the text you want marked as a block.**

2. **Hold down the Shift key and use the arrow keys to mark the block.**

Suggestions for sample files to type

Drumming up ideas for sample text files to type in is the bane of the computer book author. I've seen some real losers in my time. To assist my fellow authors, as well as budding MS-DOS Editor enthusiasts, the following list contains some suggestions for li'l sample text files you can type in. Only titles are offered; it's up to you to devise content.

Four famous-but-not-dead people I'd like to invite over for dinner

Nasty nicknames for the losers on those hair-loss TV commercials

What if Democrats ran the afterlife

Thoughts Freud might have on the things I doodle when I talk on the phone

If I were in charge of building a VCR, what I would put on the knobs

Why walking through a sandbox with wet socks on makes my skin crawl

Ten common, household objects a 2-year-old could stick in his ear

A promo for the new *Sports Illustrated* famous groin injuries football video

Ten things you'd find in an airplane lavatory

Several convincing reasons why aliens would prefer to land in your state instead of anyplace else.

Either way, the marked block appears highlighted on the screen, typically shown with inverse text (such as blue text on a white background). After that block is highlighted, you can do the following things to it:

- ✔ Press Ctrl+C to copy the block, and then move the cursor to where you want to paste the copy and press Ctrl+V to paste it.

- ✔ Press Ctrl+X to cut the block, making it vanish from the screen. Move the cursor to where you want to paste the block, and then press Ctrl+V to paste it.

- ✔ Yes, these are the same Ctrl+C, Ctrl+X, and Ctrl+V keys used in Windows for Copy, Cut, and Paste.

- ✔ Alas, there is no Ctrl+Z "undo" command for the Editor. (Notepad and WordPad have it.)

- ✔ Delete the block by pressing the Delete key.

Searching and Replacing

To search for a specific tidbit of text in your document, press Alt+S, F. This move drops down the Search menu and selects the Find command. A magical box then appears, where you can type in the text you're looking for. Type **Uruguay** to find all references to that South American nation. Press Enter to scope it out.

- ✔ The Find command locates text from the cursor's position to the end of the document. If the text isn't found, Find then starts looking at the start of the document. And if the text doesn't exist, you'll see an `Edit was unable to find a match` box displayed. Sigh deeply and press the Esc key.

- ✔ To find the next occurrence of your text tidbit, press the F3 key.

Information about the Editor not worth reading

The Editor uses drop-down menus to contain its commands. You activate the menu by pressing Alt and then the first letter of the menu you want to use. You can also press both the Alt key and the letter key at the same time; Alt+F drops down the File menu.

Each menu contains menu items, all of which pertain somehow to the title of the menu. For example, the File menu contains file commands. You select these commands by typing the highlighted letter in their name.

If you have a mouse, you can select menu items with it. This involves using a whole lot of mousy terms, which I don't really care to get into in this book.

Printing with the Editor

To print your prose, use the Print command found in the File menu. Start by making sure you have a printer turned on and all ready to print. Then press Alt+F to get the File menu; then press P for the Print command. You'll see a li'l box displayed on the screen. Press Enter to print your whole ding-dang file. Zip, zip, zip. It's done.

✔ If the printer isn't turned on, or it's goofy or something, you'll see a *Printer error on LPT1* type of error box. Fix the printer and try again.

Printing Any Text File without Having to Bother with the Editor

You can print any text file by using the DOS Editor to edit it and then using the Editor's Print command as described above. You can also print any file at the handy DOS prompt by using the following command:

```
C> COPY ARNOLD.TXT PRN
```

Yes, this is the typical COPY command, which in this case is used to print the text file ARNOLD.TXT. First comes COPY, a space, and then the name of the file you want to print. Follow the file's name with another space, and then PRN. Make sure your printer is on and ready to print, and then press Enter.

✔ The COPY-PRN command can be used to print any text file on disk, not just those created by the Editor. These are the same files you can view with the TYPE command. Refer to Chapter 2 in the section "Looking at Files."

✔ You might also want to check out "Printing a Text File" in Chapter 9.

✔ If the printer isn't ready to print (such as when you forget to turn it on), you'll probably see a "Write fault error writing device PRN" error. Gadzooks! Turn the printer on and carefully type **R.** That should do the trick. If not, press A and you'll be safely back at the DOS prompt.

Saving Your Stuff to Disk

Before you quit the Editor, you need to save your file back to disk. If you don't do this, all that work and your many precious words will not be saved for posterity.

To save your stuff, press and release the Alt key and then press F. This action *drops down* the File menu at the top of the screen.

Press S to save the file.

If you're editing a new file, a Save box-thing appears where you can type the name of the file you want to save. Type in the name; be sure to use something memorable. Press Enter to save the file to disk.

- ✔ The file you save to disk is a text file, which means it contains readable text as opposed to unfathomable stuff or information only the computer can digest.

- ✔ The Editor does not automatically give your file a .TXT extension. You'll need to type that into the Save box if you want your files to end in .TXT.

- ✔ Refer to Chapter 12 for more information on naming files.

- ✔ If you're using the Editor to create a DOS batch file, you must type **.BAT** as the extension. The Editor won't do this automatically for you, and Notepad and WordPad cannot put the .BAT extension on the files they create.

- ✔ If a box appears proclaiming that the file already exists, type **N** and select a different name. If you type **Y**, you'll overwrite the file already on disk. If that's what you want, OK. Otherwise, select another name because you may not be certain of what you're overwriting.

- ✔ Other application programs, text editors, and word processors can easily read the text files you create using the DOS Editor. Unfortunately, the Editor can only deal with basic, no-frills text files. You cannot edit a document from your word processor using the Editor unless you save it in the *plain text*, *DOS text*, or *ASCII* format first.

Quitting the Editor

You should quit the Editor only after saving your file to disk; refer to the preceding section for the details on this operation. After the file is saved, you quit the Editor so that you can return to DOS and spend more time enjoying life at the DOS prompt.

To quit the Editor, press and release the Alt key, and then press F. This action drops down the File menu.

Press X to select the Exit item. This quits the Editor and returns you to the safe-but-not-warm-and-fuzzy DOS prompt.

- ✔ If you haven't saved your file before quitting, a message box or window appears asking if you want to save. Press Y in that instance; follow the steps listed in the previous section on saving a file.

- ✔ You cannot quit the editor by closing its window on the screen. This is an example of one of those programs you must properly quit or Windows will get all steamed.

Part III
The Non-Nerd's Guide to Disks and Files

The 5th Wave   By Rich Tennant

In this part...

The D in DOS stands for Disk. It's a *Disk* operating system, which seems kind of silly today when every computer is sold with both floppy disks and hard drives. Back in the olden days, it just wasn't so. It's now a trivia question that the first IBM PC had a hole in the back for plugging in a cassette recorder and, in fact, you could use it if you wanted to save or load a file. (I'm not sure if anyone ever did that or not.)

But now everyone has disks. Disks and drives. Drives and subdirectories. Pathnames and filenames. It can get pretty confusing, which is why this chapter was written: to defog the air surrounding your disk drives and files and all the strange and wonderful things that could possibly go wrong with them.

Chapter 9

File Fitness (Stuff You Do with Files)

A file is basically a collection of stuff on disk, usually stuff you want to keep. One of DOS's main duties (right after confusing the hell out of you) is to work with files. For a filing cabinet, this is obvious. Under DOS, it's not.

This chapter is about working with files — duplicating, copying, deleting, undeleting, moving, and printing them — everything you want to know about files in DOS.

Duplicating a File

Duplicating a file is done with the COPY command. You need to know the name of the original file and the new name you want to give the duplicate.

Suppose the file you have is named MUSHY.DOC. You want to make a duplicate file named CRUNCHY.DOC. Here's what you type:

```
C> COPY MUSHY.DOC CRUNCHY.DOC
```

A common reason for creating duplicates is to make a backup file of an original. For example, if you work on CONFIG.SYS and AUTOEXEC.BAT:

```
C> COPY CONFIG.SYS CONFIG.BKD
```

Here the file CONFIG.SYS is duplicated and given the name CONFIG.BKD.

Both the original and the duplicate files will have the same contents but different names, because no two files in the same directory can be given the same name.

- ✔ If the operation is successful, DOS responds with the message `1 file(s) copied`. If not, you'll most likely receive a `File not found` error message. That's OK. You probably just mistyped the original filename. Try again.

- ✔ To find out which files are on disk, you use the DIR command. Refer to "The DIR Command" in Chapter 2.

- ✔ For information on naming new files, refer to "Name That File!" in Chapter 12. Generally speaking, files can contain letters and numbers. Beyond that it gets confusing, which is why you should read Chapter 12.

- ✔ If the duplicate file already exists, DOS will properly warn you. For example, if the file CRUNCHY.DOC already exists, DOS tells you so:

```
Overwrite C:CRUNCHY.DOC (Yes/No/All)?
```

This statement means the file CRUNCHY.DOC already exists. Rather than clobber it without so much as a thought, DOS is asking first. My advice is to type **N** here — N for "No thanks." (Press Enter after typing **N**.) Then try the COPY command again and use another name for the duplicate.

Copying a Single File

Copying a file is handled by the COPY command. You need to know the name of the original file and the destination (the place where you want to put the copy).

For example, to copy a file to another drive, specify that drive's letter plus a colon:

```
C> COPY OVERTHAR.DOC A:
```

In the preceding example, the file OVERTHAR.DOC is copied to drive A. On drive A, you'll find an identical copy of the file OVERTHAR.DOC; both files will have the same name and contents. To copy a file to another directory on the same drive, specify that directory's pathname. For example:

```
C> COPY OVERTHAR.DOC \WORK\STUFF
```

Here the file OVERTHAR.DOC is copied to the subdirectory \WORK\STUFF on the same drive.

To copy a file to another directory on another drive, you must specify the full pathname, including the drive letter and a colon:

```
C> COPY MENU.EXE B:\MAIN
```

Here the file MENU.EXE is copied to the MAIN directory on drive B.

If another file with the same name exists, DOS asks the `Overwrite (Yes/No/ All)?` question. Type **N** and press Enter. (Refer to the preceding section's checklist for more information.)

✔ Copying a file in DOS doesn't work like it does in Windows 95. In Windows 95 you select the file, copy it, and then paste it. In DOS, you just copy it using the COPY command; no pasting occurs (which would just gum up the keyboard).

✔ If you want to copy a file to the same directory as the original, you must specify a different name. Refer to the earlier discussion "Duplicating a File."

✔ For more information on pathnames and subdirectories, refer to Chapter 11.

✔ Copying a file to a floppy disk in Windows is done by right-clicking the mouse on that file's icon and choosing Send to⇨3¹/₂ Floppy (A).

Copying a File to You

A short form of the COPY command can be used to copy a file from another drive or directory to your current directory. In this format of the COPY command, you specify only the original file (which cannot already be in the current directory). This shortcut just can't be done in Windows, no way, no how.

For example, suppose the file DREDGE is located on drive A. To copy that file to drive C (your current drive), type:

```
C> COPY A:DREDGE
```

To copy the BORING.DOC file from the \WORK\YAWN subdirectory to your current location, you can type :

```
C> COPY \WORK\YAWN\BORING.DOC
```

- ✔ Copying a file in this manner only works when you're not in the directory containing the file. Of course, after the COPY command, the file will be in the current directory.

- ✔ You cannot duplicate files using this command; you can only copy them from elsewhere to the current directory. If you try this command and the file is in the current directory, you'll get a `File cannot be copied onto itself` error message.

- ✔ For more information on directories, refer to Chapter 11; information on the *current directory* is offered in the section "Finding the Current Directory" in that chapter.

Copying a Group of Files

You can copy more than one file with a single COPY command. This is done by using *wildcards*.

The * wildcard replaces a group of characters in a filename.

The ? wildcard replaces a single character in a filename.

For example, if you want to copy all files with the .DOC extension to drive A, you would use the following command:

```
C> COPY *.DOC A:
```

Here the *.DOC matches all files ending in DOC: BABY.DOC, EYE.DOC, EAR.DOC, WHATSUP.DOC, and so on. Note that both the period and the .DOC ending are specified after the asterisk. The files are copied to drive A (as shown by the A:).

To copy all files, use the *.* (star-dot-star, which is less of a tongue twister than asterisk-period-asterisk) wildcard:

```
C> COPY *.* A:
```

This command is commonly used when you are copying all the files from the floppy drive to your hard drive:

```
C> COPY A:*.*
```

TECHNICAL STUFF

Copying? Duplicating?
What's the diff and why should I care?

True, copying and duplicating a file are the same thing. In both instances, you have two copies of the same file, each containing the same information. The difference is only in the vernacular: A duplicated file is usually on the same drive in the same directory and has a different name. A copied file is usually created on another drive or in another directory.

Note that you can copy a file with a different name, which is like duplicating it. For example:

`C> COPY SILLY.DOC A:DROLL.DOC`

Here, SILLY.DOC is copied to drive A — but it's given a new name, DROLL.DOC.

In this example, you're copying the files *to you* from the floppy drive. (Refer to the previous section for the gory details.)

The ? wildcard is used to represent a single character in a filename. For example, assume you had ten chapters in a book, named CHAP01.DOC through CHAP10.DOC. You can copy them to drive A using the following command:

```
C> COPY CHAP??.DOC A:
```

✔ For more information on wildcards, refer to the section "Wildcards (or Poker Was Never This Much Fun)" in Chapter 12.

✔ Refer to Chapter 11 for information on the current directory and pathnames.

Creating a Shortcut

Shortcuts are like copies of files, but they don't take up as much disk space. For example, if your annoying neighbor's house burned down and you wanted to put a copy of that graphical image in both your GRAPHICS and LETTERS/XMAS directories, you need only keep the original in one and stuff a shortcut copy into the other. That way the file doesn't take up twice as much room on disk.

You can only create a shortcut in Windows, not in DOS. In fact, shortcuts are particularly useless in DOS. They should have a large, glowing neon sign over them blinking "Don't Bother." Personally, I avoid them like the plague.

Deleting a File

Deleting a file is done with the DEL command. You follow DEL with the name of the file you want to delete:

```
C> DEL SAMPLE.BAK
```

There is no feedback; the DEL command is like the midnight assassin, silent and quick.

If the file you're deleting isn't in the current directory, you must specify a drive letter and colon or a pathname:

```
C> DEL A:MEMO
```

Here the file MEMO is deleted from drive A.

```
C> DEL \WP51\DATA\XMASLIST.95
```

Here the file XMASLIST.95 is deleted from the \WP51\DATA directory.

- ✔ Never delete any file named COMMAND.COM. While you're at it, don't delete any file in your WINDOWS directory or any of its subdirectories. If you're using DriveSpace to compress your hard drive, never, ever delete any file that starts with DBLSPACE, DRVSPACE, or STAC.

- ✔ Be careful with the DEL command! Delete files you've created, files you know about, and files you've copied. Don't go on a spiteful fit of vengeance and delete files whose purpose you don't know.

- ✔ The ERASE command can also be used to delete files. ERASE and DEL are exactly the same command and do the same things. (I know, it's redundant. But that's what you should expect from DOS.)

- ✔ If the file doesn't exist, you'll see a `File not found` error message.

- ✔ Information on using pathnames is covered in Chapter 11.

Deleting a Group of Files

To delete more than one file at a time — truly massive, wholesale slaughter — you use the DEL command with wildcards. This can get nasty.

The * wildcard replaces a group of characters in a filename.

The ? wildcard replaces a single character in a filename.

Extra verbiage on why you would want to delete files

Deleting a file with the DEL command seems like a drastic thing to do — especially when you've invested all that time in creating the file. But there are reasons. The first is to clean up space. Some files may contain unnecessary copies of information; some files may be old versions or BAK (backup) duplicates. Deleting them gives you more space.

Zapping extra files is also a part of disk maintenance or "housekeeping." If you've ever created a TEMP, KILL, or JUNK file, you'd use the DEL command to delete them. (Oh, TEMP, KILL, or JUNK may contain information you had to save to disk but now no longer need — stuff like today's bets at the track, the rough draft of your letter to your congressperson, or that second copy of the books before the auditor comes.)

For example, to delete all files with UP as their second part (the extension), you would use the following command:

```
C> DEL *.UP
```

In this example, *.UP matches all files ending in UP, such as FED.UP, SHUT.UP, THROW.UP, and so on. Note how both the period and the UP ending are specified after the asterisk.

As with deleting a single file, the feedback from this command is nil. Yes, even as a mass murderer, DEL makes no noise.

An exception to DEL's silence is when you use the *.* wildcard. Because this deletes all files in the directory, something must be said:

```
C> DEL *.*
```

DOS will heed you with the following message:

```
All files in directory will be deleted! Are you sure (Y/N)?
```

Don't be too quick to press Y here. Ask yourself, "Am I certain I want to ruthlessly destroy those innocent files?" Then, with a demented "Yes" gurgling from your lips, press Y and Enter. Boom! The files are gone.

- ✔ For more information on wildcards, refer to "Wildcards (or Poker Was Never This Much Fun)" in Chapter 12.

- ✔ You can also delete groups of files on other drives and in other directories. Wow! Run amok! But be sure to specify the proper locations for the files, disks, and pathnames as needed.

Some background stuff I shouldn't tell you about ATTRIB

The ATTRIB command is used to modify special features of a file that are called *attributes*. One of these attributes is the *read-only* attribute. When a file is marked as read-only, you can only read from the file. Any attempt to modify it, rename it, or delete it will be met with an Access denied error message.

To make a file or group of files read-only, the ATTRIB command is used with a +R:

```
C> ATTRIB NOKILL.ME +R
```

In this example, the file NOKILL.ME will be read-only protected. Of course, the protection offered here is minimal: Any dolt can use the ATTRIB command to remove the read-only protection and delete the file. Go figure.

The File! I Cannot Kill It!

Suppose that one day, when you're feeling rather spiteful, you decide to delete that useless BARNEY.LUV file. You type the following with wicked staccato fingers:

```
C> DEL BARNEY.LUV
```

But upon pressing Enter, you see that DOS tells you Access denied. Ha! Will that spoil your mood, or what?

Generally speaking, when you see Access denied, it means that someone somewhere doesn't want you to delete the file. There are some very important files on your system. Some may not have names obvious to you. So it's never a good idea to go out stomping on files like a kid through a flower bed. Tsk, tsk, tsk.

Shhh! (Whisper this if you're reading aloud.) If you really want to delete the file, you must first type the following, using the proper filename or wildcard:

```
C> ATTRIB BARNEY.LUV -R
```

That's the ATTRIB command, followed by the name of the file, space, then a minus sign (–), and an R. There cannot be a space between the minus sign and the R.

By pressing Enter, you're removing the *access* protection from the file(s). You can now delete it (or them):

```
C> DEL BARNEY.LUV
```

Need I mention it again? Files are protected for a reason. Only use the ATTRIB and –R when you badly want to delete a file.

Undeleting a File

Be careful with what you delete! DOS has no UNDELETE command in Windows 95, nor can you use the Windows Recycle Bin to recover any files you delete in DOS. When a file is killed off at the DOS prompt, it's pretty much gone for good.

Now, as usual, there are some exceptions and tips here:

Exception: If you've upgraded to Windows 95 from an older version of Windows or DOS, you still have an UNDELETE command you can use. However, this command will be run in the special MS-DOS-Only mode (see Chapter 7). Even then, it may not recover the files.

Exception: Some third-party UNDELETE or UNERASE commands may recover any files you deleted, so don't live in total despair.

Tip: My advice is to do all your major file deleting in Windows instead of at the DOS prompt. That way you can take advantage of the Windows Recycle Bin to recover any deleted files you want back.

Tip: You can always recover a deleted file from a recent hard disk backup — providing you bother to back up your hard disk in the first place.

If you do attempt to run the UNDELETE command, Windows displays a warning dialog box telling you it has to switch into MS-DOS mode to continue. Scary stuff. Type **N** for No to keep on working in Windows.

Moving a File

To move a file from hither to thither, you use the MOVE command. To move the file BEKINS.VAN to drive A, you type this in:

```
C> MOVE BEKINS.VAN A:
```

DOS takes the file BEKINS.VAN, copies it to drive A, and then deletes the original. After all, that's what a move operation is: copy and then delete. Something like the following message is displayed:

```
C:\BEKINS.VAN => A:\BEKINS.VAN [ok]
```

That means the file was moved, OK. OK? Good.

- ✔ DOS's MOVE command is the same as a Cut and Paste file operation in Windows 95.

- ✔ The MOVE command's song goes like this, *Move this file to there*. You type the place you're moving the file — the destination — last. Files can be moved to another disk drive or another directory.

- ✔ The MOVE command can also be used to rename directories, though you can also use the REN to do that.

- ✔ If a file with the same name already exists DOS displays a warning. For example:

```
Overwrite A:BEKINS.VAN (Yes/No/All)?
```

This statement means a file with the name BEKINS.VAN already exists on drive A. Type **N** and press Enter, and the MOVE command won't stomp it.

- ✔ Remember: The MOVE command deletes the originals. If you want to copy a file, use the COPY command instead.

Renaming a File

DOS enables you to plaster a new name on a file using the REN command. The file's contents and its location on disk stay the same. Only the name is changed (like they used to do on "Dragnet" to protect the innocent).

For example, to rename CHAPTER1.WP to CHAP01.WP, you can use the following:

```
C> REN CHAPTER1.WP CHAP01.WP
```

The old name is specified first, followed by a space, and then the new name. No sweat.

If the file isn't in the current directory, you must specify a drive letter or pathname. However, the new filename doesn't need all that extra info:

```
C> REN B:\STUFF\YONDER THITHER
```

In this example, the file named YONDER is on the disk in drive B, in the STUFF subdirectory. The file is given the new name THITHER by the REN command.

You can also rename a directory (a.k.a. *folder*) using the very same REN command:

```
C> REN TEMP JUNK
```

The above command renames the TEMP directory to JUNK, a more apt description of the contents.

Renaming a group of files is possible — but tricky. No, the REN command cannot rename all files (*.*) individually. It can, however, rename a group of files all at once. For example :

```
C> REN *.OLD *.BAK
```

Here, all files ending in OLD are renamed. They'll keep their original filenames (the first part), but each will be given the new second name, BAK.

- ✔ REN has a longer version, RENAME. Both are the same command; you can use either, though REN is quicker to type.

- ✔ For information on file-naming rules, refer to "Name That File!" in Chapter 12.

- ✔ You can also refer to Chapter 12 for information on renaming your old DOS files with the new, longer, and more descriptive Windows filenames.

- ✔ You can only use wildcards with the REN command when you're renaming a group of matching files. Generally speaking, the same wildcard must be used for both the original filename and the new name. For more information on wildcards, refer to "Wildcards (or Poker Was Never This Much Fun)" in Chapter 12.

- ✔ Information about accessing other disks and pathnames is covered in Chapter 11.

Printing a Text File

You can use DOS to print any text file with the handy COPY command. Yeah, it sounds odd — but it works. First, a few rules:

1. **Try the TYPE command on the file first.**

   If you can read it, it will print OK. If you can't read the file (if it looks "Greek"), the same garbage you see on your screen will be sent to your printer. That's probably not what you want.

2. **Before printing the file, make sure your printer is connected, *online*, and ready to print.**

3. **Use the COPY command to copy the file from your disk to the printer:**

   ```
   C> COPY PRINTME PRN
   ```

   PRN is the name of your printer. After pressing Enter, DOS makes a copy of the file PRINTME (my example) on your printer.

4. If a full page doesn't print, you'll need to eject the page from your printer.

This is done by typing the following command:

```
C> ECHO ^L > PRN
```

That's the ECHO command, followed by a space and then the Ctrl+L character (the eject page command). You produce that character by holding down the Ctrl (control) key and typing an **L** — do not type in ^L (the hat and L characters). Then type a space, the greater-than symbol (>), another space, and then **PRN**. Press Enter, and a sheet of paper magically ejects from your printer. Neat-o.

✔ Text files typically have names that end in .TXT. The most common text file is named READ.ME or README. Some files ending in .DOC are text files, but that's not always the case; TYPE the file first to be sure.

✔ It's usually best to print a file using the application that created it. DOS can print only text files.

✔ If you upgraded to Windows 95 from a previous version of DOS, you may have the old PRINT command hanging around. If so, avoid it. The PRINT command *does not* print files and, in fact, is wholly unnecessary with Windows 95.

✔ You can also print any text file using the DOS Editor. Visit Chapter 8 for information.

✔ For more information on the TYPE command and looking at files, refer to "Looking at Files" in Chapter 2.

✔ If you need general information about using a printer with your computer, refer to my book *PCs For Dummies*, also available from IDG Books Worldwide.

Cosmic drivel about ECHO ^L > PRN

The ECHO command is DOS's "display me" command. Anything you type after ECHO is echoed to the screen. This command is primarily used in batch files, which are quasiprograms written by advanced DOS users who think they're really cool.

Ctrl+L is a special control character, actually a single character that you produce by pressing the Ctrl+L key combination. On the screen, this character may look like the ankh symbol, but every computer printer sees this as the direct command to toss out a sheet of paper. For laser printers, that's often the only way you can see your work.

The cryptic (very cryptic) > PRN is what's called *I/O redirection*, and it's leagues beyond what's in this book. Basically, the greater-than sign (>) tells DOS to send its output, the Ctrl+L in this case, to another device, something other than the screen.

The named device is PRN, the printer. In the end, the eject-page command (Ctrl+L) is sent to the printer (> PRN) via the ECHO command. And they all live happily ever after.

Chapter 10

Playing with Your Disks

• •

In This Chapter

▶ Preparing a disk for use by DOS (formatting)

▶ Formatting different size disks

▶ Checking how much of a disk has been used

▶ Changing a volume label

▶ Reformatting an already formatted disk

▶ Duplicating disks

• •

*B*oth computers and humans have two kinds of long-term storage. The internal storage in a human is provided by a wet slimy thing called a brain. It's fast on the uptake and can store volumes of information but is sluggish on the retrieval. Inside a computer, the hard drive provides fast but limited storage and retrieves quickly.

Humans supplement their brain-storage device with storage media, such as scraps of paper with things written down on them. Computers use floppy disks, on which information can be written and removed from the computer, taken elsewhere, or just stored. Both systems have their pluses and minuses.

This chapter is about using *floppy disks,* the removable long-term storage devices used by computers. You use floppy disks to make safety copies of your important files, move files between computers, back up information from the hard disk, or play a limited-distance version of Frisbee. Floppies can be frustrating or fun, but above all they must be formatted (see "Formatting a Disk," next in this chapter).

Formatting a Disk

Before you can use a disk, it must be formatted. This isn't as much of a hassle as it was a few years back. Today, most diskettes come pre-formatted. Buy a box, they're ready to use. If not, then you must format them yourself. It's just another one of those burdens we as computer owners must shoulder.

The reason floppy disks come "naked" out of the box is because you can use floppy disks on a variety of computers — not always DOS computers. For DOS to use the disk and store information on it, you must format that disk the way DOS likes. You do this with the FORMAT command.

To format a disk, first place it label side up and toward you and insert it into drive A. If you're using a $5^1/_4$-inch disk, you'll have to close the drive's door latch after inserting the disk; $3^1/_2$-inch disks just suck right in. Type the following:

```
C> FORMAT A:
```

After pressing Enter, you'll be asked to insert the disk. That's already done, so press Enter again, and the disk begins formatting.

After formatting is complete, you'll be asked to enter a *volume label* for the disk. Press Enter (unless you want to type a label name; it's optional).

Wow! It's statistics time. Feel free to ignore the numbers and technical descriptions that follow the volume label question. On the screen:

```
Format another (Y/N)?
```

If you want to format another disk, press Y and then Enter when it asks you. Remove the first disk and replace it with another. If you don't want to format another disk, press N and then Enter.

You can also format disks in drive B, providing your PC has a drive B. Here is the command you use:

```
C> FORMAT B:
```

Follow the same steps as listed for drive A.

- ✔ Never format any drive other than A or B; you should always use the two FORMAT commands listed here when formatting disks.
- ✔ The disk you format must be the same size and capacity of the drive you're using: high-capacity disks for high-capacity drives; low-capacity disks for low-capacity drives. (See *PCs For Dummies* [IDG Books Worldwide] for more information on disk capacities and whatnot.)
- ✔ If you see the message Track 0 bad or Disk unusable, refer to Chapter 16.
- ✔ You can format a low-capacity disk in a high-capacity drive; refer to the next section.

Formatting a Low-Capacity Disk in a High-Capacity Drive

It's possible to format a disk of lower capacity in a high-capacity drive. You would do this to be compatible with computers that have only the lower capacity drives or if you're using cheaper, low-density disks. If that's never your situation, there's no need to do this.

To format a low-capacity disk in a high-capacity drive, you must first get the low-capacity disk. Never format a high-capacity disk to a lower format. (It renders the disk useless.)

Insert the low-capacity disk into your high-capacity drive, label up and toward you. For a 5¹/₄-inch drive, latch the drive's door shut after you've inserted the disk.

If you're formatting a low-capacity (720K) disk in a high-capacity 3¹/₂-inch drive, type this FORMAT command:

```
C> FORMAT A: /F:720
```

That's FORMAT, followed by a space, A and a colon (meaning drive A), a space, / F and a colon, and then the number 720. Press Enter and follow the instructions on the screen. Keep in mind that if you answer Y when asked to `Format another?`, you will still be formatting the low-capacity disks.

If you're formatting a low-capacity (360K) disk in a high-capacity 5¹/₄-inch drive, type the following FORMAT command:

```
C> FORMAT A: /F:360
```

This is the same FORMAT command as listed in the preceding example, save for typing the number 360 instead of 720. Follow the same instructions listed in the section "Formatting a Disk" just before this one. Remember that any additional disks you format by answering Y will be formatted at 720K.

If you have an extended-density (2.8MB) drive, you can use the following FORMAT to format a 1.4MB high-capacity disk:

```
C> FORMAT A: /F:1440
```

Follow the instructions on the screen. (Technically, this is formatting a high-capacity disk in a higher-capacity drive. Silly? Yeah, I know.)

✔ If you want to format the low-capacity disk in drive B, substitute B: for A: in either of the preceding commands.

✔ If the FORMAT command refuses to format the disk for any reason, you can force it to format by adding the /U option. Here are the modified commands:

```
C> FORMAT A: /F:360 /U
C> FORMAT A: /F:720 /U
C> FORMAT A: /F:1440 /U
```

Again, *do not* use these commands to force-format a high-capacity disk to a lower capacity. Always use low-capacity disks when you format low capacity.

Checking a Disk's Size and Other Trivia

In one corner of the land of long, complex computer numbers is the cottage of Disk Statistics. These are values that tell you how much of your disk is being used and how much you have to go. Good numbers to know if you want to see how much room you have left for the next really huge Windows application.

Checking disk size with the DIR command

One tiny bonus of the DIR command is that it gives you some brief, though confusing, disk statistics at the end of its output. For example:

```
86 file(s)      4,496,581 bytes
 2 dir(s)   1,623,556,096 bytes free
```

This message tells you the DIR command listed 86 files that eat up some 4 million bytes (4 megabytes) of disk space. Two directories (folders) were also listed. The last big number tells you how much space is available or "free" on the hard drive. In this example, that's 1 billion 623 million-odd bytes, or 1.6 gigabytes in computerspeak.

Of course, big numbers like that don't really tell you anything. Like that sign that lists the accumulated debt of the United States, a few billion here or there doesn't really have any value. What you really want to know is how much of your hard drive is used as a percentage. To find that out, type the following DIR command:

```
C> DIR /V
```

Type DIR, a space, then slash-V. Press Enter.

A whole lotta files will whiz by, and then you'll see the impressive statistical results displayed. Something like this:

```
86 file(s)        4,496,581 bytes
 2 dir(s)          6,225,920 bytes allocated
               1,623,556,096 bytes free
               2,145,058,816 bytes total disk space, 24% in use
```

More gobbledygook. But the last value is the most important. It tells you 24% (or whatever number you see on your screen) of your disk is being used. In this example, some 76 percent of the disk is still available — up for grabs by the programs and data files that need it.

- ✔ If your percentage-in-use value is above 90 percent or more, you should probably do some massive disk reorganization, removing old programs and files, or break down and buy a second, larger hard drive for your computer.

- ✔ To check the percentage of disk space used on a floppy disk, use the following DIR command:

```
C> DIR A: /V
```

Type DIR, a space, A, colon, another space, slash-V. To check disk space on a floppy disk in drive B, substitute B: for A: above.

- ✔ Some would suggest you run Window's DriveSpace or the Stacker program to increase your disk space. While this is an option, I don't recommend it; newer, larger hard drives are inexpensive and avoid the hassles such disk-expanding programs induce.

- ✔ The slash-V option is the *verbose* option. It tells DOS to spew forth more information than is humanly necessary.

- ✔ If it were up to me, I'd remove the words *allocated* and *default* from the computer lexicon.

Using the CHKDSK command

You can also use the old, but still handy, CHKDSK command to determine a disk's size. The CHKDSK command is known as *check disk,* which is kind of what CHKDSK looks like without all the superfluous vowels. Basically, this command reports information about your disk, most of it technical.

To see how much information you can store on a floppy disk, and therefore see its size or capacity, type **CHKDSK** at the DOS prompt, followed by **A:**, indicating the drive currently holding your floppy disk. Press Enter, and prepare to be overwhelmed:

```
C> CHKDSK A:
```

After pressing Enter , you'll see something like this:

```
Volume DOS HAPPY    created 09-05-1996 8:16p
Volume Serial Number is 0D1B-0FF8

   1,457,664 bytes total disk space
     832,000 bytes in 38 user files
     625,664 bytes available on disk

         512 bytes in each allocation unit
       2,847 total allocation units on disk
       1,222 available allocation units on disk

     655,360 total bytes memory
     617,552 bytes free


Instead of using CHKDSK, try using SCANDISK blah blah blah
            blah
```

There are four chunks of information here, most of it trivia. The most important is the first number value, which tells you the size of your disk. In this example, it says there are 1,457,664 bytes of *total disk space.* That means this disk is a 1.4MB, formatted floppy disk. Other values are divulged in the following chart:

Floppy Disk Size	*Long, Involved Number Displayed*
360K	365,056
1.2MB	1,228,800
720K	730,112
1.4MB	1,457,664
2.8MB	2,915,328

✔ To check the capacity of a disk in drive B, substitute B: for A: in the CHKDSK command.

✔ The value bytes available on disk tells you how much space is left on the disk for storing files.

✔ If you see any errors, refer to Chapter 11 for information on the ScanDisk program.

✔ CHKDSK is pronounced *check disk*. Don't even attempt to pronounce it without any vowels — unless you're fluent in Russian.

✔ If you see something about "bad sectors" in CHKDSK's output, you have a bum disk. Copy whatever files you want to keep off of that disk. Then throw the disk away. A bad disk is bad eternally.

Changing the Volume Label

When you format a disk, the FORMAT command asks you to enter a *volume label*. This is an electronic name encoded on the disk — not the sticky label you should apply later. Giving your disk a volume label can be a good idea, especially if your sticky label falls off the disk. In that case, you could find out the name of your disk electronically using the DIR command. The volume label appears at the top of the DIR command's output, and you can use the handy VOL command to find a disk's volume label. Type:

```
C> VOL A:
```

or

```
C> VOL B:
```

The VOL command reports back the disk's volume label, or it may tell you that the disk has no label.

After you've formatted a disk, you can change the volume label using the LABEL command. Type **LABEL** and then follow the instructions on the screen:

```
C> LABEL
```

After pressing Enter, you'll see the current label for the drive, as well as the cryptic volume serial number. DOS asks you to enter a new label up to 11 characters long. The label can contain letters and numbers. If you want a new label, type it in. If you don't want to change the label, don't *type* anything, but *do* press Enter.

If you enter a new label, DOS changes it on the disk. You can use the VOL command again to verify the new label.

If you just pressed Enter and your disk already had a label, DOS will ask if you want to delete the old label. If so, press Y. Otherwise, press N and you'll keep the original label.

To change the label on a disk in any drive, follow the LABEL command with that drive letter and a colon. Here's an example:

```
C> LABEL A:
```

Here, the label is examined/changed for drive A. Substitute B: for A: in our example to replace the label on drive B.

- ✔ The VOL command can be followed by any drive letter and colon. You use this to see the volume label for any other disk in your system, including your hard disk.
- ✔ Remember to insert a floppy disk in drive A or B before using the LABEL or VOL command on those drives.

Reformatting Disks

Disks must be formatted before your computer can use them. But once formatted, you can reformat them. This can be done under two circumstances: when you want to totally erase the disk and all its data, or accidentally.

Obviously, you shouldn't erase a disk that you don't want to erase. All the data on the disk goes bye-bye. The only way to avoid this is to be careful: Check the disk with the DIR command first. Make sure that it's a disk you want to reformat.

Personally, I erase disks all the time. I have stacks of old disks that I can reformat and use. The data on them is old or duplicated elsewhere. So reusing the disk is no problem. Here's the FORMAT command you want to use:

```
C> FORMAT A: /Q
```

That's the FORMAT command, a space, and then A and a colon, which directs the FORMAT command to format a disk in drive A. That's followed by another space and a slash-Q. That tells DOS to *Quickformat* the disk. It's very fast.

If DOS refuses to Quickformat the disk, try the following FORMAT command:

```
C> FORMAT A: /U
```

This is the same command as the last one but with a slash-U instead of a slash-Q. This command tells DOS to *unconditionally* format the disk. It takes longer than the Quickformat, but it generally works.

✔ If you want to reformat a disk in drive B, substitute B: for A: in these examples.

✔ Note that you cannot Quickformat a disk to a different size. In fact, you shouldn't be reformatting disks to a different size anyway. But if you must, use the /U option as shown here.

✔ Quickformat only newer disks. If a disk has been sitting around a while, use the FORMAT command without the /Q. That takes longer, but the FORMAT command will do a better job to ensure that the disk is still usable.

✔ After formatting a disk, you'll see a list of statistics. If one of the statistics mentioned is xxxx bytes in bad sectors, you have a bum disk on your hands. My advice: Toss the sucker. If you still have the receipt, and the store said they were "fully guaranteed," you can try to get your money back. Good luck!

✔ You can recover accidentally reformatted disks by using the UNFORMAT command. Refer to "I Just Reformatted My Disk!" in Chapter 14.

Duplicating Disks (the DISKCOPY Command)

To make a duplicate of a file on disk, you use the COPY command. (Refer to "Duplicating a File" in Chapter 9.) To make a duplicate of a floppy disk, you use the DISKCOPY command. DISKCOPY takes one floppy and makes an exact duplicate of it, even formatting a new disk if it was previously unformatted.

There are two things you cannot do with the DISKCOPY command:

1. You cannot DISKCOPY two disks of different size or capacity.

2. You cannot use DISKCOPY with a hard disk or a *RAM drive.* (If you don't know what a RAM drive is, go to the refrigerator and reward yourself with a cool, carbonated beverage.)

When you copy disks, DOS refers to the original disk as the *SOURCE.* The disk to which you're copying is the *TARGET.*

To make a copy of a disk, first write-protect the original, the SOURCE: On a 5¹/₄-inch disk, cover the notch with a sticky tab; on a 3¹/₂-inch disk, move the sliding tile so that you can see through the hole. Put your write-protected original into drive A. Close the drive's door latch for a 5¹/₄-inch disk.

About the ol' "Insufficient space for the MIRROR image file" message

Sometimes you may try to reformat a diskette and end up with the following message:

```
Drive X error. Insufficient space
for the MIRROR image file.

There was an error creating the
format recovery file.

This disk cannot be unformatted

Proceed with format (Y/N)
```

What DOS is trying to tell you here is that the magic it does to allow a disk to be unformatted can't happen. The disk you're reformatting is very full. Therefore, you must be doubly sure you want to format it because it can never be unformatted. My advice is to press Y here if you're certain. Otherwise, use another disk.

Type the following command at the DOS prompt:

```
C> DISKCOPY A: A:
```

That's DISKCOPY, a space, and then A: twice (meaning drive A mentioned twice and separated by a space). Press Enter. DOS asks the following:

```
Insert SOURCE diskette in drive A:
Press any key to continue
```

Since you've already stuck the proper, write-protected disk into drive A, you can safely whack the Enter key here.

Next, DOS examines the disk, spews out some technical mumbo-jumbo, and then:

```
Reading from source diskette . . .
```

The drive churns away for a few anxiety-filled moments. Then you're asked to insert the target diskette:

```
Insert TARGET diskette in drive A:
Press any key to continue
```

Remove the source disk and insert your duplicate disk, the TARGET. Close the door latch if you have a 5¹/₄-inch disk. Press Enter.

```
Writing to target diskette . . .
```

Take a few seconds to put the original (the source) back in a safe place. When the operation is complete, you'll see:

```
Do you wish to write another duplicate of this disk (Y/N)?
```

DOS is asking if you want to make another copy, another TARGET. Press Y if that's what you want to do, and then heed the instructions on the screen (same as the preceding example). If not, press N to be asked:

```
Copy another diskette (Y/N)?
```

Press N again to return to the comfy, cozy DOS prompt.

You can use the duplicate disk instead of the original.

- ✔ The original disk = SOURCE.
- ✔ The duplicate disk DISKCOPY makes = TARGET.
- ✔ You can do a DISKCOPY in your B drive by substituting B: for A: in the preceding command.
- ✔ You can use the following DISKCOPY command if and *only* if your drives A and B are of the same size and capacity:

```
C> DISKCOPY A: B:
```

   This command is faster because you don't have to swap disks. The SOURCE goes in drive A, the TARGET in drive B. Remember to remove your SOURCE when you're done.

- ✔ If the target disk is unformatted, DISKCOPY formats it. If it's already formatted, DISKCOPY replaces the original contents with the copy.
- ✔ The DISKCOPY command is the only accurate way to duplicate a disk. Even the COPY command cannot always make a full copy of all the files on a disk.
- ✔ Refer to *PCs For Dummies* for more information on write-protecting diskettes.
- ✔ Use DISKCOPY only to copy disks for your use, not for friends — it's illegal to copy licensed programs for others.

Chapter 11

The Hard Drive: Where You Store Stuff

I've always been fascinated by the hard disk. Why isn't it an *easy* disk? Computers are supposed to make life easier, not harder. Yet computer nerds are fascinated by hard disks. They've even come up with a whole row of verbal hurdles to leap over for anyone who attempts to understand what goes on in those spinning storage whatchamagizmos.

Using your hard drive means organizing all the massive amount of stuff you can put there. That's where the funky terms come into play. This chapter describes the ugly terms you'll encounter when you use a hard drive, what they mean, and why the heck you'd ever want to use them. This stuff is really important. If you learn only one thing — how to find your way around a hard disk — it will be worth the price of this book.

What Is a Subdirectory?

A *subdirectory* is workspace on a disk. It's almost like a disk within a disk. You can copy files and programs into a subdirectory or workspace, and you can use DOS commands. The advantage to subdirectories is that you can store information in a subdirectory and keep it separate from other files on the same disk. That keeps the disk from getting file-messy.

Any disk can have subdirectories, though they're used primarily on hard drives to keep files separate and your programs organized. So rather than let you suffer through a hard drive with bazillions of files all in one place, the subdirectories enable you to organize everything by placing information into separate, special areas.

✔ In Windows 95 parlance, a subdirectory is called a *folder*. Since this is a book about DOS, the term subdirectory is used instead.

✔ Actually, subdirectories should just be called *directories*. The prefix *sub* means *under,* just as submarine means any large naval vessel that a Marine is standing on. All the workspaces on a disk are really directories. However, when you refer to one directory in relation to another, the term *subdirectory* is used.

✔ If you want to create a directory to keep some of your files separate from other files, refer to "How to Name a Directory (the MKDIR Command)" in Chapter 12.

✔ All the directories on your disk create what's called a *tree structure*. For information, refer to "The Tree Structure" later in this chapter.

The Root Directory

Every disk you use on your computer has one main directory, called the *root directory*. The root directory (often just called *the root*) exists on all disks; it happens naturally, created when the disk is first formatted.

The symbol for the root directory is the single backslash (\). This is an abbreviation — shorthand — that DOS uses in reference to the root directory. It also plays an important role in the *pathname,* which is covered later in this chapter.

Additional directories on a disk are subdirectories under the root directory. They branch off of the root like branches of a tree. In fact, if you map out the directories on a disk linking each subdirectory, it looks like a family tree of sorts (see Figure 11-1).

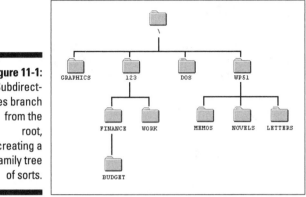

Figure 11-1:
Subdirect-
ories branch
from the
root,
creating a
family tree
of sorts.

- ✔ In Figure 11-1, file folders are used to represent each directory on disk. This is very Windows-ish, and I apologize for it.

- ✔ Funny thing: Even though Windows calls them folders, they still call the root directory the root directory.

- ✔ The \ (single backslash) is also the abbreviation for the root directory in Windows as well.

- ✔ The FORMAT command is used to prepare disks for use under DOS. It also creates the root directory. For more information, refer to "Formatting a Disk" in Chapter 10.

- ✔ Whenever you're using a disk, you're *logged to* or currently using a directory on that disk. To change to another subdirectory, refer to "Changing Directories" later in this chapter; to change to another disk, refer to "Changing Drives" in Chapter 2. To see which directory you're currently logged to, refer to "Finding the Current Directory" later in this chapter.

You are not required to know this stuff

Subdirectories are often called *child* directories. And from a subdirectory's point of view, it has a *parent* directory. For example, in Figure 11-1, DOS is a subdirectory of the root directory (\). DOS is the root directory's child directory. The root directory is the parent of the DOS directory.

If you were logged to or using the 123 directory in Figure 11-1, its parent directory would be the root. The 123 directory also has two child directories — or two subdirectories. They are named FINANCE and WORK.

The visual representation shown in Figure 11-1 is only for your head; you'll *see* nothing of the sort as you use your computer. However, it's a good visual representation of the relationships among various directories on a disk. The TREE command, covered later in this chapter, enables you to see the representation in a different, more DOS-ish format.

That Funny <DIR> Thing

To find a subdirectory on a disk, you use the DIR command. Directories are listed there, along with other files. The way you identify a directory name is by the <DIR> thing shown after its name (where other files would have their file size in bytes).

For example, consider the following output from the DIR command:

```
Volume in drive C is WINDOWS SAD
Volume Serial Number is 16CE-9B67
Directory of C:\
123          <DIR>         03-18-92  9:33p
COMM         <DIR>         08-07-92  9:37p
DOS          <DIR>         09-20-93 10:52p
GAMES        <DIR>         09-22-93  5:18p
WINDOWS      <DIR>         07-11-95  9:50a
WP60         <DIR>         09-21-93  5:12p
AUTOEXEC BAT          574  09-05-93 10:04a AUTOEXEC.BAT
COMMAND  COM       54,928  08-11-93  6:20a COMMAND.COM
CONFIG   SYS          464  07-25-93 10:20a CONFIG.SYS
WINA20   386        9,349  08-11-93  6:20a WINA20.386
         9 file(s)         65,315 bytes
         6 dir(s)     636,468,736 bytes free
```

The *files* 123, COMM, DOS, GAMES, WINDOWS, and WP60 are actually directories on disk. At the top of the output in the preceding example, Directory of C:\ tells you that you're looking at a directory of drive C (that's the C:), the root directory (shown by the backslash). The <DIR> entries in the listing are all subdirectories of the root directory.

- ✔ Subdirectories appear in the DIR command's listing because they're part of your disk, just like files. In fact, directories are named just like files and can even have an extension like a file. Refer to "How to Name a Directory (the MKDIR Command)" in Chapter 12 for more information (if you're curious).

- ✔ For more information on the DIR command, refer to "The DIR Command" in Chapter 2.

- ✔ For information on finding a lost directory on disk, refer to "Finding a Lost Subdirectory" in Chapter 12.

- ✔ The C:\ you see at the start of the DIR command's output (Directory of C:\) is actually a pathname.

- ✔ The final part of the DIR command's output is just DOS's attempt to overwhelm you with large values.

- ✔ If you just want to see a list of directories, you can type the following DIR command:

```
C> DIR /A:D
```

Type DIR, a space, slash, A, colon, D. I remember this by thinking "All (colon) Directories." However, that's not what the A stands for. (You don't want to know what the A stands for.)

What Is a Pathname?

A *pathname* is just a really long filename. A filename is a name given only to a file, the file's title, which should also tell you something about the file's contents. A pathname, on the other hand, tells you where a file is located — it tells you on which disk the file has been saved and in which subdirectory.

A file's pathname is like a path to the file. It tells you how to get to a specific file or subdirectory — an exact location. For example, the following is a pathname, a full pathname to a specific file on disk:

```
C:\WORK\CHAP12.DOC
```

The filename CHAP12.DOC identifies a file on a disk. In the preceding example, the full pathname says it's a file on drive C, as seen by the C: at the start. Furthermore, the file CHAP12.DOC is located in the WORK subdirectory. The backslashes (\) in the pathname are provided as separating elements, keeping the drive letter, subdirectories, and filename from running into each other.

Dot to dot

How many times have you seen something like the following in the DIR command's listing?

```
.   <DIR>        08-13-96  9:06p
..  <DIR>        08-13-96  9:06p
```

Doesn't that just bug you? A single period, or dot, isn't the name of a file, and dot-dot isn't the name of a file either. (Filenames, legal and illegal, are covered in "Use These Filenames, Go Directly to Jail!" in Chapter 12.) By now you know that these are both directories on disk. Where are they? What are they?!

The dot and dot-dot entries are abbreviations. Dot, the first entry here, is an abbreviation for the current directory. Dot-dot refers to the parent directory.

You can use these abbreviations to refer to the current or parent directory in various DOS commands. This, however, is an advanced and secretive subject, best left up to the loftier books on using computers. But if dot and dot-dot ever bugged the heck out of you, now you know what they represent.

This breaks down as follows:

```
C:                          Drive C
C:\                         The root directory
C:\WORK                     The WORK subdirectory
C:\WORK\CHAP12.DOC          The file CHAP12.DOC and its full
                            pathname
```

Pathnames don't always have to end with a filename. They can also be used to identify a directory located somewhere on a disk. In that case, the pathname tells you which drive it's on and all its parent directories on up to the root. For example, consider this pathname:

```
C:\WP60\DATA
```

To break this pathname down, you have:

```
C:                          The drive letter, C
C:\                         The root directory of drive C
C:\WP60                     The WP60 subdirectory on drive C, a
                            subdirectory of the root
C:\WP60\DATA                The DATA subdirectory under the WP60
                            directory
```

✔ Even though Windows uses all these friendly, cuddly terms like folder and desktop, pathnames crop up more often than you'd like.

✔ The backslash is used both as a symbol for the root directory and as a separator. A backslash always separates subdirectories from each other. No spaces are used in a pathname.

✔ A pathname that starts with a drive letter is called a *full pathname*. (Pathnames don't always need the drive letter.)

✔ The drive letter is optional in a pathname. However, I recommend using it because it's more specific.

✔ When you use the CD command by itself to locate the current directory, what it returns is a pathname; refer to the next section.

Finding the Current Directory

To find out which directory you're currently using (or *logged to*), type the CD command:

```
C> CD
```

The directory you're using will be displayed on the next line. (Actually, what you will see is a pathname of the current directory.) You can change to any other subdirectory on the same drive by using the CD command followed by that directory's pathname. Refer to the next section for the specifics.

> ✔ CD has a longer form, CHDIR. Both do the same thing, but CD is quicker to type (and you can say *current directory* or *change directory* in your head instead of *chiddur*).
>
> ✔ For more information on changing drives, refer to "Changing Drives" in Chapter 2.
>
> ✔ For more information on pathnames, refer to "What Is a Pathname?" earlier in this chapter.
>
> ✔ The PROMPT command can be used to tell you the current directory at all times. Refer to "Prompt Styles of the Rich and Famous" in Chapter 3.

Changing Directories

To change to another directory, type the CD (Change Directory) command followed by the pathname of the directory to which you want to change. In computer jargon, this *logs* you to that new directory.

For example, suppose you want to change to the root directory. Type this in:

```
C> CD \
```

Technical background junk

Whenever you use a computer, you're using, or attached to, some specific disk drive. Though your system may have several drives, you're actually using only one of them at a time. That drive is said to be the *currently logged drive*. (*Logged* in computer lingo means *using*.) The same holds true with directories on a disk; you can use — or be logged to — only one directory at a time.

When you first use a disk, you're automatically logged to its root directory, the main directory on disk. After you've been using the computer for a while, you'll probably wind up elsewhere on the disk, say in some subdirectory somewhere. To find out the pathname of that subdirectory, use the CD command as just described.

In Windows 95, whenever you start a DOS window it uses a specific directory — not necessarily the root directory — as the current directory. Refer to Chapter 7, "The definition of a 'working' directory" for more information.

That's the CD command, followed by a space and the root directory's name, the backslash.

To change to the \WP60 subdirectory, type

```
C> CD \WP60
```

Try to type in a pathname that includes the root directory. This kind of pathname always starts with a backslash, which indicates the root. If you know the full pathname of the directory, type it in. Otherwise, you can refer to "Finding a Lost Subdirectory" in Chapter 12 for finding lost directories.

You can use the DIR command to find the name of a subdirectory to log to. If you find a name, a full pathname isn't needed. For example, if you use the DIR command and see the DATA directory (marked by <DIR> in the directory listing), you can log to (use) it by typing

```
C> CD DATA
```

Because DATA is a subdirectory, or child, of the current directory, there's no need to specify a full pathname.

You can take another shortcut to log to the parent directory:

```
C> CD ..
```

The dot-dot is an abbreviation for the parent directory — no matter where you are. This is much quicker than typing out the full pathname for the parent directory.

- ✔ You cannot use the CD command to change to a subdirectory on another drive. You must first log to that drive and then use the CD command. Refer to "Changing Drives" in Chapter 2 for how to log to another drive.

- ✔ If you see an `Invalid directory` error message, you didn't type in a full pathname or you mistyped something. It could also be that you're not logged to the proper drive. Refer to "Finding a Lost Subdirectory" in Chapter 12 for finding lost directories.

- ✔ You can also use the CHDIR command, the longer form of the CD command. CHDIR stands for Change Directory, supposedly.

- ✔ Refer to "What Is a Pathname?" earlier in this chapter for information on pathnames.

The Tree Structure

All the subdirectories on a disk make for a fairly complex arrangement. I know of no one, nerd or non-nerd, who actually knows exactly what's where on his or her system. So to find out, to get a view of the big picture, you can use the TREE command. In Windows, you can use the Explorer. Both show you the tree, but with different purposes.

Using the TREE command

Type the following command:

```
C> TREE C:\
```

That's the TREE command, a space, C, a colon, and a backslash character. The TREE command is followed by a pathname; C:\ means drive C's root directory. Press Enter and the TREE command displays a graphic representation of your tree structure, how your subdirectories are organized for drive C.

If you get a Bad command or filename or Incorrect DOS version error message, take heart. Windows probably destroyed the TREE command when you updated. Oh, well.

The display scrolls off the screen for a time. If you want to pause the display, press the Ctrl+S key combination; to continue, press Ctrl+S again. You can also use the following command:

```
C> TREE C:\ | MORE
```

That's the same command as before, followed by a space, the pipe character (|), another space, and the word MORE. This inserts an automatic *more prompt* at the bottom of each screen. Press the spacebar to look at the next screen.

If you want to print a copy of the output, turn on your printer and type this command:

```
C> TREE C:\ > PRN
```

That's the same TREE command described in the preceding example, a space, a greater-than symbol (>), another space, and the word PRN. Press Enter. If the printed output looks gross, try this variation of the command:

```
C> TREE C:\ /A > PRN
```

That's a slash-A in the middle of the command, surrounded by a space on each side. (Well, as you make more demands on DOS, it gets more cryptic. But at least your printed copy won't look so gross.)

Using the Explorer to view the tree

In Windows 95, you can see the same tree structure displayed by the TREE command, but in the Explorer. To start the Explorer, right-click the mouse on the My Computer icon on the desktop and choose Explore from the shortcut menu. The Explorer appears on the screen, looking similar to what you see in Figure 11-2.

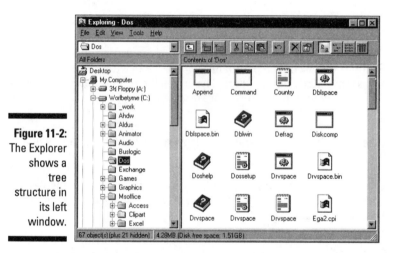

Figure 11-2:
The Explorer shows a tree structure in its left window.

What you should look for is the tree structure displayed in the Explorer's left window. Actually, in the Explorer, it's more like an outline with collapsible topics. These "topics" are really branches in your hard drive's subdirectories.

- 🖝 To open a branch, click on a + (plus) by a folder's name.
- 🖝 To close a branch, click on the – (minus) by a folder's name.
- 🖝 To see the contents of a folder (directory), click on that folder's name.
- 🖝 To learn more about the Explorer, refer to your favorite Windows book.
- 🖝 Close the Explorer's window when you're done by clicking on its X close button.

Is My Disk Okay?

Computer disks are nothing like melons. You can't thump them to hear if they're ripe. You can't see any soft spots. And you can't slice into them to find a soupy-white mush of maggots to realize a disk is rotten. Instead, you have an interesting disk-prodding tool called ScanDisk that can do the thumping, looking, and slicing for you — plus a bit of repair.

Scanning the disk with ScanDisk

I'm not trying to fool you here, but ScanDisk isn't a DOS program. It's a Windows program. Even if you remember running it from the DOS prompt, forget it! ScanDisk now runs in Windows, but there are still a few advantages to running it from a DOS prompt.

What ScanDisk does is take a close look at your disk, and if it finds anything awry, it fixes it on the spot. Nifty, even if it is a Windows-only program.

To use ScanDisk, type the following command at the DOS prompt:

```
C> SCANDISK /A /N
```

Type SCANDISK, a space, slash-A, another space, slash-N. Press the Enter key.

After pressing Enter, ScanDisk — the Windows program — runs (see Figure 11-3). The options you typed tell ScanDisk to run automatically, which means you don't have to mess with the ScanDisk dialog box and that ScanDisk does everything you need it to do without any extra effort on your behalf. Basically, ScanDisk proceeds to smell, squeeze, and thump your disk, looking for any soft spots.

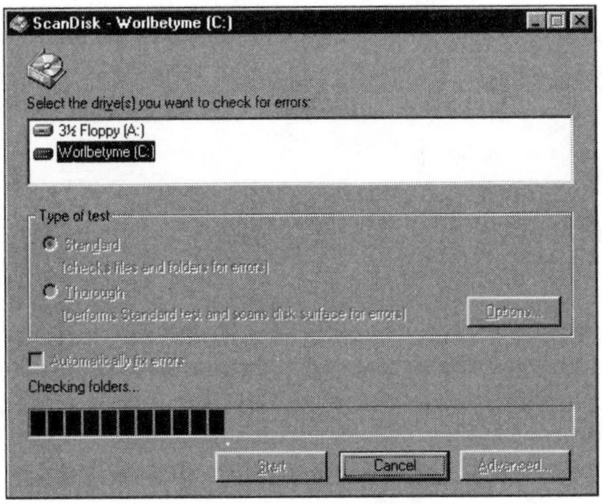

Figure 11-3:
ScanDisk
at work.

ScanDisk's final duty is to offer you an annoyingly complex summary screen. The first line of this screen is all you need to read. In Figure 11-4 it says ScanDisk did not find any errors on this drive. Cool. Neat-o. You passed the SAT! Press the Enter key to close the statistical window and get back to the DOS prompt.

Figure 11-4:
The results
are in.

✔ You should run ScanDisk to check your disk drives at least once a month, more often if you're getting any disk errors.

✔ Refer to the next section for information on what to do when ScanDisk finds an error.

✔ The /A option tells ScanDisk to check all of your disk drives automatically. *A* could mean All or Automatically, or maybe even Alabama.

✔ To use ScanDisk on a specific disk drive, follow the SCANDISK command with that drive letter. For example

```
C>SCANDISK A:
```

The preceding command scans a floppy disk in drive A. Substitute your favorite drive letter for A: to scan that drive.

✔ The /N option tells ScanDisk to start and finish itself automatically, reducing any futzing you need to do in the ScanDisk dialog box. I have no idea what N stands for.

Having ScanDisk fix your disk

When ScanDisk finds something amiss with the disk it's scanning, it lets you know. A box appears on the screen detailing the error, similar to the box shown in Figure 11-5. The box does its best to explain what's wrong and offers you several options at fixing the problem. Most of the time, when you're faced with such a box, pressing Enter patches things up nicely.

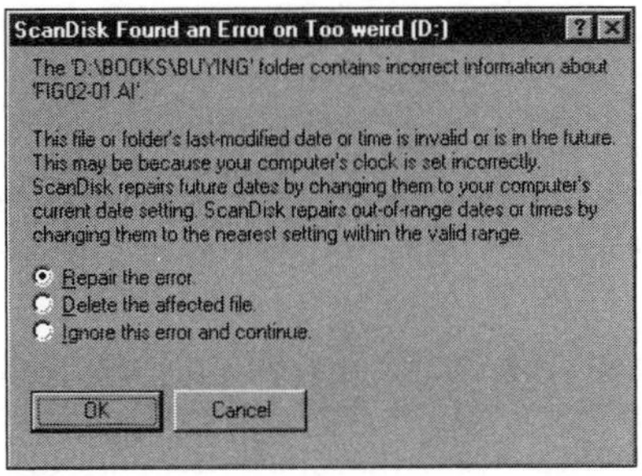

Figure 11-5:
ScanDisk
fixes a
boo-boo.

✔ A common disk boo-boo that ScanDisk locates is the old "lost files or directories" error. When that happens, choose the option to Delete the files. Sure, you can save them. But nearly all of the time they contain stuff you don't need. And when they do contain useful information, it takes someone with a computer science Ph.D. to pull the information out of the recovered files into a useable form. My advice: Delete 'em and forget 'em.

✔ Don't bother with an "undo disk" if ScanDisk asks you. Having one sure sounds safe, but it slows up the disk repair operations and — I'm sorry to report — if your disk is that bad off, the undo disk isn't going to help you anyway.

Backing Up

Backing up is making a safety copy of your data, typically the data on your hard drive. You make a copy of all the files on your hard drive on a large stack of floppy disks or, more preferably, to a snazzy tape backup unit. Either way takes about the same amount of time, but the tape backup unit takes less of your effort. And the software to handle that job is called Backup, which proves that cleverness must ooze from the pores of the creative types at Microsoft.

Alas, backing up just isn't a DOS thing anymore. The Backup program is now Windows-only, which is good since Windows is (*sniff, sniff*) in charge now. Therefore, the following check marks provide some background pointers on using Backup. I'll leave the nuts-and-bolts of running the Backup program to your favorite book on Windows.

✔ You should back up the files you create or use everyday. I do this religiously and haven't lost anything I have been writing in more than nine years (since my Big Blue period).

✔ Backing up today's work, or all of the changed files today, is called an *incremental backup.*

✔ Every week or every other week, back up the entire hard drive. The whole dang doodle. All of it.

✔ Use several sets of backup diskettes or backup tapes. Always keep the old ones in a safe place. In my office, we have a fire safe where we store our backup disks and tapes.

✔ You can back up a single file if you like. In fact, this is one of the best ways to transport a large file to another computer; the backup file can span several diskettes.

✔ The process of copying your backup files from the backup disk or tapes back to the hard drive is called *restore*. This can be done to recover an older version of a file or to restore an entire hard drive should something unspeakable happen to it.

✔ No one has to back up. Since there is no rigid penalty, few people do. Only those who've lost everything on their hard drive due to some mishap back up every day without fail. I'm among that group, and since the Big Hard Disk Crash of '87 I've backed up every day, without fail, and haven't lost a byte of data since. Don't let something stupid like losing your entire hard drive force you into the backup habit.

✔ By the way, you must manually install the Backup program onto your computer. Again, I'll leave it up to that other Windows book to explain the details.

Freeing Up Space on a Hard Disk

Your main weapon in the battle of shrinking disk space is to buy another hard drive. As an alternative you can meddle with disk compression, but I don't recommend it. Another way to fight the battle is just to delete files. No, not randomly; every hard drive has a few extra gross of files just lying around that aren't needed for anything, and that can quickly vanish with deft use of the DEL command. The problem is knowing which files you can safely delete without fouling up the whole system.

Generally speaking, you can delete any of the following types of files:

✔ Backup files (ending with the .BAK extension)

✔ Temporary or junk files

After deleting those types of files, you can free up disk space by doing what the nerds call *archiving*. That's taking old data files that you don't need anymore but don't want to delete and copying them to floppy disks.

For example, if you store all of last year's budget files and proposals in a specific place, copy them all to floppies, properly label the floppies, and then delete the old files from your hard drive. That way you'll still have the files on floppy disks, but lots more room will be made available on your hard drive. This technique usually frees up the most space, and you can use the Windows Backup program as discussed in your favorite book on Windows.

You can also archive old programs and especially games from your system. I found a copy of an old disk utility on my hard drive that was eating up 8 megabytes — and I hadn't used the program in over a year!

Chapter 12
Files — Lost and Found

Did you know that the word *file* can be anagrammed into the words *life* or *lief?* Aside from that, there's really nothing interesting about files. Well, actually only two things: The first is the good news that under Windows 95 you can actually name a file pretty darn much anything you like. No more are you stuck with a task akin to getting a 14-letter last name on a 7-character vanity license plate. The second, and unfortunate thing, is that files, like certain socks, occasionally get sucked into some parallel universe since the last time you saw them. It's like the car-keys gremlin who goes around snatching up your keys for a few seconds. There's also a file gremlin who steals files — even though you just saved them to disk.

This chapter contains instructions for defeating the file gremlin, whose name is probably Lief. Actually, this chapter contains tidbits of information about using files, naming files, and all that file stuff. It doesn't contain information on copying, renaming, or deleting files, which is conveniently stored in Chapter 9.

Name That File!

When you create a file, you give it a name. The name should reflect what's in the file or somehow be able to describe the file's contents. After all, it's that name that gives you the clue as to what the file is when you are looking at a directory listing.

One of the blessings of Windows 95 is that you're now no longer limited to the lousy eight-character filename limit. On the downside, this technique requires that you always bookend your filenames with double quotes. So it's a six-of-one/half-dozen-of-the-other solution.

✔ Actually, your files now have *two* names! One is the long name and the other is the shorter, abbreviated DOS name. Of course, this dichotomy doesn't present itself if you stick with less-than-eight character filenames.

✔ **dichotomy** (di-kot'-e-mee) *n.,pl.* **1.** Something divided into two conflicting or contradictory parts. **2.** A filename now legal under DOS. See also DICHOT~1.

General file-naming rules

You can name a file just about anything — providing you always put that name into double quotes. The filenames can contain spaces, periods, and a veritable salad bar of other characters. But you must enclose everything in double quotes. To wit

```
"LETTER TO MOM"
```

That's a proper filename in DOS under Windows 95. It doesn't start with a double quote, by the way. The filename is LETTER (space) TO (space) MOM (end of file name). The double quotes merely contain the filename.

The following are all also considered okey-dokey filenames:

```
"WordPerfect 5.1 Documents"
"alt.adjective.noun.verb.verb.verb"
"Here, there, and everywhere!"
"Six of one; half dozen of the other"
"The longest filename you can type in is 255 characters,
 though my advice is always to be brief."
"This could really drive you NUTS!"
"+"
"Alicia Silverstone.jpg"
```

If this drives you nuts, you can always use the older, traditional way of naming files (covered later). However, as long as you enclose your DOS files in double quotes, just about anything goes.

✔ There are a few characters you cannot use in a filename. See "Use These Filenames, Go Directly to Jail!" later in this very same chapter.

✔ Upper- and lower-case letters are seen the same by DOS. So the following long filenames all represent the same file on disk:

```
"get out of the house!"
"Get out of the house!"
"GET OUT OF THE HOUSE!"
```

✔ Always surround your long filenames with double quotes!

✔ Since directories (folders) can have long names too, you'll have to enclose full *pathnames* in double quotes if *any part* of them contains a long name.

For example:

```
"C:\MY DOCUMENTS\LETTER.DOC"
```

See Chapter 11 for more information on pathnames.

✔ Here's a list of characters formerly forbidden in a DOS filename that are now utterly okey-dokey:

```
. [ ] + = ; ,
```

Also included in that list is the space character (it's up there, but you just can't see it).

✔ Filenames can be up to 255 characters long. For the sake of brevity, however, it pays to keep your filenames short and to the point.

✔ See the section "The old, traditional DOS way" for the other way you can name files, a shorter way minus the double quotes.

Using long filenames with your DOS commands

All DOS commands can work with the longer filenames. Again, the only thing you need to remember is the double quotes. For example:

```
C> REN LTR2MOM.DOC "Tuesday's letter to Mom.DOC"
```

The REN command renames a shorter DOS filename to a longer Windows filename.

```
C> COPY "Bogus company report 16.WKS" A:
```

The above COPY command copies the file named BOGUS COMPANY REPORT 16.WKS to the floppy disk in drive A.

```
C> DEL "I'm sick of this, let's do something else now."
```

The DOS command deletes the file named I'M SICK OF THIS, LET'S DO SOME-THING ELSE NOW.

- ✔ See "Wither goest thy filename extension?" for more information on the filename extensions.
- ✔ See Chapter 9 for more information on the REN, COPY, and DEL commands.

Using long filenames with your applications

When it comes to using long filenames with your favorite DOS programs, don't! They won't recognize them. Alas, for DOS programs — save for a few exceptions — you're stuck with using the shorter, traditional, eight-character filenames.

- ✔ When you do use long filenames in an application, in WordPad for example, do not specify the double quotes. They are only needed at the DOS prompt.
- ✔ The MS-DOS Editor now accepts long filenames. See Chapter 8.
- ✔ Any DOS program that doesn't specifically support Windows 95 features cannot accept the longer filenames. Oh, you can try. But I'll bet it probably won't work!

Recognizing a long filename in a DIR command

Long filenames appear two ways in the DIR commands output:

```
SALLY'~1        355  08-19-96 10:25p Sally's job
```

First comes what's called the *truncated DOS filename*. This is a traditional, old-style DOS filename. It's a shorter version of the longer filename (and one you can freely use without the double quotes).

Next come the file's size, date, and time. Finally comes the long Windows 95 filename.

- ✔ Both filenames are OK to use.

- ✔ If you use the long filename with a DOS command, remember to enclose it in double quotes. The DIR command doesn't put it in double quotes (probably just to confuse you).

- ✔ The shorter, truncated, traditional DOS version of the filename will not display any of the following characters:

```
. [ ] + = ; ,
```

Instead of the above, you'll see an underline character in the shorter DOS filename. For example, you could have a file named the following:

```
64+64.TXT
```

This file will look like this in the DIR command's output:

```
64_64~1.TXT    355  08-19-96 10:25p 64+64.txt
```

Why? I dunno. But don't be surprised when you see such a filename. And remember that both versions — 64_64~1.TXT or 64+64.TXT — work.

Don't bother with this trivia about truncated DOS filenames

Oh, I could go into the **what's** and **why's** of the truncated DOS filenames, even telling you how Windows cheats to create long filenames, but why bother? What you might care about is that the truncated file contains the first six letters of the long filename, a tilde, and then a number or letter. The number allows you to have several long filenames that each start out the same. For example:

```
"Here's a joke about religion"
```

This file would have a truncated version named HERE'S~1.

```
"Here's a joke about politics"
```

This file would have a truncated version named HERE'S~2.

The numbers after the tilde keep the shorter versions unique. You can use the DIR command to see which name matches up to which file.

Also, when you access Windows 95 files over a network from an older DOS machine, you'll only see the truncated filenames listed. This keeps everyone happy.

Whither goest thy filename extension?

A filename extension is a period followed by the last three characters of a filename. It's used by both DOS and Windows to identify a file of a certain type. This remains true even if you use a long filename; the last three characters after a period are the extension.

```
"Chapter 27.DOC"
```

The above filename has the extension .DOC, probably a document file created by a word processor.

```
"TIC.TOC.TXT"
```

The above filename has an extension .TXT. Even though a period is used before the extension in the filename, only the last three characters after a period count.

Here are some common file extensions:

.ANI	Animated cursor file
.AVI	Video clip file
.BAK	A copy of a data file as a backup
.BAT	A special type of program; a batch file
.BFC	Briefcase file
.BMP	Bitmap image file
.COM	A command program or command file (program file)
.CUR	Cursor file
.DBF	A database file
.DCX	Fax file
.DOC	WordPad document
.EXE	An executable file or another type of program
.FON	Font file
.GIF	Graphics file (CompuServe naked lady format)
.HLP	Windows help file
.ICO	Icon file
.INI	Configuration file
.JPG	JPEG graphic file
.MID	Midi file

.PCD	Kodak PhotoCD graphic
.PIC	A picture file
.SYS	A system file
.TGA	Targa graphic file
.TIF	Graphics file (TIFF)
.TXT	A text file
.TXT	Text document
.WAV	Sound file
.WKS	A worksheet file
.XLB	Excel worksheet (also XLS)

Windows uses these extensions to identify certain files as belonging to certain programs. Therefore, you must be careful when you use them. However, for DOS programs it doesn't really matter.

You may not see these extensions at all when browsing files using the Explorer or My Computer. Windows sometimes shuts off the extensions so as not to confuse people (or to confuse people, I forget which). To turn on the extensions, start up the Explorer and choose View➪Options. In the Options dialog box, View panel, click the mouse to remove the check mark by Hide MS-DOS file extensions for file types that are registered. That way Windows will show all filename extensions.

The old, traditional DOS way

You need to bother with double quotes only if you're going to give a file a name longer than eight characters. If you're under the eight-character limit, you can name things the old-fashioned way, without the double quotes. In that mode you'll be using the traditional and much-hated *eight-dot-three* file naming pattern:

```
FILENAME.EXT
```

The first part of the filename can have up to eight characters. This can be followed by an optional dot (period) plus up to three additional characters. This is where they get the eight-dot-three (which really sounds like Mr. Spock calling out photon torpedo spreads).

The first eight characters of a filename are the descriptive part. These characters can be any number or letter — but no spaces! For example, the following are all OK filenames, none requiring double quotes or other voodoo:

```
TEST
A
80PROOF
HELLO
1040
LETTER
KINGFISH
```

If you want to add an extension to a filename, you must specify the dot (or period) and then up to three more characters. Here is the same group of rowdy files with extensions added:

```
TEST.OUT
A.1
80PROOF.GIN
HELLO.MOM
1040.X
LETTER.DOC
KINGFISH.ME
```

Again, the only limitation here is to avoid using a space in the filename. If you must have a space in there, the filename *must* be enclosed in double quotes. It doesn't matter how long it is. But if you stick with just letters and numbers, eight characters or less mean no double quotes.

Use These Filenames, Go Directly to Jail!

If you goof when you name a file, you'll usually get some pleasing error message or an idle threat. Generally speaking, as long as you put your filename in double quotes, you'll be OK.

You cannot, however, under any circumstances — even if the building were on fire and St. Peter appeared to you, winked, and said it was OK just this once — use the following characters in a filename:

```
" / \ : * | < > ?
```

Another warning: Even though you can have a number of periods before, after or amidst a filename, a file cannot be named with all periods. The following are all forbidden filenames:

```
.
..
...
....
```

And so on, up to 255 dots for a filename.

The reason here is that DOS believes the single dot or period to be an abbreviation for the current directory. Therefore, if you try to name a file in this manner, you'll get a `Duplicate file name` or `file in use` or `Path not found` error. The following filename is OK:

```
ANTICI.........PATION!
```

And a filename can start with any number of periods as well:

```
...WHATEVER
```

- ✔ Yes, periods and spaces can be used in your filenames, providing you keep everything between double quotes, and heed the earlier warning about periods.

- ✔ The double quote is a forbidden character? Yes! They're only used to enclose long filenames. You cannot have a double quote in your file name, no, not never. Heavens!

- ✔ DOS uses the slash character for optional switches after a command. See Chapter 5, "About the Darn Command Formats."

- ✔ The backslash is used by DOS as a separator in a pathname. See Chapter 11 for the details.

- ✔ The colon (:) is only used after a letter of the alphabet to identify a disk drive, so it cannot appear in a filename.

- ✔ The special characters asterisk (*) and question mark (?) are actually filename wildcards, covered later in this chapter.

- ✔ The special characters less-than (<), greater-than (>), and the pipe character (|) are all used by DOS for other confusing purposes.

Significant Filenames

Filenames that end with a .COM, .EXE, or .BAT extension are special. Those are actually programs that do things on your computer. As such, please don't name any of your files with those extensions. You can use any other extension or three-letter combination you can dream up. But .COM, .EXE, and .BAT are for programs only.

How to Name a Directory (the MKDIR Command)

Directories are given names just like files. You can give any directory just about any name, providing you keep it all comfy and cozy in double quotes. Traditionally, directories aren't given names longer than eight characters and rarely will they have an extension.

Directories are named as they're created. You do this by using the MD command. Here's an example:

```
C> MD MISC
```

This command is MD, for *Make Directory,* followed by a space and the name of the directory to create. In this case, DOS creates a subdirectory named MISC. (For more on subdirectories, refer to Chapter 11.)

If you're in a long-file naming mood, use the following:

```
C> MD "MISCELLANEOUS"
```

But since few people can remember how to spell MISCELLANEOUS, I'd stick with MISC.

✔ There is no visual feedback for creating a directory.

✔ Remember, stick with eight characters or less, letters and numbers only, and you don't have to use the double quotes.

✔ If you don't like your directory's name, you can rename it using the REN command. All the rules for renaming files apply; see Chapter 9 for the details.

✔ Creating directories is a job best left to someone else. However, you can create your own directories to store your favorite files, thus keeping them together. More information on subdirectories is offered in Chapter 11.

Using the DIR Command

The DIR command is used to see a list of files on disk. You just type **DIR** and press Enter:

```
C> DIR
```

The files are listed in a special format, shown with their size and date and time of creation or last update.

The filename is shown twice. The first filename is the short, truncated DOS name. And in the DIR command's output you'll see that the filename is separated from the extension, like this:

```
AUTOEXEC  BAT
CONFIG    SYS
```

They do this so that all the extensions are lined up in one column. Although this makes the directory listing look all nice and pretty, it doesn't show you how to accurately type in that filename.

The second filename is shown after the time and it doesn't have any unnecessary spaces. That filename, long or short, appears as its wholesome self:

```
AUTOEXEC.BAT
CONFIG.SYS
```

To see a list of files on another drive, use the DIR command with the drive letter and a colon:

```
C> DIR A:
```

In this example, you'll see a listing of all files on the disk in drive A. Substitute B: for A: if you want to look at drive B.

To see a list of files in another directory on the same disk, specify that directory's pathname after the DIR command:

```
C> DIR \WP60\DATA
```

Here the DIR command lists all the files in the \WP60\ data subdirectory.

To see a single file's information, just type that file's name after the DIR command:

```
C> DIR BLOOP.NOF
```

Here the DIR command is followed by the file named BLOOP.NOF. Only that single file (and its associated and miscellaneous information) will be displayed.

To see only a specific group of files, follow the DIR command with the proper, matching wildcard:

```
C> DIR *.COM
```

In this example, DIR is followed by a space, an asterisk, a period, and then .COM. This command displays only those files with the .COM extension.

- ✔ There are no double quotes around the second filename in the DIR command's output. Why? Because the double quotes aren't part of the filename!

- ✔ For more information on subdirectories and pathnames, refer to Chapter 11.

- ✔ For more information on using wildcards, refer to "Wildcards (or Poker Was Never This Much Fun)" later in this chapter.

The wide DIR command

When you long for the wide open spaces of the Big Sky country, you can use the following DIR command:

```
C> DIR /W
```

That's the DIR command, a space, and slash-W. Pressing Enter displays the directory listing in the wide format, with only the truncated (short) filenames marching across the screen five abreast.

If you want to display a wide directory of another drive or a subdirectory, sandwich the drive letter or subdirectory pathname between the DIR and the /W. For example:

```
C> DIR A: /W
```

or:

```
C> DIR \WP60\DATA /W
```

Refer to the previous section for more details.

Making DIR display one screen at a time

When the DIR command scrolls and scrolls, rolling up and up the screen and you cannot find the file, you can use the following DIR command at the next DOS prompt:

```
C> DIR /P
```

That's the DIR command, followed by a space and a slash-P. The P means *page* or *pause*, and DOS will insert a friendly "press any key" message after each screen of filenames. Press the spacebar to continue.

✔ To cancel the listing, press Ctrl+C. Refer to "Canceling a DOS Command" in Chapter 3.

✔ If you're just hunting down a specific file, follow the DIR command with that filename. Refer to "Using the DIR Command" earlier in this chapter.

✔ If you're looking for a group of files that can be matched with a wildcard, refer to "Wildcards (or Poker Was Never This Much Fun)" later in this chapter.

✔ You can use this DIR command to see a directory listing of another drive or subdirectory. Just sandwich that drive letter or subdirectory pathname between DIR and the /P. Here's an example:

```
C> DIR A: /P
```

> or:

```
C> DIR \WP60\DATA /P
```

Refer to the section "Using the DIR Command" earlier in this chapter if you care to fondle the DIR command further.

Displaying a sorted directory

Have you ever gotten the impression that DOS could just care less? It's true. When DOS displays a list of files, it shows them to you in any old order. To sort the files in the listing alphabetically, use the following DIR command:

```
C> DIR /O
```

That's the DIR command, a space, and then slash-O. The O must stand for *Oh, sort these,* or maybe the word *sort* in a foreign language. (It may mean *order* — naaa.)

Finding a Lost File

In some cases, losing a file is worse than losing a pet or a small child in the mall. Pets and children have legs and wander off. Files? Where do they go? (And would one expect to find them in the video arcade?)

The first step in locating a lost file is knowing its name. If you want to copy a file and are greeted with the happy `File not found` error message, you may have mistyped the name. (It happens.) Check your typing. Furthermore, you may want to check the directory listing to see if the file is there. Type this command:

```
C> DIR /P
```

The slash-P pauses the listing, enabling you to scan each entry. Even the author of this book has transposed filenames as he's saved them. (Here's a hint: The new files are usually listed at the end of the directory, though that's not a hard-and-fast rule.)

If the file still doesn't show up, use this command:

```
C> DIR \WHERE.AMI /S
```

That's the DIR command, followed by a space, and then a backslash and the filename. In this example, the filename, WHERE.AMI, is used. After the filename comes a space and then slash-S. For finding long files, remember the double quotes:

```
C> DIR "\WHERE AM I" /S
```

The double quotes surround the entire filename, including the \ (which is part of the *path*).

By pressing Enter, you tell DOS to search the entire hard drive for the file you've specified. If it's found, you'll see it on the screen as follows:

```
Directory of C:\LOST\FOUND
WHERE AMI   574 08-01-94 10:04a WHERE.AMI
  1 file(s)   574 bytes
```

Here DOS has found the lost file in the subdirectory \LOST\FOUND. You then need to use the CD command to move to that subdirectory and from there you can get at the file. (The CD command is covered in "Changing Directories" in Chapter 11.)

 ✔ If any additional matching files are found, they're listed as well, along with their directory.

 ✔ When you find the lost file, consider copying it to the proper location, or use the REN command to rename the file to the name you originally thought you used. Refer to "Copying a Single File" in Chapter 9 for information on the COPY command; refer to "Renaming a File," also in Chapter 9, for information on REN.

Finding files in Windows

Windows comes with a nifty — and thorough — Find command you can use to find files all over creation. You can access it by pressing the F3 key when you see Windows desktop, or choose Find⇨Files or Folders from the Start thing's menu. The Find dialog box appears, where you can type in the name of the file, the last time you accessed it, plus maybe any text you may remember in the file. Click the Find Now button and maybe — just maybe if you're really good — Windows will locate the file.

Unlike finding a file in DOS, if you're hunting for something with a long filename, you don't have to put it in double quotes in the Find: All Files dialog box.

✔ If the list scrolls off the screen, you can tack on the slash-P option. Here's an example:

```
C> DIR \WHERE.AMI /S /P
```

Everything else in the command remains the same.

✔ If the file still isn't found, it may be on another disk drive. Log to another drive and then type the same DIR command again.

✔ If you still cannot find the file on any drive, you probably saved it under a different name. Because I don't know what that name is, it's up to you to scour your drive looking for it. Use the CD and DIR commands to move around and find the file.

✔ Don't rule out the possibility that you deleted the file using Windows. If so, check Windows Recycle Bin for the file. See your favorite Windows book for clean and effortless file recovery.

Finding a Lost Subdirectory

A lost subdirectory is a bit harder to find than a lost file, especially when you know that it's somewhere on the drive — but where? As with finding a lost file, the first step is to use the DIR command. Look for the telltale <DIR> in the listing. That shows you all the subdirectories.

If you don't find your subdirectory, you can use the DIR command to search for it. Type in the following (this is bizarre, so watch your fingers):

```
C> DIR \*.*/A:D /S | FIND "MARS PROBE"
```

That's the DIR command, a space, and then a backslash and star-dot-star. That's followed by another space, a slash-A, a colon and D, and then a space and a slash-S. A space follows slash-S, and then the pipe or vertical bar character, another space, the FIND command, a space, and then the name of the subdirectory you're looking for (MARS PROBE in the example). The subdirectory name *must* be in uppercase (all caps) and have a double quote character (") on either side whether or not it's a long filename.

Press Enter and DOS scours the drive, looking for your subdirectory. If it's found, it is displayed as follows:

```
MARSPR~1  <DIR>  09-23-97 7:23p mars probe
Directory of C:\LOST\mars probe
```

The subdirectory's name comes first — as it would in a directory listing. That's followed by the pathname. To change to that subdirectory, you would type in the pathname following the CD command. In the example, that would be:

```
C> CD "\LOST\MARS PROBE"
```

Or if you're an old DOS fanatic (or just enjoy using that out-of-the-way tilde key):

```
C> CD \LOST\MARSPR~1
```

✔ If more than one subdirectory appears, you may have to log or change to each one in turn to find the one you're looking for.

✔ There is a chance that this command may not find your subdirectory. In that case, you can use the TREE command to view your hard disk's tree structure. Refer to "The Tree Structure" in Chapter 11.

✔ Refer to Chapter 11 for more information on the CD command and pathnames.

Wildcards (or Poker Was Never This Much Fun)

Wildcards enable you to manipulate a group of files using a single DOS command. The object here, just like using wildcards in poker, is to specify wildcards in a filename in such a way as to match other files on disk. That way you can wrangle a group of files — the whole lot of them — with only one command. This is the convenience aspect of computers they promised in the brochure.

For example, if you've named all the chapters in your Great American Novel starting with CHAPTER, you can treat all of them as a group using a wildcard. If all your special project files start with PROJ, you can do things to those files en masse — even if the rest of the files are named something completely different.

There are two wildcards DOS uses, the question mark (?) and the asterisk (*). They are covered in the following two sections.

REMEMBER

- ✔ Wildcards are generally used with DOS commands. They can seldom be used inside programs.

- ✔ Remember, if you're using long filenames, to enclose the whole filename — including the wildcards — in double quotes.

- ✔ Not all DOS commands will swallow wildcards. The TYPE command, for one, must be followed by a single filename. Refer to "Looking at Files" in Chapter 2.

Using the ? wildcard

The ? wildcard is used to match any single letter in a filename. It can be used by itself or in multiples of however many characters you want to match. For example:

The wildcard filename TH?? matches all four-letter filenames starting with TH, including:

```
THIS
THAT
"THURSTON HOWELL III"
```

The wildcard filename CHAP?? matches all files starting with CHAP and having one or two more letters in their name. This includes:

```
chap00
CHAP01
CHAP02
```

On up through:

```
CHAP99
```

and any other combination of characters in those two positions.

You can also use the ? wildcard in a filename extension:

The wildcard filename BOOK.D?? matches all filenames starting with BOOK and having D as the first letter of their extension:

```
BOOK.DOC
BOOK.DIC
BOOK.DUH
BOOK.DOO
```

You can even mix and match the ? wildcard:

The wildcard filename JULY????.WK? matches all files starting with JULY that have WK as the first two letters of their extension:

```
JULY13.WKS
"JULY 4TH.WKD"
```

All of these wildcard combinations can be used with DOS's file exploitation commands: DIR, DEL, COPY, REN, and so on. Refer to Chapter 9 for more information on manipulating groups of files.

Using the * wildcard

The * wildcard is more powerful than the single-character ? wildcard. The asterisk is used to match groups of one or more characters in a filename. Here are the examples:

- ✔ The wildcard filename *.DOC matches all files that have .DOC as their extension. The first part of the filename can have any number of characters in it; *.DOC matches them all.

- ✔ The wildcard filename PROJECT.* matches all files with PROJECT as their first part, with any second part — even if they don't have any second part.

The * wildcard can also be used in the middle or start of a filename to match things in a rather strange manner.

The wildcard filename *ER matches all filenames that end with ER, including:

```
PACKAGER
RECORDER
PLAYER
VIEWER
```

In the middle of a filename, B*ING would match all filenames :

```
BORING
BEDDING
BEGINNING
"BOTTLE FEEDING"
```

Note that B*ING will match "BOTTLE FEEDING" even though B*ING isn't in double quotes. Clever that DOS, eh?

Quirky yet easily skippable stuff

If you want to match all filenames that start with B, use this wildcard:

```
B*
```

This matches all files, whether or not they have a second part. True, you could use B*.*, but DOS matches the same files, so why bother with the extra dot-star?

The wildcard *. (star-dot) matches only filenames *without* an extension. This is the only time under DOS that a command could end in a period. Here's an example:

```
C> DIR *.
```

In this example, the DIR command shows only files without any extension (typically only the subdirectories).

*Using *.* (star-dot-star)*

The most popular wildcard is the "Everyone out of the pool!" wildcard, *.*, which is pronounced *star-dot-star*. It means everything, all files, no matter what their name (but usually not directories).

Since star-dot-star matches everything, you should be careful when using it. This is that one rare occasion in your life when you can get everyone's attention. It's like: You can't fool all of the files some of the time, but you can fool all of them all of the time with star-dot-star.

- ✔ The COPY *.* command copies all files in the directory. Refer to "Copying a Group of Files" in Chapter 9.
- ✔ The DEL *.* command is deadly; it ruthlessly destroys all files in the directory; refer to "Deleting a Group of Files" in Chapter 9.

✔ The REN command with *.* is tricky. You must specify a wildcard as the second part of the REN command; you cannot give every file in the directory the same name. Here's an example:

```
C> REN *.DOC *.WP
```

In this example, all files with the .DOC extension are renamed to have a .WP extension. That's about the most you can do with the REN command and wildcards.

✔ Shhh! Technically speaking, you really need to use only * (a single star) with Windows 95. The DIR * command and DIR *.* both now mean the same thing since a period in the middle of a file is no longer special. Even so, I'd stick with *.* since it will be compatible with your old DOS programs and utilities.

Part IV

Yikes! (or Help Me Out of This One!)

The 5th Wave By Rich Tennant

"OH SURE, $1.8 MILLION DOLLARS SEEMS LIKE ALOT RIGHT NOW, BUT WHAT ABOUT RANDY? WHAT ABOUT HIS FUTURE? THINK WHAT A COMPUTER LIKE THIS WILL DO FOR HIS S.A.T. SCORE SOMEDAY."

In this part...

Computers have an attitude. They induce dread and fear, mostly because when something goes wrong, it does so without any foreshadowing. Without motivation, your computer just suddenly doesn't work. "I mean, I used this stupid thing yesterday, and today it won't work!" Don't worry, even the DOS gurus have these problems.

The good news is, of course, that your computer won't explode. But it will do some unfriendly things that make your heart drop a few flights. Some of this stuff isn't serious at all, which is what this part of the book tries to explain. But sometimes it pays to call in an expert. This part is where you'll learn how to tell the difference between the two situations.

Chapter 13

When It's Time to Toss in the Towel (and Call a PC Guru)

Computers, like anything made by the human hand, aren't perfect. For the most part, they work flawlessly. But suddenly you feel that something is wrong — like when you're driving your car and it feels a little sluggish or when you eat one last piece of pizza and then you hear *that noise*.

Computers won't usually act sluggish or make noises when they go south, but they will start behaving oddly. This chapter tells you what you can do in those situations, and it gives you an idea of when it's time to yell out for a professional to deal with the situation.

My Computer's Down and I Can't Get It Up!

You have a problem. Your computer isn't working the way it should. Something is definitely amiss.

The first step is to analyze the problem. Break everything down and find out what is working. Even if you can't fix the problem, you're better prepared to tell an expert about it and have him or her deal with it.

Check the following items first:

- ✔ Is the computer plugged in? Seriously, check to see if it is. If the computer is plugged into a power strip, make sure that the power strip is plugged in and switched on. Furthermore, you may want to check other items plugged into the same socket. Bad sockets happen. And check the circuit breaker.

- ✔ Is everything else plugged in? Monitors, modems, and printers all need to be plugged in. Are there power cords attached? Are they turned on?

- ✔ Note that most power cords on your computer have two connections: One end plugs into the wall (or a power strip) and the other plugs into the computer, printer, modem, and so on. Believe it or not, *both* ends need to be plugged in for the computer to work. One end is *not* built into the computer the way it is in an iron or TV set.

Check the following connections:

- ✔ Computers have a ganglia of cables attached. There are power supply cables, and then there are data cables. A printer has two cables: a power cable and a printer cable. The power cable connects to the wall socket; the printer cable connects to the computer.

- ✔ Modems can have three or four cables attached: a power supply; a data line between the modem and the computer's serial port; one phone line from the modem to your telephone; and, often, a second phone line from your modem to the phone company's wall socket.

- ✔ By the way, your modem has two places to plug in the phone jack. One hole is for a phone cord that goes to the wall, often labeled *Line*. The other hole, for a phone you can use (obviously) when your computer isn't using the modem, is often labeled *Phone*. The modem cannot dial out if the phone cords are switched, but — and this is odd — a phone plugged into the wrong hole *will* work. Strange.

- ✔ Make sure that all the cables are connected to their proper *ports* on the PC's rump. You may have to trace each cable with your finger, seeing as how the back of a PC resembles the tail end of a squid. Also, serial and parallel ports look similar on some PCs. If your modem or printer isn't working, try swapping the plug around a few times (of course, this is assuming that it worked once before).

- ✔ Keyboard cables can come loose, especially given the unique design of most PCs where the keyboard is connected to the back (which never made sense). But be careful here; plug or unplug the keyboard connector only when the computer is turned off.

Here are some other things to check:

✔ Is the computer locked? There's a key on the front of most PCs. It must be turned to the unlocked or open position for you to use the computer.

✔ Is the monitor off or dimmed? Monitors have their own on/off switches; make sure that the monitor switch is on. Also, monitors can be dimmed, so check the brightness knob. Furthermore, some operating systems, such as OS/2 and Windows, have _screen dimming_ programs. Try pressing the spacebar to see if the monitor comes back on.

✔ Is there a blackout? If so, you won't be able to use the computer. Sorry.

✔ Is there a brownout? A brownout happens when the electric company isn't sending enough juice through the power lines. A computer won't turn on if the required number of volts isn't present. If the system is already on, a brownout will force the system to shut itself off. This is unusual because, during a brownout, the lights in the room and all your clocks may continue to work.

The following items are all general things to look for and quick items to check if you're not a professional computer doctor. They're also all hardware items. If your problem is in software, refer to the discussion under "It's Just Acting Weird" later in this chapter.

✔ If possible, you can further narrow the problem down to a specific part of the computer: the computer box, disk drives, keyboard, monitor, printer, or some other peripheral. If everything works OK except for one part of the computer, you've narrowed down the problem far enough to tell the repair person about it over the phone.

✔ Fixing this stuff isn't hard. Most repair places or computer consultants will simply replace a defective part with a brand new one. In fact, I would go out on a limb here and say: Never trust anyone who claims to be able to fix what you have without needing to replace anything. I speak from personal experience here. Some bozo claimed he could fix my $4,000 (1987 model) laser printer. After $600 of his attempts, it ended up costing me another $1,000 to fully replace the defective part. An expensive lesson, but one worth passing on.

It's Just Acting Weird

Computers act weird all the time. Sometimes, however, they act more weird than usual. If you've gone through the previous section and have determined that your hardware works fine, then what you may have is a software problem.

The best thing to check for with a software problem is any recent changes made to the system. With Windows now, you make changes typically using the Control Panel or often by right-clicking something and changing its Properties. These changes can drastically affect how the system works: You could lose disk drives, some programs won't find enough memory, and some applications will refuse to work. To remedy the problem, undo your changes, or call someone else for help.

Frequently, weirdness can occur after a period of time. The longest I've been able to continuously run my word processing software (without shutting the computer off) is about three days. (OK, I slept a little every night.) After three weeks, mold must grow on the circuits because the computer suddenly stops working. The same thing happens to other programs as well, but with different time periods involved. Windows itself usually needs to be reset once a week or so to keep it happy.

✔ Windows has a "safe" startup mode in case things get entirely weird on you, such as you've messed with the Control Panel and suddenly everything on the screen comes in two shades: dark and green. If that happens, exit Windows (if you can) and start it up in the "Safe mode": press the F8 key when Windows first starts, just after the Starting Windows message (see "The polite way you're supposed to do it" in Chapter 1 for the details). Pressing the F8 key displays a startup menu of sorts (see Figure 1-6). Choose option 3, Safe mode, to start your computer in a way that will undo any potentially damaging changes you may have made. Then undo your deleterious changes and reset Windows to start normally.

✔ Don't be surprised if you suspect a hardware problem and it turns out to be software. For example, losing your hard drive is really a software problem; the physical hard disk hasn't left your computer to go outside and frolic through the garden. Instead, Windows may have mislaid its map of what equipment it's got on board.

✔ Any program you're just learning will act weird until it's used to you. You'll experience at least three confounding, unreproducible errors that your guru never heard of in the first month you use a program intensively — then they'll never occur again. Try not to get too mad at the machine or the software.

The Computer Has Lost Track of the Time

About 99 percent of the computers sold today have battery-backed-up clocks inside. They keep the time no matter what, even if you unplug the PC. So when you notice that the time isn't correct — or the computer thinks it's January 1, 1980 (and Jimmy Carter is still in office!), you need to check your battery.

Replacing a computer's battery is as easy as replacing the battery in a clock or camera. Of course, if you don't particularly think that's easy, make someone else do it for you.

✔ The date and time are set in Windows by right-clicking on the date on the right side of the taskbar. Choose A̲djust Date/Time from the pop-up menu that appears, and then set the current date and time using the Date/Time Properties dialog box. See your favorite book on Windows for the details.

✔ Not only will bad batteries change the time, but computers just lose track of the time for the heck of it. For example, my PC is currently 10 minutes fast. If I don't check it every two weeks or so, it would soon be off several hours in a few months. It's just a PC-nutty thing.

✔ There's also the annoyance of daylight saving time. Just about everyone (outside of Indiana) has to change their PC's clock twice a year. You think computers would do this automatically being computers and all. But, no.

✔ Windows will remind you that the clock needs resetting — and reset it itself — for daylight saving time. But this works only when you first turn your computer on after the clocks change. If you keep your PC on all the time (like I do), you get no gentle reminder.

✔ You can change or set the date using DOS's DATE command. For example, to set today's date to June 11, 1996, type:

```
C> DATE 6-11-96
```

If you type the DATE command by itself, DOS displays what it thinks today is and then gives you a chance to type in a new date, or press Enter to keep the date as it is.

✔ The time can be changed at the DOS prompt using the TIME command:

```
C> TIME 9:22a
```

The above TIME command sets the computer's clock to 9:22 in the a.m., or "morning" as humans call it.

As with the DATE command, you can type the TIME command at the DOS prompt to have the computer tell you what it thinks is the current time.

Gulp! The Hard Drive Is Gone!

Hard drives do have a tendency to wander. Normally, no one would care, but hard drives do contain all sorts of important information. So concern over their whereabouts is justified.

Read this if you care about your data

Buy a new drive when the old one starts to go. Sure, you can run special software utilities to fix these intermittent problems. But that's not going to do much for a hard drive that's truly on its way south for retirement at a reef off Florida. Look at it this way: An old, failing hard drive is like a bald tire. You need a new tire to replace it — not a toupee.

Keeping the old, worn-out hard drive around is a bad idea as well. Even if it's only marginal, there's no sense in keeping it for games or as a "temporary" files disk. That's like keeping your old bald tire as a spare.

There are two reasons a hard drive suddenly disappears. The first is related to the computer's battery. In addition to maintaining the current time, the battery keeps a special area of memory active. In that area of memory, the computer remembers a few things about itself, including whether or not it has a hard drive. When the battery goes, the computer forgets about the hard drive. Oops!

To fix the battery problem, replace the battery. This requires opening up the computer, so it's OK to pay someone else to do this if the thought of opening up the computer makes you wince.

After the battery is replaced, you need to run your computer's hardware setup program. You'll need to tell the computer all about itself again; give it the current time, tell it about its floppy drives, memory configuration, and what *type* of hard drive is installed. Most hard drives are type 46 or 47, which are the "anything goes" types since types 1 through 45 are for old IBM drives no one has used since 1984. If you're in doubt, make someone else do this.

The second reason a hard drive suddenly disappears is age. The average PC hard drive can run flawlessly for about four years. After that, you're going to start experiencing problems, typically Access, Seek, Read, or Write errors. This is a sign that the hard drive is on its last legs. If you see these ominous words, back up all your work and start hunting for a new drive.

A Record of Your Hardware Setup Program

Because your hardware setup program's information is so important, run that program right now and jot down this important information. If running the hardware setup isn't obvious to you, refer to Chapter 15 on running diagnostic programs and get the information from there.

Program name to run SETUP: _____

Keys to press to run SETUP: _____

First floppy drive: _____

Second floppy drive: _____

First hard drive (type): _____

Second hard drive (type): _____

Main (motherboard memory): _____

Extra memory: _____

Total memory: _____

Monitor/display: _____

Keyboard: _____

Serial port 1: _____

Serial port 2: _____

Printer port 1: _____

Printer port 2: _____

Math coprocessor: _____

Other stuff: _____

Other stuff: _____

Other stuff: _____

Note that not every computer has all of these items. If there are any extra items mentioned, write them down on the blank lines provided.

Steps to Take for a Locked Computer

The Reset button is not a panic button, but it's the next best thing. When your computer is all locked up and the programs appear to have flown to Orlando, try the following steps:

Steps: Dealing with a computer that is locked up

Step 1. Press the Esc (Escape) key.

Or if the program uses a different cancel key and you know what it is, press it. For example, the old WordPerfect program uses F1.

Step 2. Press the Ctrl+C (Control+C) or Ctrl+Break (Control+Break) key combination.

This step usually (and safely) cancels any DOS command.

Step 3. In Windows, you can press the Alt+Esc key combination to leave a window and move to the next window.

Step 4. To get rid of a Windows program run amok, press Ctrl+Alt+Delete — those three keys — all at the same time.

Doing so brings up a Close Program dialog box (covered in Chapter 14). Click on a stubborn program in the list, preferably one Windows recognizes as "not responding," and then click on the End Task button to close the highlighted task (program).

Step 5. If none of these tricks work, press Ctrl+Alt+Delete again to bring up the Close Program dialog box.

Choose the Shut Down option or press Ctrl+Alt+Delete again to reset your computer. If that doesn't work, or if your keyboard is beeping at you, punch your Reset button.

Note that you only resort to resetting after trying all the alternatives. Resetting is such a drastic measure that you should really run through your options before trying it. Never act in haste.

✔ If your system lacks a reset button and Ctrl+Alt+Delete doesn't reset, you'll have to turn off your computer. Flip its power switch, wait at least 20 seconds (for everything to calm down — I'm serious!), and then turn the computer back on again.

✔ Information on using the Ctrl+C cancel key is covered in "Canceling a DOS Command" in Chapter 3.

✔ What does the Reset button do? It interrupts power to the main chip, which causes it to restart. It's kinda like a whack on the head.

"I Had to Reset My Computer"

OK. So you had to reset. This is a horrid thing to do to Windows, but given that operating system's flaky nature, it's something you may have to do often. In fact, I reset my computer twice today trying out a new DOS game. (Gotta run it in the MS-DOS Only mode; see Chapter 7 for the lowdown.)

Resetting your computer using the proper reset option in the Shutdown dialog box is OK. Don't panic! But whenever you must reset suddenly, or after a power outage or something, you should run the ScanDisk program to check out your disk. Windows may or may not do this automatically (I'm not certain), but it's a good idea to run ScanDisk yourself just to be sure.

✔ Alas, a panicked reset usually means you'll lose some data. Hopefully it won't be that much. As long as you remember to save every once in a while as you work you won't have that much to redo.

✔ Refer to Chapter 11, "Scanning the disk with ScanDisk," for information on running ScanDisk.

✔ To reset properly, choose the Shutdown command from the Start thing's menu; press Ctrl+Esc, U. The second option in the Shut Down Windows dialog box is Restart the computer? Choose it and click Yes to reset your PC, should you really need to do so.

When to Scream for Help and Who to Scream At

There comes a time when you must scream for help. When that happens, and when you've exhausted all other options mentioned in this book, be a good computer user and obey the following:

✔ First, get mad. Get it out of your system.

✔ Know the problem. Be able to offer a full report on what you were doing, what you just did, and what happened. If you've narrowed down the problem, don't be afraid to say what you suspect it is.

✔ *It's voodoo I tells ya!*

✔ Be at the computer when you call for help. They'll always ask you questions you can only really answer while at the computer.

✔ Tell the person you're begging for help from about anything new or changed on your PC. Always let him or her know if you attempted to modify something or changed something yourself.

Freely skip this stuff on why you need to reset

When you reset in the middle of something, you often catch some programs with their pants down, so to speak. These programs may have created temporary files or may have some files that are "half open" on disk. Resetting leaves the files on disk, but not officially saved in any directory. The result is the lost chains or lost clusters that the ScanDisk command is designed to look for.

Running ScanDisk as described in Chapter 11 scours the drive and puts missing clusters and file fragments into real files on disk. They're named FILE0000.CHK, FILE0001.CHK, and on up through however many files were found. There's nothing most of us can do with these files, so they're OK to delete. (If you follow the directions in Chapter 11, you'll have ScanDisk delete them as they're found.)

- ✔ In order of preference, contact the following people: your office computer specialist or MIS manager, a friend who knows something about computers (and is still willing to help you), your computer dealer, the manufacturer, or the Almighty.

- ✔ If the problem cannot be fixed over the phone, take the computer to the shop. If possible, try to back up your data before you do so (refer to your favorite Windows book for the details). Remember to bring along cables and any necessary peripherals. Ask the computer fix-it person what he or she would like you to bring in, just to be sure.

- ✔ Always opt for the diagnostic first. Typical repair places will do a look-see for about $30 to $60. Then they should call you with an estimate. If they fix anything else "voluntarily" (for example, items not mentioned in the estimate or items they have not phoned you about), then it's free. Check with the laws in your state or county, but, generally speaking, repairing a computer is covered by the same laws that protect people at car repair places.

- ✔ Replacing something is easier than fixing it. If possible, try to order a bigger, faster, and better version of the thing you're replacing.

I Just Spilled Java into the Keyboard

I've added this as a special section because, believe it or not, many people spill things into their keyboards. Maybe not coffee (my personal favorite is lemonade), but something liquid that makes your eyes bulge out for a few comic moments.

OK. Suppose you've just spilled something into your keyboard. (You'll be reading this fast, so I'll type it in as quickly as I can.)

Just turn the computer off!

Never, under any circumstances, should you unplug the keyboard with the computer light still on!

Depending on the size of the spill, you may be able to save your information and quit the application. It's always better to turn off the PC properly; choose Shutdown from the Start thing's menu and wait until Windows says it's OK to turn the computer off before you do so. If not, it's OK to just flip the power switch. Try to pour any excess liquid out. Use a paper towel to sop up any remaining excess liquid.

Let the keyboard dry out. For coffee, this should take about 24 hours. After that time, turn on your PC and refer to the section "I Had to Reset My Computer" earlier in this chapter. Everything else should work as before.

If you've spilled something sugary into your keyboard, the dry-out time is still 24 hours. However, sugary stuff tends to create a sticky film. It won't interfere too heavily with the electronics, but it will make your keys stick. I've heard of people giving their keyboards a "bath" in a special solution. However, I recommend taking the keyboard to a pro for cleaning. In fact, this is a good thing to do on a regular basis, given all the cookie crumbs, chip fragments, and hair (ugh!) that end up in your keyboard.

✔ If you have to unplug your keyboard, do it with the computer turned off.

✔ If you're accident-prone and you expect to spill other liquids into your keyboard from time to time, you can buy a clear plastic cover molded to fit the keyboard's contour. You can still type and use the keyboard, but it's sealed.

Chapter 14

After You Panic, Do This

. . . .

In This Chapter

▶ Determining where you are when you suddenly find yourself there

▶ Returning to where you were before

▶ Finding a lost file

▶ Finding a lost program

▶ Recovering from DEL *.*

▶ Undeleting an entire subdirectory

▶ Unformatting a disk

. . . .

*I*f you're still in a panicky mode, refer to the preceding chapter. That's more of a panic-stricken chapter. This chapter is about what to do *after* you panic. The situation can always be resolved, no matter what. Even if the system is making popping noises and you see smoke, there's nothing to worry about (unless the drapery catches fire).

Where Am I?

Has this ever happened to you: You're driving your car and suddenly you realize that you've been under *highway hypnosis?* What happened during the last few miles? Where are you? Well, that's never happened to me. But sometimes I do wake up in the middle of the night screaming (if that makes you feel any better).

Getting lost is part of using a computer. If you ever find yourself lost, try one of the following remedies:

✔ If you are using a familiar program and suddenly find yourself in the unfamiliar — but still in the program — try pressing Esc to *back out* (or press whatever the cancel key is, such as F1 in the old WordPerfect).

✔ If pressing Esc doesn't work, check the keyboard. Type a few keys. If the keyboard starts beeping, the system is locked. See "I Just Can't Quit This @#$%?! DOS Window!" later in this chapter.

> ✔ If you're suddenly out at the DOS prompt, refer to the next section.
>
> ✔ If you find yourself lost at the DOS prompt, use the CD command to find out where you are. Typing **CD** tells you the current drive and directory, and it may explain why the program you were trying to run doesn't work. Refer to Chapter 11 for more information.

How Do I Get Back?

Sometimes you may find yourself in a different place. Say you are working in Lotus 1-2-3 and trying to save a worksheet when suddenly you find yourself at the DOS prompt. What happened? Or maybe you were at the DOS prompt just a moment ago, and now there's a strange program on the screen.

First trick to try:

```
C> EXIT
```

Type the EXIT command at the DOS prompt. This may return you to your program, or it may just close the DOS window and return you to Windows where you can become frustrated in a different color.

Second trick to try:

Press Alt+Tab. Just once; press and hold the Alt key and tap the Tab key. Release the Alt key. This may switch you back to your program if, perchance, you accidentally multitasked away. (It's one of the perils of a multitasking operating system).

Third trick to try:

Press the Escape key. You may have brought up a *pop-up* program by accident. These programs are triggered by certain key presses and you may have stumbled across one of them. Or you may have dropped down a menu or activated some Windows doohickey. Press Esc to exit. This should work and return you to the DOS prompt.

Fourth trick to try:

Press the F3 key and then Enter. This may restart a program that accidentally threw you out. If you press F3 and don't see anything, try typing **MENU** or whatever command you normally type to use your computer (or the application you were so rudely ejected from).

Some programs require you to type in two things when the program starts. For example, if you were running an accounting package in Basic, you may have to type:

```
C> BASIC GL
```

or:

```
C> QBASIC /RUN GL
```

dBASE also requires you to type in two things to run a dBASE program. If you know the name of the program to run, put it after DBASE at the DOS prompt:

```
C> DBASE PAYROLL
```

✔ Refer to "The Handy F3 Key" in Chapter 3 for information on using the F3 key.

✔ The section "Running a Program" in Chapter 2 has a list of popular program names and the commands required to run them.

"I Just Can't Quit This @#$%?! DOS Window!"

Drastic times call for drastic measures. Get a shotgun and blow a hole right through the monitor.

No wait! There are better ways to "blow away" something that's really bugging you, a locked-up program or stubborn DOS window that refuses to close. Your job is to play Arnold Schwarzenegger and *terminate* the program.

Start by pressing the Ctrl+Alt+Delete key combination. In the olden days, this reset the computer. In Windows days it brings up the Close Program, or the "If they move, shoot 'em," dialog box (see Figure 14-1).

Locate the name of your DOS program in the list, or look for MS-DOS Prompt. Highlight that program using the ↑ or ↓ arrow keys or click on it once with the mouse. Then click on the End Task button.

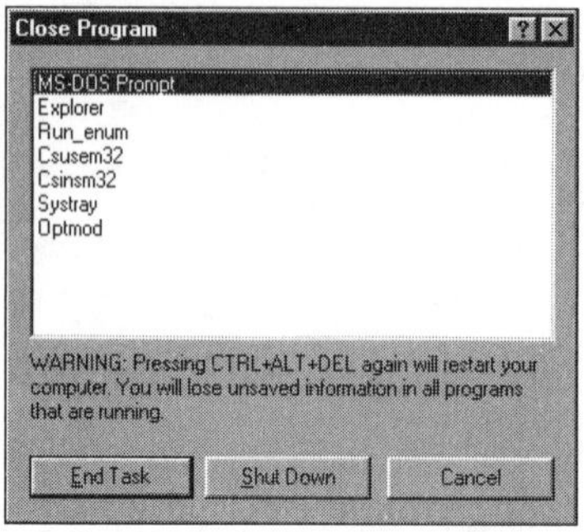

Figure 14-1:
The Close
Program
dialog box.

Windows may warn you before killing off the program. It may say the program cannot be shut down and you'll lose any unsaved information blah-blah-blah. That's not a problem since the reason you're here is that the darn thing is stuck in the mud anyway. Click the Yes button.

(If you wait while reading the dialog box, you may see a second dialog box displayed, one with the program name in the title. Click the Cancel button since this dialog box doesn't know what the heck it's talking about.)

Closing a file in this drastic way doesn't damage Windows, DOS, or your program one iota. You may, however, lose any unsaved information. And I highly recommend running the ScanDisk program after shutting down any DOS program in the *drastic* measure. See Chapter 11 for information on ScanDisk.

Where Is My File?

If you just saved a file or are looking for one you absolutely know exists somewhere, it may just be out of sight for now. Refer to the section "Finding a Lost File" in Chapter 12 for details on getting the file back.

Where Is My Program?

Programs are harder to lose than files, but it happens. The approach to finding a lost program depends on how you run the program.

If you run a program manually, you may just be lost on the disk. The manual way usually involves typing in a CD command and then typing in the name of the program at the next DOS prompt. If you type in the CD command and get an Invalid directory error message, you're probably in the wrong place. Type this command:

```
C> CD \
```

This command logs you to the root directory. Try running your program again. If it still doesn't work, try logging to the proper drive. For example, to log to drive C, type in the following:

```
D> C:
```

That's C and a colon. To log to any other drive, type its letter and a colon, and then type the preceding CD command. That should get you on the proper footing.

If you normally run your program by typing its name at the prompt, and you get a Bad command or file name error message, DOS may not remember where it put your program. This usually happens because, somehow, the *search path* has been changed. I won't explain how that can be undone here; simply reset your computer to get the proper search path back. Press the Reset button or Ctrl+Alt+Delete.

✔ If you notice that the computer loses your files a lot, yet resetting seems to bring them back, tell someone about it. Let that person know that some program on your system is "resetting the search path" and that you aren't particularly fond of it. He or she should be able to fix the problem for you.

✔ Information on the CD command and your disk's directory structure can be found all over Chapter 11.

The Perils of DEL *.*

Yeah, deleting all your files can be a drastic thing. The DEL *.* command will raze every file in a directory like loggers felling trees in an environmentalist's nightmare. However, there is a warning before this happens. DOS will tell you that all files in the directory are about to be churned to dust. It asks you if this is OK. You must type a Y to go on. Simple enough; you've been warned. Yet too many DOS beginners and experts alike are quick to press the Y key.

Before typing **DEL *.*** make sure you're in the proper directory. Use the CD command if the prompt doesn't display the current directory. (Refer to "Finding the Current Directory" in Chapter 11 and to "Prompt Styles of the Rich and Famous" in Chapter 3.) All too often you mean to delete all the files in one directory, but you happen to be in another directory when that happens.

✔ When they "fixed" DOS in Windows they forgot about the UNDELETE command. There is no way to undelete a file killed at the DOS prompt with the DEL command.

- ✔ Heavens, don't even mess with the DELTREE command! It's nasty, vile, and cannot be stopped. Only those "in the know" will bother with DELTREE. I shudder to think of anything otherwise.

- ✔ If you're really going to do some massive file deleting, do it in Windows.

I Just Deleted an Entire Subdirectory!

Neat. This result really requires effort on your behalf. Not only must you delete all files in a subdirectory, but you also have to use the RD (or RMDIR) command to peel off a directory (or the wicked DELTREE command). That command isn't even covered in this book! Congratulations.

The only way to recover a subdirectory is to *restore* it from a recent backup. Depending on how recent your backup is and how new the files were in the subdirectory, you may or may not get a full recovery.

Since backing up is done in Windows, I'll leave it up to your favorite book on Windows to go into the details on restoring a subdirectory. I wish you luck, and be more careful in the future.

I Just Reformatted My Disk!

This is why disks are labeled: so you know what's on them. Before you reformat a disk, check to see that it's empty. Refer to "Reformatting Disks" in Chapter 10. But if you do reformat a disk, type the following:

```
C> UNFORMAT A:
```

If you're unformatting a disk in drive B, substitute B: for A: here. Press Enter and follow the instructions on the screen. Be patient; it takes a few minutes to unformat a disk.

Your disk may not be in the best of shape after it's unformatted. For example, most of the files in the root directory may be gone. If they're found, they will probably be given generic names, as will any of your subdirectories. On the bright side, the data in your subdirectories, and all the subsubdirectories, will be totally intact.

Unformatting a disk only works if you use the UNFORMAT command on the disk before putting any new files on it.

Chapter 15

Diagnosing, Disinfecting, and Getting Help

In This Chapter

▶ Using a diagnostic program

▶ Scanning for viruses

▶ Using DOS's feeble online help

▶ Getting technical support

▶ Letting Windows help you

This chapter covers a broad canvas but does it with color, style, and a boldness even Bob Ross can't match.[1] First comes the majestic back-ground — diagnostic programs that tell you what's what inside your PC. These programs are followed by some bold foliage, the anti-virus programs. The anti-virus programs can help you fight the viral plague we're supposed to be having all the time (at least according to the media). Finally, I've added a waterfall and lots of "little friends" — the various ways DOS gives you help. There. I painted that whole thing without once using the words *Titanium White* or *Burnt Umber*.

What's Up Doc?

No matter how long you stare at the computer, you just can't tell what's inside it. This is why the medical profession invented X-rays. Doctors just couldn't tell what was wrong inside you unless they cut you up and poked around. Then, after they found out, they'd have to stitch you back together again and hope you'd live so you could pay the bill. Then along came X-rays and the ever-popular MRI scan, and they could see inside you, well-assured that you'd live to pay the bill. Computers are different.

[1]Bob Ross was the frizz-headed guy whose half-hour painting program on PBS enlightened millions. May he rest in peace.

First off, computers can't be X-rayed unless you take them to the airport. I'm not going to drone on here about how airport security people go all verclempt when they see a computer. Rule out X-rays. Secondly, computers can't talk. People can talk. "Doctor, my appendix is on my front side." Computers can barely muster "Hello, I'm now going to be rude to you" — so that's out as well.

On the upside, though, computers are pretty self-aware. Given the right type of program, they can fill you in on all sorts of internal tidbits without your ever having to wield a screwdriver (or an MRI scanner). This is done by using a program called a *diagnostic utility*.

Many diagnostic utilities exist in the DOS universe. OK, the *Windows* universe. Whatever. Chances are you already have one and don't even know it; both PC Tools and the Norton Utilities come with diagnostics. More likely than not, however, you probably have the MSD, Microsoft Diagnostic, program that came with older versions of MS-DOS and Windows. The only problem with this is that it's dated and the results don't reflect what kind of guts dwell inside today's computers. Keep reading and you'll witness a first-hand example.

✔ Alas, if Windows 95 came on your PC straight up, you don't have the MSD diagnostic. That's OK since it's not very Windows-specific and there are better things out there.

Running MSD (if you can't find anything else)

You start MSD by typing **MSD** at the command prompt:

```
C> MSD
```

After you press Enter, the computer will rummage around inside itself for a few tense moments (no need to step behind the lead wall here).

If you get a `Bad command or filename` error, check your spelling. If your spelling is OK, you probably don't have MSD on your computer. Sniff, sniff.

If you have MSD, it will inform you that it's running under Windows and the results will be less than accurate. OK. Press the Enter key to continue.

Don't be alarmed if MSD shifts your PC into text mode. Press Alt+Enter to switch back.

MSD will pronounce its prognosis in a screen that looks dreadfully like Figure 15-1. This screen shows you only the basics: `Computer` tells you which micro-processor lives in your PC (maybe); `Memory` gives a cryptic memory summary; `Video` tells you about your display; and so on.

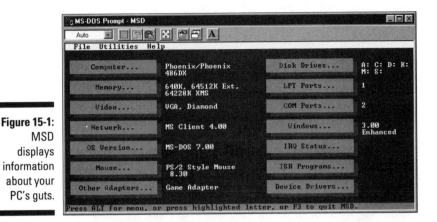

Figure 15-1:
MSD
displays
information
about your
PC's guts.

And now the warning: MSD is an *old* program so its results will be somewhat less than accurate. For example, Figure 15-1 explains — much to my chagrin and contradicting my outstanding VISA balance — that my Pentium computer only has a measly 486DX processor in it. What a rip off! I'm phoning David Horowitz right now. . . .

The truth is that MSD lies a bit. It's accurate to many extents, but since it's an older DOS program, it may not reliably tell you what lives in your new Windows computer. In fact, you'll even see the Windows button proclaiming you have Windows version 3.0 installed. Yup. Bill Gates was worth only $4 billion back then.

- ✔ You can select a specific area, such as pressing P for Computer (or clicking on that button with your mouse); you'll see more detailed information. Most of the stuff displayed is pretty nerdy, so proceed at your own risk.

- ✔ To quit MSD, press the F3 key. You may have to first press the Esc key a few times to close any open windows or panels.

Better diagnostic utilities cost you the Big Buck$

I'm not trying to sell anything, but since Microsoft laid off the MSD staff, Windows no longer comes with a decent diagnostic utility. You'll have to look elsewhere to find out that information your computer already knows about itself.

One such program is Quarterdeck's WINProbe, visage seen in Figure 15-2. It accurately spots my PC's Pentium running 133 MHz. (OK, 132 MHz. Who's counting?) It also monitors many Windows-specific items, plus offers suggestions for running your system faster, testing individual components, running faster, jumping higher, getting better SAT scores, and the whole barrel.

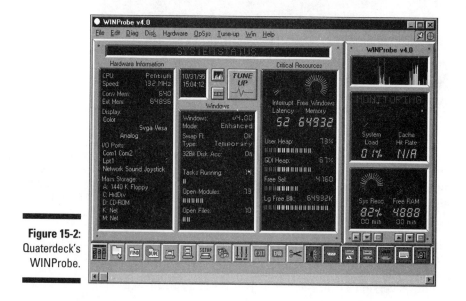

Figure 15-2: Quaterdeck's WINProbe.

✔ Other diagnostic programs exist for Windows. Refer to your local computer store or mail-order catalog for the variety.

✔ You may already have a diagnostic program available. One may have come with the Norton Utilities or other program you purchased.

✔ I don't favor WINProbe over any other product out there. But, hey, Quarterdeck did send it to me free. And I didn't even have to beg.

More Than Bugs: Viruses

Protect your system against the evil virus. Wicked they are! Chances you'll get one? Not as great as you fear. Viruses are real, but unless you're swapping a lot of disks that contain illegal or *pirated* software — especially games — you'll probably never see a virus.

We have the mainstream media to thank for the proliferation of virus phobia among computer users. The hype may be a bit heavy, yet sadly, viruses aren't a myth. On the upside, there is something you can do about them. Many companies now sell anti-virus software. These programs (utilities) will go out and hunt for viruses infecting your files and painlessly remove them.

✔ Even more bad news? Windows comes without any virus-scanning software. Neither does the DOS that comes with Windows. Microsoft is leaving you unprotected — naked in the bitter cold of the computer flu season.

✔ Of course, if you've upgraded from an older version of DOS, you may have the handy Microsoft Anti-Virus (MSAV). MSAV devours viruses quite nicely, and I'll ramble on about it here at length.

✔ What is commonly called a *computer virus* could really be one of a hoard of nasty programs that all do sad things to your computer, specifically the files you store on your hard drive. There's no need to go into the detail or all the cutesy names given these programs. Suffice it to say that you don't want one.

Some common questions about computer viruses

What can I do to prevent viruses from invading my computer? Safe computing practices are listed in the nearby sidebar "Steps to avoid nasty programs." Most important among them is to never boot (start your computer) using a strange floppy disk.

How can I tell if my PC is infected with a virus? Don't be too quick to blame quirkiness on a "virus." Unfortunately, most viruses are specifically nasty and display appropriate messages telling you of your peril — *after* the damage is done. Before doing any damage, most viruses lurk inside your PC. The only way to be sure is to run a virus-scanning program.

I hear my PC caught a virus in the Orient. Should I wear a mask while I compute? No, the bugs the PC catches are electronic. People don't "catch" computer viruses. Spray some Lysol around your computer room if it makes you feel good.

Will copying files from my friend's disk infect my PC? Probably not. However, it's a good idea to scan the disk with your anti-virus software before you copy the files. Most viruses infect your computer when you run an infected program, so merely copying files doesn't have a risk. Running an infected program or booting from an infected floppy disk — this is the most deadly way — is what leads to infection.

How can I be sure that files I download with my modem don't have viruses?
Run your anti-virus program and scan the files. If the files are contained in a ZIP
file or other archive, "explode" them first and then run your anti-virus software on
the lot. You'll know in a matter of seconds whether the files are free from infection.

How do I get rid of a virus? There are many techniques for virus removal, from
"peeling" the virus from your disk to utterly destroying the infected file. Most
anti-virus software handles the removal process for you should any infected
files be found. After that, you'll be safe from impending doom (unless your PC
becomes infected again).

If I have a virus, should I restore from a backup to delete it? Generally
speaking, no. The reason is that the virus may have been backed up, and
restoring the file would restore the infection. You should first remove the virus,
and then do an immediate, full, hard-disk backup.

It's said that a virus affects your computer's behavior, making it run slowly and
often impeding your ability to get work done. If so, then isn't Microsoft Windows a virus? No comment.

Steps to avoid nasty programs

1. **Never start your computer using a strange or unmarked floppy disk.**

   Even if a well-meaning friend gave you the disk (to examine some game or leer at some graphics files), never start your computer with it. This is the number one way viruses are spread among PCs. (Also, such un-marked floppy disks are usually pirated cop-ies of software, and their use is illegal.)

2. **Avoid software that comes on unlabeled diskettes.**

   Software that you buy in the store should come in a shrink-wrapped box and be prop-erly labeled. Some shareware software or freebie stuff may come crudely labeled — but be careful; run a virus-scanner on that disk. Again, software on an unlabeled dis-kette is probably pirated, and you shouldn't use it anyway.

3. **Okay, enough beating around the bush: Pi-rated software, stuff that people copy and distribute illegally, is often rife with viral infections.**

   Don't pirate; don't get a virus.

4. **If possible, ensure that you're the only per-son who uses your computer.**

   If the PC is out in the open, someone may happen by and ungraciously infect it for you. (Indeed, around my former office, computer pranks were popular to the point of memo-randum and condemnation by The Powers That Be.) When someone asks to borrow your PC, just say no!

5. **Run virus-scanning and removal software often.**

   How often? Once a month, at least. Right after you install any new software, definitely.

Running Anti-Virus

MS-DOS 6 came with a program called MSAV, the Microsoft Anti-Virus. If you upgraded from that operating system, you'll still have MSAV on your computer. You can use this program to check for signs of viral infection.

To run MSAV and scan your computer for viruses, type the following at your DOS prompt:

```
C> MSAV
```

Type **MSAV** and press Enter. The program starts and displays all sorts of wondrous information (see Figure 15-3). Pressing the F5 key makes it look for and remove any virus-infected files on the hard drive.

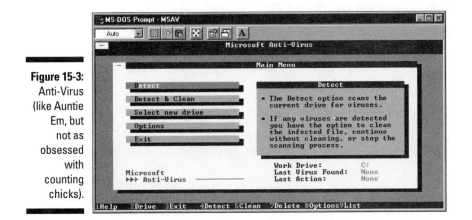

Figure 15-3: Anti-Virus (like Auntie Em, but not as obsessed with counting chicks).

➤ If MSAV finds a virus, follow the instructions on the screen for virus removal. Then phone up a friend and brag that you had a virus but MSAV saved your butt.

➤ I don't have any infected files, otherwise I'd show you what the "I found one and would you like it removed" screen looks like.

➤ Press F3 followed by Enter when you're ready to quit MSAV.

➤ Run MSAV as often as you like. But chances are, as long as you don't use illegal software or run programs somebody gave you "for free," you'll be safe from the virus.

➤ Information on the Windows-based version of MSAV is covered in the next section.

Yes, Virginia, there is a Windows version of MSAV

Figure 15-4 shows you the Windows version of MSAV, which you may or may not have depending on if the old version of Windows on your computer had it. In fact, I wouldn't even know how you could find it using the Windows interface, but the following command will start it from the DOS prompt (sneaky, aren't I?):

```
C> MWAV
```

Type **MWAV** and press the Enter key. DOS will start the Windows Anti-Virus program (if you have it).

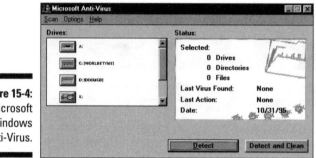

Figure 15-4: Microsoft Windows Anti-Virus.

Start by clicking on the hard drive you want to scan. For most of us mortals, that would be drive C. Click on the drive C icon in the Drives list. Then click on the Detect and Clean button to do the whole job.

Have a cup o' joe. This takes a while.

  ✔ If any viruses are found, you'll be alerted to their presence and informed of their deletion. Since this has never happened to me, my advice is to follow the suggestions on the screen to peel the virus free of your system.

  ✔ Click the OK button when the scanning is done. Then choose Scan⇨Exit Anti-Virus to quit the MWAV program.

Running the IBM version of Anti-Virus

If you upgraded to Windows 95 from a computer infected, er, set up with PC DOS instead of MS-DOS, the program you need to run is IBMAVD. Type the following:

```
C> IBMAVD
```

Keeping your anti-virus software up-to-date

To scan for viruses, most anti-virus software looks for what are called *virus signatures*. These are telltale pieces of computer code that identify viral infections. Most anti-virus software can recognize hundreds of computer virus signatures. Unfortunately, the deviants are out there busily dreaming up new viruses whose signatures your software may not recognize.

Don't panic about this! As fast as they're churning out new viruses, the boys and girls who write anti-virus software are working on solutions that recognize those new virus signatures. To obtain this new information, you need to either fill out and return the update coupon that came with your anti-virus software or you can use a modem to access the software developers (or often their *forum* on CompuServe) and grab the new signature files. Using a modem to get the files can be easy, though I recommend that you have your guru do it.

This anti-virus program does the same thing as the MS-DOS version, though you just press the Enter key or click on the Big Blue button to start.

OK. Enough information for PC DOS users.

> ✔ The Windows version of IBMAVD is called IBMAVW. Type that command at the prompt if you want to run the Windows version of the IBM virus checker.

Yes, You Can Believe It, DOS Has Lots of Help for You

DOS was ridiculed for years, not only because it was cryptic but because everyone would call it *dose* instead. Not only that, the cryptic commands had options that only God and Bill Gates knew by heart. The rest of us? We had to look in the manual or use some crusty old book to see what options were available. Well, that's no longer the case.

Starting with DOS version 5, there is some help available. Not much, but some. DOS 5 was the first version of DOS to even think about offering help. Not only do you get the nifty /? command line help (covered next), but there's a program called HELP that lists all the DOS commands and can display more information on each of them. It works like this:

```
C> HELP
```

Type in **HELP**. Avoid the temptation to type an exclamation point after that. Then press Enter. You'll see a list of all of DOS's commands plus a brief description of what each does.

With MS-DOS 6, the HELP program offered even more advice and options, working almost like a Windows help program, but in the text mode. (By the way, PC DOS 6 still uses the old DOS 5 help — in case you're a strange weirdo like me who still uses PC DOS.)

If you upgraded from either DOS version 5 or 6, then your HELP command still exists. Alas, the help doesn't apply to the DOS in Windows. In fact, there is no native HELP command for DOS in Windows; so if you upgraded, typing **HELP** at the prompt gives you a dreaded Bad command or filename error. And we all know how helpful that can be.

Fortunately, the /? command-line switch still works, no matter what DOS you upgraded from.

The /? command-line switch

For DOS's command-line commands, there is the universal /? option or *help switch*. You use this dealie after any DOS command to see a list of requirements and options for that command. This is what the techno-types call the *command format*. To see it, follow any DOS command with /? and no other options. Here's an example:

```
C> COPY /?
```

Here the COPY command is followed by a space and then slash-question mark. Instead of copying anything (or displaying the "huh?" error message), DOS instead spits out a list of command options and formats for the COPY command.

The good thing about /? help is that it's there! It works with all DOS commands! The bad thing is that the help is no more useful than the DOS manual. Hey! It *is* the DOS manual! Right on the screen. How con*veee*nient.

- ✔ The information /? displays is rather terse — not friendly at all. If you want something more friendly, refer to the next section on the HELP command.

- ✔ Actually, the best guarantee for help would be to find a good DOS reference, such as the little book that's a companion to this one, *DOS For Dummies Quick Reference* (IDG Books Worldwide, Inc.).

> ✔ What? The /? switch doesn't work? Then what you probably have isn't a DOS command. Some third-party utilities work on the command line just like DOS commands. If /? doesn't work, most likely you've found one of those. Refer to its manual for the help you need.
>
> ✔ Refer to Chapter 5, the section "About the Darn Command Formats," for more information on deciphering the darn command formats.

The F1 Help key

DOS has two types of commands. First are the traditional commands, such as COPY, MOVE, and REN. Then come commands that should really be called *utilities*. These include Anti-Virus, the Editor, and a few others. For those commands, you can get helpful information by pressing the F1 key. This is a standard help convention for most applications: Press F1 and you get help. Easy 'nuff.

The full-on, high-power, calmly desperate HELP command

Providing you upgraded to Windows from an MS-DOS 6 PC, you have a full-screen HELP program at your disposal. (Everyone else, read this and turn green with jealousy.) With DOS 6 you had what was essentially the manual — nerd meat and potatoes — right on your hard drive. Yet the HELP command was actually better than having a real manual because it's very specific, provides lots of good examples, and doesn't smell as bad as the real manual. And you still have it under Windows.

Two ways to use the HELP command are available. First, you can just type **HELP** at the DOS prompt:

```
C> HELP
```

Do not follow HELP with an exclamation point. Just type **HELP** and press Enter.

When you type HELP by itself you'll see a list of DOS commands plus some "topics" on which you can get extra help (see Figure 15-5). Use the arrow keys or the Tab key to highlight the various help subjects and press Enter to see the helpful information. You can also double-click on the topics with your mouse.

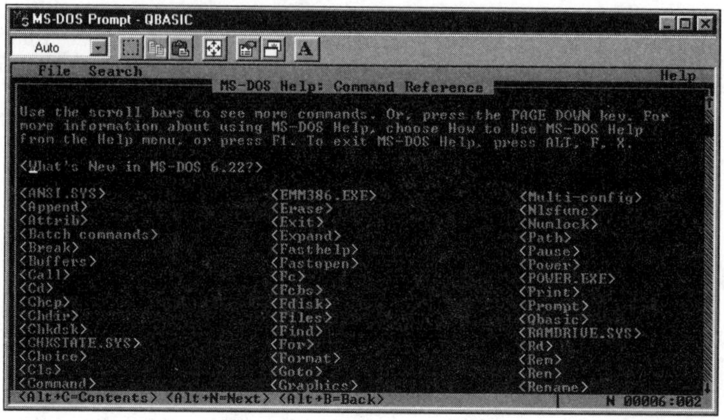

Figure 15-5:
HELP as
MS-DOS 6.2
dishes it up.

When you need help with a specific DOS command, type **HELP** and then that DOS command. Here's an example:

```
C> HELP MSAV
```

Type **HELP**, a space, then the DOS command or topic of interest. Above, HELP is followed by MSAV. After pressing Enter, you'll see oodles of information about the Anti-Virus program and all that.

- ✔ To quit HELP, press Alt+F, X. This action selects the Exit item from the File menu and returns you back to the cozy DOS prompt.

- ✔ As you read the helpful information, there will be two items at the top of the HELP screen, just below the menu bar. The items will be two of the following: Syntax, Notes, or Examples. The Syntax item displays a screen that describes the command's format and options; Notes displays information about using the command, plus tips; and Examples shows you how the command can be used and what it can do. Always look to the Examples screen. In most cases, what you're looking for will be illustrated right there.

- ✔ You move around in the HELP program using the Tab key. Press Tab to highlight an item on the screen; press Enter to see more information. Other key combinations are displayed on the bottom of the screen.

- ✔ HELP's Find command can be used to find itsy-bitsy information on specific subjects. For example, if you see the STACKS=0,0 thing in your CONFIG.SYS file, you can start the HELP command and press Alt+S, F to bring up the Find box. Type **STACKS** into the Find What box and press Enter. DOS will scour the HELP command's archives for matching information and display it right there on the screen.

✔ If you have the HELP command from MS-DOS 6, then you also have the FASTHELP command. Typing **FASTHELP** at the prompt displays the same results as the HELP command under DOS 5. Does that make sense? Well, anyway, just be thankful you get *some* kind of help.

✔ Any DOS commands that deal with CONFIG.SYS are no longer valid for DOS under Windows. Don't bother with 'em, since Windows does things its own way and pretty much ignores any changes you make in CONFIG.SYS.

Windows tries to help you

Windows actually has some decent help available, especially in the form of its Troubleshooter programs. For example, if your printer is acting weird, you can use the Printer Troubleshooter to help narrow down the problem. Same thing with DOS and the MS-DOS Troubleshooter.

To see the Troubleshooter, you'll need to fire up the Windows Help thing. From the start menu choose <u>H</u>elp, or press Ctrl+Esc, H. The Help dialog box appears (see Figure 15-6). Click on the Index tab to make sure that panel is in front.

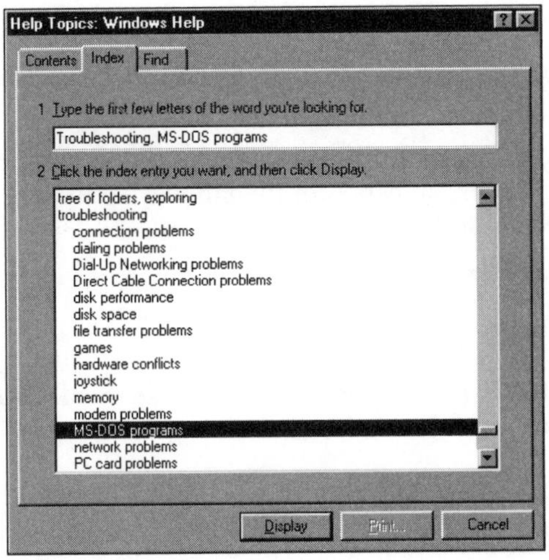

Figure 15-6:
The
Windows
Help thing.

Into the first box, type the following (just like Figure 15-6):

```
Troubleshooting, MS-DOS programs
```

Type **TROUBLESHOOTING,** a comma, then **MS-DOS**. That's all you need to type for the proper item to be highlighted in the window.

Press the Enter key. The MS-DOS Troubleshooter is then displayed for your amusement (see Figure 15-7). You work the Troubleshooter as follows:

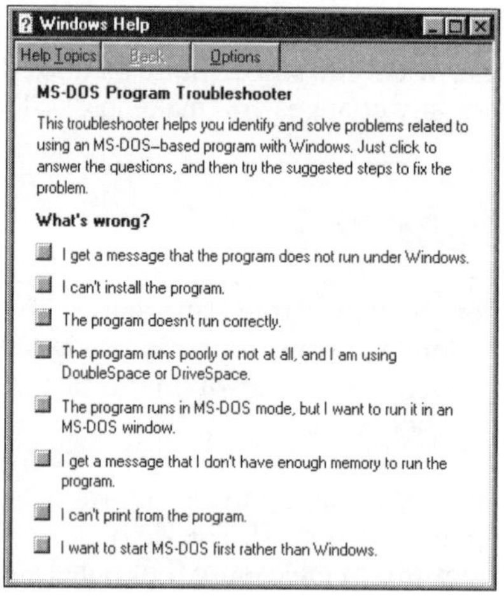

Figure 15-7:
The MS-
DOS
Trouble-
shooter.

> **Windows Help**
>
> Help Topics | Back | Options
>
> **MS-DOS Program Troubleshooter**
>
> This troubleshooter helps you identify and solve problems related to using an MS-DOS–based program with Windows. Just click to answer the questions, and then try the suggested steps to fix the problem.
>
> **What's wrong?**
>
> ☐ I get a message that the program does not run under Windows.
>
> ☐ I can't install the program.
>
> ☐ The program doesn't run correctly.
>
> ☐ The program runs poorly or not at all, and I am using DoubleSpace or DriveSpace.
>
> ☐ The program runs in MS-DOS mode, but I want to run it in an MS-DOS window.
>
> ☐ I get a message that I don't have enough memory to run the program.
>
> ☐ I can't print from the program.
>
> ☐ I want to start MS-DOS first rather than Windows.

1. **Read over the questions.**

2. **Click the mouse on the box next to the question that describes your situation.**

   For example, you could click the little box by `The program doesn't run correctly`. The troubleshooter then moves on to either ask more questions or divine a solution.

3 a. **If you see more questions, start over at Step 1.**

3 b. **Heed the instructions.**

When the Troubleshooter displays a series of steps, take them. Those are the steps to solving your problem. Hopefully.

After performing the steps, there are Yes and No choices. Pick `Yes!` If your problem was solved, or `No` for more troubleshooting.

Close the Troubleshooter when you're done by clicking on its X close button.

✔ The final question the troubleshooter asks is, `Did this fix the problem?` It's like the folks at Microsoft *really care!*

✔ If you click the mouse on the Troubleshooter's Options button a menu drops down. Choose Options➪Print Topic to get a hard copy of any steps the Troubleshooter may ask you. This will help if you can't see the Troubleshooter while you're taking the proper steps to solve the problem.

✔ Some buttons in the Troubleshooter will start other programs, some of which you may need to run to solve your problem.

✔ There are also various help topics under the MS-DOS heading. Just type in **MS-DOS** when you see the Index in the Windows Help thing.

✔ You may see steps telling you to edit Window's startup files or the CONFIG.SYS file. It might be a good idea to have your guru make any changes in that case. (I don't recommend messing with that file at all, as discussed in Chapter 7.)

Your Last Resort: Calling for Technical Support

There is no rule that says a company must offer you phone support for your computer or its software. However, some companies are nice and offer it to you — sometimes for free — when you need it. For this you should be thankful.

Never use tech support as a *first* resort.

Support lines are often flooded with jokers asking lame questions, which bogs down support for those people who are really in a bind. This book contains the answers to most of your questions and will help you piece together quite a lot of PC puzzles. Still, when the time comes, and you feel the urge to call technical support, do them a favor and run through this list first:

1. **Look up your question in this book or your software manual.**

   Use the index. Refer to the table of contents. Don't be lazy and just read the first few sentences or just pieces of paragraphs. In this book, related information is always listed in the check marks that conclude each section.

2. **Ask your guru for help.**

   If it's your office, then that's what they pay the gurus for. At home, call your crazy neighbor Earl and see if he's still willing to help you.

3. **Check the online help.**

   Most modern software gives you help by pressing the F1 key. In DOS, you can use the HELP command, as discussed earlier in this chapter. Don't neglect scoping out the "Examples" in the HELP for DOS 6.

4. **Refer to the README file.**

   Nearly every software program sold today comes with a lengthy README.TXT file, which you're usually exposed to right after installation. Refer to it again if you need to — especially for hardware (computer or printer) problems. There's a lot of specific information in there.

5. Try the situation again and take notes.

Providing you've been diligent to this point, try the operation again. For some dumb reason, it almost always works the second time. If not, take some notes. Write down any error messages or numbers. Also, recall the last thing you did to your PC. I have a friend whom I won't name (OK, it's Tom), and he always messes with his PC and then seems surprised when things foul up afterwards. If you mess, expect weirdness. The two *are* related.

6. Run a diagnostic program.

This step isn't meant to solve any problem. Instead, the diagnostic comes in handy when telling tech support people what's where inside your PC. (Don't forget the MSD program that comes with most versions of DOS and Windows.)

7. Dial tech support.

- Most software manuals bury the tech support numbers. If so, write them down on the blank pages provided in the back of this book or right in the front of that software manual.

- Note that several ways often exist to get tech support. The best is to call up and talk to a real live human. However, some automated tech-support systems ("voice menus") exist that are quite good. Consider calling those first because the lines aren't as busy as the real human type of tech support.

- Tech support calls come in three types: Free 800 number lines; toll calls (where you pay for the phone call); and expensive calls, where you pay for the call *and* for the person's time on the other end of the line.

- Printer problem? Call your printer's tech support. DOS problem? Call whoever sold you DOS. Word processor problem? Call the word processor developer. Windows problem? Hey, give up now! Seriously, call Microsoft. But don't bother Microsoft for problems with other hardware or software; they only do Windows.

- Pay attention when you call! Be at your computer with it on and ready to go. The tech support people can help you best when you're helpful to them as well.

- Be careful when dialing any 1-900 tech support numbers. If you misdial you might get the 1-900 Tech Guy Party Line or the Psychic Nerds Network.

- Tech support hours are usually from Monday through Friday (but not on holidays) during business hours. Check to see whether the times are Eastern, Central, Mountain, or Pacific.

- Modem support is available from the majority of computer companies. You can download files or pose questions online. Many developers also have forums on CompuServe. You can also find FAX lines for tech support questions, as well as FAX-back lines, where the other computer calls your FAX machine and sends you the information you requested.

- Software companies often sell more than one product. Make sure that you're calling the right number for that product. Also, Microsoft sells both DOS and Windows. Only call those support lines with your specific DOS and Windows questions. If you're having a problem with a Lotus or Borland product, call them instead.

- For heaven's sake, don't call up and play "Stump the Support Guy."

- Don't forget to have your serial number handy! Many places ask for a product's serial number before you get support.

The 5th Wave   By Rich Tennant

"No thanks. But I would like one more chance to see if I can edit my AUTOEXEC. BAT file so my programs will appear when I start up my computer."

Chapter 16

DOS Error Messages (What They Mean, What to Do)

- -

In This Chapter

▶ Typical, annoying DOS error messages (nearly two dozen of them!)

▶ Some messages that blurt themselves out in graphical mode (fewer, but more annoying)

- -

*T*he list of possible error messages you may see DOS display is massive — truly huge. This isn't because DOS is riddled with mistakes; it's because DOS is so vast. When you consider the bonus programs included with DOS, such as the Editor, the potential for error messages is staggering. But rather than have you stagger about, this chapter contains 20-something common error messages you might see while you're running DOS under Windows on your PC. Each error message is explained according to its meaning and probable cause, with a suggested solution for each. Nothing here is really fatal, though a few of the error messages will scare the bejesus out of you. Never fear, a solution is always at hand.

Note that DOS error messages tend to be kind of vague. This is because neither DOS nor the PC hardware is built to perform the kind of defaulted diagnostics that would result in messages like, "There's no disk in drive A; please put one in," or "Press A to cancel that last command." Oh well.

You'll find extended discussions of some issues or solutions in other chapters. I've cross-referenced them here.

Various DOS Error Messages (Text Mode)

First come the standard DOS text mode error messages. These are some of the over 500 error messages you may see more often than not (hopefully not).

Abort, Retry, Fail?

Meaning: The latest missile launched by the Air Force is careening out of control toward Moscow. Actually, this is a generic response to a variety of what DOS calls *fatal errors*. DOS has taken its best stab at doing something and just can't figure out what's wrong.

Probable cause: Typically, this message is preceded by a line of text explaining what DOS tried to do: read from a disk, write to a disk, touch its toes, and so on. Nine times out of ten you'll see this message when you attempt to access a floppy disk in drive A or B and the drive door is open or there is no disk in the drive.

Solution: If you can remedy the situation, such as closing the drive door or putting a disk into the drive, do so. Then press R to Retry. If nothing can be done, press A for Abort (which means Cancel, but most programmers don't know if Cancel has one or two *l*'s in it).

Pressing F, the Fail option, can be used in a few rare circumstances. For example, suppose you type **A:** to switch to drive A and there's no disk in there. When that happens, the Abort, Retry, Fail error appears and you'll never see a DOS prompt again — unless you type **F** to fail. Then you'll see Current drive is no longer valid. OK. Type **C:** to log back to drive C.

Most often I get the Abort, Retry, Fail error message when I type **A:** instead of **B:** and there is no disk in drive A. My solution is to have a formatted disk (any disk will do) handy. I slip that disk into drive A and then press R to retry. After the DOS command is done (or whatever), I retype the command again specifying **B:** or whichever letter I originally meant to type.

Access denied

Meaning: You're a mere mortal and lack the mental key to unlock some digital door. Actually, you've tried to change a file that DOS is not allowed to change.

Probable cause: The file you specified, or one of several files in a group, has its read-only file protection set. You cannot rename the command with REN; you cannot delete it with DEL; and you cannot use any applications to change the file's contents. This error may also occur if you specified a subdirectory name in a command that normally manipulates files.

Solution: Just ignore the file. Chances are the file's not meant to be touched, anyway. (You can refer to "The File! I Cannot Kill It!" in Chapter 9 if you're desperate.)

WARNING!

Skip this only if you don't take the hard drive seriously

When you get the `Abort, Retry, Fail` message and the error DOS displays seems more drastic, it's time to worry a bit. Situations such as a `read error`, `write error`, or `seek error` could be the rumblings of a major disk disaster (especially if the disk you're trying to access is the hard disk). If the errors are consistent, refer to the nearest PC-knowledgeable person and scream "Help" quietly into his or her ear.

Bad command or file name

Meaning: DOS doesn't understand the command you just typed.

Probable cause: You mistyped a command name, misspelled the name of a program on disk, or DOS cannot find the named program. This is also DOS's typical response when you type in a dirty word or hurl it an insult via the command line.

Solution: Check your typing. You can also refer to "Where Is My Program?" in Chapter 14 if you're certain the program worked before.

Divide overflow

Meaning: This never was a DOS error message. It's actually a PC hardware error that DOS begrudgingly displayed. The DOS-in-Windows version goes like this:

```
Your program caused a divide overflow error.
If the problem persists, contact your program vendor.
```

The program will quit and you'll see a DOS prompt hanging there.

Probable cause: A program — not necessarily DOS — has tried to divide some number by zero. On a calculator, that produces the infamous E error. On your PC, it's called a *divide overflow* error.

Solution: The program screwed up. Yeah! This isn't your fault. In fact, it's usually a sign that the program wasn't very well written or tested. If you care, see if you can duplicate the error, and then proudly call up the software developer to report a *bug*. (This is real advanced user stuff — your guru will be jealous.)

Because this error message usually is followed by a DOS prompt, it means your program is done and anything unsaved is lost. You can try to run your program again, but you'll need to re-create all your data. Another reason to hate computers!

Drive not ready error

Refer to the section "Not ready, reading drive *X*."

Duplicate file name or file in use, or File not found — filename

Meaning: You've used the REN command to rename a file and something went wrong.

Probable cause: You've specified the new name and that file already exists; or the file you want to rename doesn't exist.

Solution: Try the command again. Check to see that a file with the new name doesn't already exist. DOS gives you a hint with the File not found error in that it's usually followed by the name of the file not found. (Also refer to "Renaming a File" in Chapter 9 for more information.)

File cannot be copied onto itself

Meaning: You've forgotten something with the COPY command. This isn't a major boo-boo. In fact, nothing bad has happened (which is ironic, given the insincere nature of the COPY command).

Probable cause: You've used the COPY command to duplicate a file and given the duplicate the same name as the original. While COPY will overwrite a file that already exists, you cannot use COPY to overwrite the source file. For example, you probably typed something along the lines of:

```
C> COPY MYSELF MYSELF
```

when what you meant to type was:

```
C> COPY MYSELF B:
```

and you left the B: off.

Solution: Don't specify the same name twice. Refer to "Duplicating a File" in Chapter 9 for the proper ways and means.

File creation error

Meaning: For some unspecified reason, DOS will not make a new file.

Probable cause: Using the COPY command to copy or duplicate a file and the filename is already used by a directory; or if a file already exists by that name, but it's a read-only file; or if the disk or directory is full and can't contain any additional files; or if you misused the > symbol. This error can also be produced by any program as it saves a file, though File creation error is an error message specific to DOS.

Solution: If the filename is already taken by a directory or some other file, try creating the file using a new name. If the file is read-only, refer to the section "The File! I Cannot Kill It!" in Chapter 9. If the disk is full, delete some superfluous files or try using another disk or making a subdirectory.

File not found

Meaning: DOS is unable to locate the file you've named.

Probable cause: You mistyped the name, or the file isn't on that drive, in the current directory, or on the path you've specified.

Solution: Check your typing. Refer to "Finding a Lost File" in Chapter 12.

General failure

Meaning: DOS has lots of specific error messages. When it tosses General failure at you, it means something bad has happened but DOS has nothing specific to say about it. This is like DOS saying "all hell's breaking loose," but it's not that serious.

Probable cause: Typical things that cause DOS to report General failure include an incompatible floppy disk; the floppy drive door being left open; an attempt to read from an unformatted disk; or the absence of a disk from a floppy drive.

Solution: Check to see if there is a disk in the drive or if the drive's door latch is open. Try again by pressing R for Retry. If there is a disk present, it's not properly formatted; press A for Abort. Use the FORMAT command to format the disk — but make sure the disk is formatted to its proper size and capacity. Refer to Chapter 10 and the sections "Formatting a Disk," "Formatting a Low-Capacity Disk in a High-Capacity Drive," and "Checking a Disk's Size and Other Trivia."

Insufficient disk space

Meaning: The disk is full. There is no more room left to create or copy any files.

Probable cause: You've used the COPY command to copy too many files to the disk. Various other DOS commands and programs may produce this error.

Solution: Use a different disk, or delete some unneeded files, or start copying to another disk. If you notice that the disk still seems to have ample space available, you've simply filled up the root directory. Delete a few files (or copy them to another disk), and then create subdirectories for the extra files. Refer to "How to Name a Directory (the MKDIR Command)" in Chapter 12. Run ScanDisk (see Chapter 11) to see if your disk is filled with loose fragments that take up space but don't do any good. Also refer to "Freeing Up Space on a Hard Disk" in Chapter 11.

Invalid directory

Meaning: You've specified a directory that doesn't exist. (DOS is big on using the term *invalid,* which it takes to mean illegal.)

Probable cause: You used the CD command to change to a directory that you don't have. If not that, then you may have specified a full pathname to a file or directory and something in the pathname isn't right.

Solution: Check your typing. Refer to "Finding a Lost Subdirectory" in Chapter 12 for hunting down lost directories.

Invalid drive specification

Meaning: What the hell kind of drive is that?

Probable cause: You've typed in a drive letter that isn't assigned to any disk drive on your system. For example, if you have drives A, B, and C, and you type **D:**, you'll get this message.

Solution: Check your typing. The colon (:) is a sacred character under DOS. It only follows a drive letter, which can be any letter of the alphabet. If that drive doesn't exist, DOS will spit back a variation of the Invalid drive specification error message.

P.S. If it gives this message when you try to log (switch) to drive C, that means DOS has lost track of your hard drive. Oops. See Chapter 13, "When It's Time to Toss in the Towel (and Call a PC Guru)."

Invalid media or Track 0 bad — disk unusable

Meaning: The FORMAT command cannot format the disk. At least, it cannot format it to the specific capacity.

Probable cause: You're trying to format a disk at the wrong capacity, for example, a 360K disk to 1.2MB or a 1.2MB disk at 360K. Or you may have successfully formatted a high-capacity disk at low capacity and now are attempting to reformat it to high capacity. Or you have a bad disk.

Solution: You can try the FORMAT command again, but add the slash-U (/U) option. If that doesn't work, try taking a bulk eraser, one that you may use to erase a videotape, and erase the disk. That may allow the disk to be formatted — but always format disks to their proper capacity. Refer to Chapter 10.

Invalid parameter, Invalid switch, Invalid parameter combination

Meaning: You typed something improperly at the DOS prompt, left something required out of a command, or mistyped an option.

Probable cause A: Usually a typo. If one of these errors pops up, you're on the right track, but you may need to check the format of the command again.

Probable cause B: You used one of the forbidden characters in a filename. The main culprit here is the / character, which DOS sees as the *switch*. That's why you get an Invalid switch error when you try to name a file something stupid.

Solution A: Check your typing. You may have forgotten a space. If you've forgotten an option with some DOS command, enter the command again but with its help switch, slash-? (/?), supplied instead. Here's an example:

```
C> FORMAT /?
```

This displays all the options and requirements of the command. Check for the one you want and then specify it properly. Refer to "About the Darn Command Formats" in Chapter 5 and "Yes, You Can Believe It, DOS Has Lots of Help for You" in Chapter 15 for more information.

Solution B: Use another filename. See Chapter 12 for more information on what you can and cannot name a file.

Non-system disk or disk error

Meaning: You're trying to start the computer from a non-boot disk. It may be formatted, but there is no copy of DOS on the disk.

Probable cause: You've left a floppy disk in drive A while starting your computer.

Solution: Make sure that drive A is empty, or open the drive door latch. Press the spacebar to allow your PC to boot from the hard drive.

Various versions of DOS, Windows, and some third-party utilities that have their own disk formatting programs, and diskettes that come pre-formatted will put subtly different error messages on their diskettes. The general gist here is `Non-System Disk`. What you see on the screen may be different than what's shown above.

Not ready, reading drive *X*

Meaning: You've tried to access or log to either of your floppy drives, and DOS found only air where it expected a disk.

Probable cause: There's no disk in the drive, or the drive door latch is open.

Solution: Stick a disk into the drive or close the drive door, and then type **R** to retry.

Sharing violation

Meaning: You cannot modify or delete that file, or you've brought one of your speeding tickets for Share Day at the office.

Probable cause: Some other program is currently using that file. This happens a lot with multitasking operating systems like Windows. The system's just being safe, making sure you know that two things cannot work on one file at the same time. (If they could, it could be chaos!)

Solution: Wait. Switch to the other program and close the file in question, or just make up your mind to start working on something else.

Write protect error

Meaning: You've attempted to write to or alter a disk that's been tagged as write-protected.

Probable cause: The disk has a write-protect tab on it, or the $3^1/2$-inch disk has its little tile off the hole. This prevents any information from being written to the disk or information on the disk from being changed.

Solution: Answer A for Abort. If you really want to change the information, remove the disk's write-protection and try again (press R for Retry instead of A for Abort).

Some More, Annoying Windows Errors

Since Windows is in charge of your computer, a few of the more vile errors are displayed as graphical dialog boxes on the screen. These Windows error messages are all specific to that thing in which we run DOS.

Major program screw-up type of error

Meaning: Your program — or even DOS itself — has tried to do something entirely forbidden or has crashed in such a way as to be caught by Windows' safety net. The error dialog box, with its overly grim message, is shown in Figure 16-1.

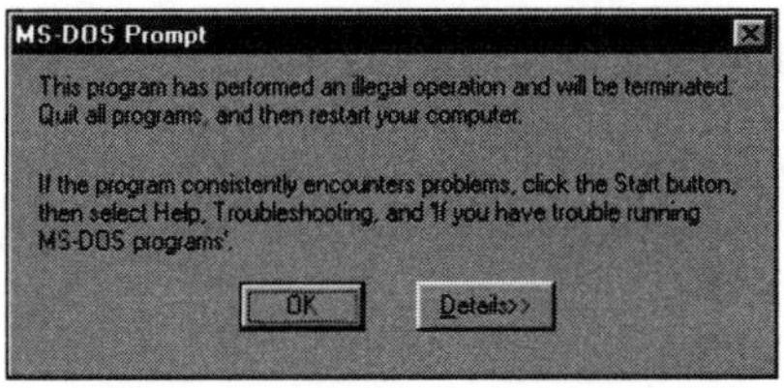

Figure 16-1: The "something nasty happened" dialog box.

MS-DOS Prompt

This program has performed an illegal operation and will be terminated. Quit all programs, and then restart your computer.

If the program consistently encounters problems, click the Start button, then select Help, Troubleshooting, and 'If you have trouble running MS-DOS programs'.

[OK]   [Details>>]

Probable cause: Who knows? Something screwed up, either you, your program, DOS, something. In any case, it screwed up in a way as to threaten Windows' very existence.

Solution: The solution (for Windows, obviously), is to kill the program. It stops dead in its tracks. You should click the OK button or press Enter. That closes the DOS program's window and returns you to Windows.

The dialog box says you should also quit and restart Windows. In my experience, that's never really been necessary, but it might be a good thing to do anyway. At minimum, I'd save all my files and kneel in the direction of Armonk, N.Y.

Don't bother clicking the Details>> button in the dialog box. It displays nerdy technical information that won't further explain what happened to anyone other than Mr. Spock.

Pasting graphics into a DOS application error

Meaning: You've used the Paste button on the toolbar to paste something into DOS, but Windows won't let you do it. The dialog box displayed is shown in Figure 16-2.

Figure 16-2:
Can't paste
a graphic
into a DOS
window.
No way.

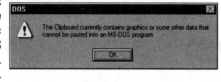

Probable Cause: You've tried to paste a graphic or some other non-text type of information into your DOS window. Only text can be pasted into a DOS window. (See Chapter 6 for more information on DOS copy and paste.)

Solution: Don't do it again! You can't paste graphical information into a DOS window. However, you can paste it into another program, such as Paint or a graphics program, and save it to disk in a file format your DOS program can read.

The thrill of sudden termination

Meaning: Your program stopped working but wasn't smart enough to close its own DOS window. So the window sits there dead and a dialog box appears like the one shown in Figure 16-3.

Figure 16-3:
You think the
computer
would be
smart
enough to
avoid
displaying a
dialog box
like this one.

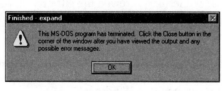

Probable Cause: No problem here. The program just stopped working and cannot close its DOS window. This happens with DOS utilities (like EXPAND in Figure 16-3) that you run in their own DOS window.

Solution: Close the window.

Part V

The Part of Tens

The 5th Wave   By Rich Tennant

"OH YEAH, AND TRY NOT TO ENTER THE WRONG PASSWORD."

In this part...

*L*ike things tend to get collected in lists. For example: Ten People Who Have Been Hit By Lightening While Yodeling, Ten Things You Don't Want to See Rolling Down the Aisle While Your Plane Takes Off, or Ten Poisonous Molds That May Be Growing In Your Refrigerator Even Now. If you love reading that type of trivia, then this part of the book is for you.

I get asked questions like this all the time: "Can you name the top five things a PC owner needs?" or "What are the ten biggest goofs people make when using a computer?" Since I love that kind of thing, I decided to put all sorts of useful information here, in this part of the book. These aren't meaningless lists of tens or "Top Ten" lists of silly things. These are interesting lists of do's and don'ts, suggestions, tips, and other helpful information for people who have computers sitting on their desks.

Note that there won't always be ten items in each category, and in some cases there may be more. After all, if there's one more mold growing in that mystery clump of aluminum foil, why leave it off the list?

Chapter 17

Ten Things You Should Do All the Time

In This Chapter

▶ Take care of your files

▶ Always quit a program properly and return to DOS

▶ Keep your disks away from magnets

▶ Keep your PC in a well-ventilated place

▶ Save your files

▶ Change your printer's ribbon or toner when it gets low

▶ Label your disks

▶ Wait at least 30 to 40 seconds before turning the computer on again

▶ Buy supplies

▶ Buy more books

---

*T*he rest of the lists of tens in this book are all fairly negative things, so why not start on an upbeat note? You may not have to do these things every second of the day, but keep each of these things in mind as you use your PC. Some of these items are elaborated on elsewhere in this book — that is duly noted here.

Care for Your Files

There are three things you should do to ensure that you, your PC, and the files you create always live in harmony: Back up, check your disk, and check for viruses. Refer to Chapter 11 for information on backing up, though more detailed information should be found in your favorite Windows book. Information on checking the disk (using ScanDisk) is in Chapter 11 as well. Checking for viruses is covered in Chapter 15.

Always Quit a Program Properly

There is no reason to quit a program by punching the Reset button — or worse, by turning the computer off and then on again. Just as in social circles, there's always a proper method of exiting any situation. Know what it is and use it to quit your programs. Believe it or not, it's faster to quit your program the right way than to reset anyway.

In the case of DOS-in-Windows, what you're quitting to in this case is Windows, not the DOS prompt. Remember that fact whenever some manual or book says "quit to the DOS prompt."

Keep Your Disks Away from Magnets

A magnet erases a disk faster than looking at Medusa turns you to stone. Magnets are everywhere, so be careful. For example, the mouthpiece on most phones and phone handsets has a big magnet in it; rest the phone down on your desktop and THWOOP! the data on the disk is gone.

Other popular desk items that contain magnets are listed below. Please try to keep your disks away from the following:

- ✔ Modems
- ✔ Paperclip holders
- ✔ Compasses
- ✔ Those things that pick up cars at the junk yard
- ✔ The planet Jupiter

Keep Your PC in a Well-Ventilated Place

PCs need to breathe. The internal fan needs to suck air in through the front of the computer box, and it needs to wheeze that air back out again through the rear of the box. Make sure nothing covers the front of the computer (where it breathes in) or the back of the computer (where it coughs it back out).

The purpose of the fan is to keep the computer cool. Just like men in the Kinsey Report, electrical components perform better under cold conditions than hot. So it may be a good idea to keep your computer out of direct sunlight — and keep your meltable disks out of the sun as well. Even for security reasons, try not to place computers directly beneath a window. (I've seen too many computers disappear from various offices thanks to the old smash-n-grab.)

Always Save Your Stuff to Disk

Whenever you start working on something new, save it to disk. *Immediately!* Then, as you're working, continue to save. When you're done, save it to disk again. The more you save, the better the chances are that you won't lose anything should the computer burp, wince, or die on you. I don't know how many times I've cursed a power outage but really should have blamed myself for not saving something a few moments earlier.

You can buy an uninterruptable power supply, or UPS, for your computer to help prevent power-outage depression (POD). All my computers are hooked up in such a manner. That way, whenever there is a brief interruption in the power service, my PCs stay on and never lose any information. Of course, I *always* save my stuff the instant it's created.

Label Your Disks

I'm in the habit of sticking a label on a disk after it's been formatted. I may just label it with the date or the word *Formatted*. Later, as the information on the disk changes, the name can be changed to reflect its contents. You can label some disks to reflect their purpose, such as *Work to Home* or *Today's Stuff*. The purpose is to help you keep track of your disks and the information on them. (Refer to Chapter 10 for more information on formatting disks.)

Wait at Least 30 to 40 Seconds Before Turning the Computer On Again

Nothing screws up a computer faster than rapidly flipping the On/Off switch a few times. Computers should be allowed time to *power down* (which is a term the Sunday Paper Grammarians love to harp on). You should allow the fan to stop spinning and those torrentially turning hard drives to gracefully wind down to silence. Only then is it 100 percent OK to turn the system back on again.

Change Your Printer's Ribbon or Toner When It Gets Low

In the Hall of I'm Too Cheap, near the Display of Irony, there's a plaque devoted to those who pay $1,000 or more for a nice laser printer but are too cheap to go out and buy a new $90 toner cartridge when one gets low. Don't do this. If your printing starts to fade, buy a new printer toner cartridge or ribbon. In most cases, using an old one has a negative effect on both the printer and your hard copy. This is something you shouldn't neglect.

Buy Supplies

In the same vein as changing a printer ribbon, you should always keep handy plenty of supplies for your computer: These include disks, labels, printer ribbons or toner cartridges, paper for the printer, and other goodies you can find hanging from the racks at any software store.

Buy More Books

Speaking from experience, and as an author of computer books, I can't recommend anything better. Seriously, keep a sharp eye out for computer books. Definitely give the computer and software manuals a try before you buy a computer book on the subject. Some books are long-winded rewrites of the manual. Avoid them. Instead, try to find books with personal insight, plenty of tips, and those written in a language you understand. The computer press reviews books but rarely keeps those items in mind. So be your own critic.

Chapter 18
Ten Common Beginner Mistakes

*G*olly, if there really were only ten common beginner mistakes, life would be so much easier with computers. Sad to say, the following only highlights a few common beginner faults, but there's nothing that can't be cured. Review this list and reduce your problems.

Assuming It's Your Own Fault

The first thing most beginners assume is that when something doesn't go right, it's their own fault. Usually it isn't. Computers don't always work as advertised. If you type in a command exactly as it's listed in the book or manual and it doesn't work, the manual is wrong, not you. How do you find out what is right? You can check the program's README file, or you can call the developer for technical support. Or experiment, especially if it's your own computer (so you delete your own files and not your co-worker's).

Mistyping Commands

Making typing mistakes is a common problem for all computer users. Beginners typically forget spaces on the command line, sandwiching separate parts of a DOS command together, which doesn't make sense to DOS. The result: You get an error message. Also, never end any DOS command with a period. Even though the manual may have a period after the command (in obeisance to English grammar), few, if any, DOS commands ever end with a period. And be aware of the differences between the forward slash (/) and the backslash (\ ), as well as the colon (:) and the semicolon (;).

Buying the Wrong Thing

Hardware and software must be compatible with your computer. In particular, this means that software must run *under DOS* (or Windows, but that's another book), and your computer must have the proper innards to support the software. The problem primarily exists with PC graphics and memory. If you don't have enough or the proper type of either, some software may not work. Don't try too hard to save money by buying bargain hardware from remainder catalogs if you don't know enough about computers to tell the difference.

Buying Too Much Software

It's fun to go crazy in a software store, wielding your VISA card like a samurai sword. Bringing home all those applications and getting started with them takes time, however. Don't give yourself too much to do, or you may neglect some of the programs you've bought. Start by buying software with the basics, maybe one or two packages. Learn those, and then expand with other programs as needed. Your brain and your monthly VISA bill will be easier to live with.

Assuming It Will Be Easy (Just Because the Program Says So)

This goes right along with buying too much software. You need time to learn a program, get comfortable with it, and become productive with it. With today's overwhelming applications, you may never master everything (no one does). Still, give yourself time to learn. You can get your work done far more quickly if you take those extra few days to experiment and play with the software, work the tutorials, and practice. (Be sure to tell the boss about that.) Most of all, don't buy software on deadline. I mean, don't think you can buy the program on Monday, install it on Tuesday, and produce the divisional report that's due on Wednesday. Programs save time only after you've learned them — until then, they eat time.

A corollary to this is: Don't expect to learn the program if you refuse to look at the manual (or a book about the program). There's no such thing as an intuitive program, no matter what they say. At least take the introductory tutorial.

Incorrectly Inserting Disks

The handy 3 $\frac{1}{2}$-inch disks can only fit into a floppy drive one way. Even though there are potentially eight ways to insert a disk, only one of them meets with success. The 5 $\frac{1}{4}$-inch disks are different. You can fit them into a drive on any of four sides both right-side-up and upside-down. The correct method of inserting both types of disks is with the label up and toward you. The notch on the 5$\frac{1}{4}$-inch disk is to the left and the oblong hole on the disk goes in first. Nothing heinous happens if you insert a 5 $\frac{1}{4}$-inch disk the wrong way — it just doesn't work.

Logging to the Wrong Drive or Directory

As you work with a computer, you'll always be using, or *logged to,* one directory on one disk drive. Never assume that you know where you are. If you do, you may delete files you don't want to delete or be unable to find files you expect to be there. Refer to "Finding the Current Directory" in Chapter 11.

Another common variant of this mistake is logging to a floppy drive that doesn't have a disk in it. If you do that, you'll see a `General failure` error message; put the proper disk into the drive and then press R to Retry.

Pressing Y Too Quickly

DOS asks a Y/N (yes or no) question for a reason; what's about to take place has serious consequences. Are you *sure* you want to go ahead? Only press Y if you really do. If you're uncertain, press N or Ctrl+C and reexamine your situation. This question happens more often than not with the DEL*.* command; make sure you're logged to the proper directory before typing **DEL*.*** to delete all the files.

Reformatting an Important Disk

Eventually, like all computer users, you will accumulate some 10,000 or so floppy disks, which you'll keep in a drawer, on a tabletop, tossed onto a shelf, or in cityscape-like piles on the floor. Grabbing one of these disks and reformatting it is cheaper than buying a new disk. But make sure that old disk doesn't contain anything valuable first. How do you do that? Label the disks properly and run the DIR command to see what's there before you format.

No Organization or Housekeeping

Organization and housekeeping are two duties that the intermediate-to-advanced DOS users learn to take upon themselves. It's routine stuff, actually part of the larger picture of hard disk management. Not performing housekeeping or being unorganized are things beginners are good at. But over the long run, picking up after yourself now can save you massive problems in the near future.

Unless you want to pick up a good book on hard disk management (which implies taking that first step toward computer nerdhood), my suggestion is to let your favorite computer expert have a crack at your computer. Tell him or her to check out the system, organize things, and clean up your hard drive. (But tell him or her not to get too fancy — you don't want to plow through six layers of subdirectories to find something.) The end result will be a faster system — and maybe even some more disk space. That's a plus, but getting more disk space isn't something beginners need to concern themselves with.

Chapter 19
Ten Things You Should Never Do

● ●

In This Chapter

▶ Don't switch disks

▶ Don't work from a floppy disk

▶ Don't take a disk out of the drive when the light is on

▶ Don't turn off the computer unless it's "safe"

▶ Don't reset to leave an application

▶ Don't plug anything into the computer while it's on

▶ Don't force a disk into the drive

▶ Never format a high-capacity disk to low capacity

▶ Never format a low-capacity disk to high capacity

▶ Never load software from an alien disk

▶ Never use these DOS commands: CTTY, DEBUG, FASTOPEN, FDISK, FORMAT C:, RECOVER

● ●

*U*h-oh. Here is a list of ten big no-nos (OK, there are 11, but who's counting?). Actually, there are a lot of bad things you can do to a nice computer. For some of them I'm hoping you don't need a written warning. For example, it's a bad idea to attempt to fix your own monitor. You can, conceivably, upgrade your computer, but being able to do something and wanting to do it are two different things.

Here, then, are ten (plus one) unhealthy things you don't even want to consider doing.

Don't Switch Disks

This isn't that obvious a warning. Basically, it means don't switch disks while you're still using the one in the drive. For example, suppose you're working on a file in drive A and you haven't yet saved the file back to disk. Then, for some reason, you switch disks and try to save the file on the second disk. The result is that you've ruined the second disk and not truly saved your file.

Always save a file on the same disk from which you've loaded it. If you want a second copy of the file on another disk, use the COPY command. Refer to "Copying a Single File" in Chapter 9.

Don't Work from a Floppy Disk

I am often amazed that people with computers that have nice, big, fast hard drives do their work on floppy disks. These days, finding a program that can be run from a floppy is almost impossible. And, for heaven's sake, don't start your PC from a floppy disk when you can start it by using the hard disk. Doing so leads to nothing but trouble.

Floppy disks are still useful. You can read and write files on a floppy, send work back and forth between two distant computers, and so on. Using floppies is slow, and floppies are less reliable than hard disks, but they work. Back up your data files to your floppies and use the floppies to move files to another machine — but do your day-to-day work on your hard drive.

Don't Take a Disk Out of the Drive When the Light Is On

The drive light is on only when the computer is writing to or reading from the disk. As with humans, the computer becomes annoyed when you remove its reading material before it's finished reading it. The result could be a damaged disk or lost information.

If you remove a disk before the light goes out, the computer displays a "What's going on?" error message. Replace the disk and press R to Retry the operation.

Turn Off the Computer When It Says It's Safe To Do So

Choose the Shutdown command from Window's Start thing menu to either reset or turn off the computer. Turn your PC off only when the computer tells you it's "safe" to do so.

Don't Reset to Leave an Application

This goes along with not turning off the PC in the middle of something. Always quit a program and return to Windows properly. Never shut something down in haste or precious data you may waste.

Don't Plug Anything into the Computer While It's On

Connect any external goodies to your computer only when your computer is off. This especially goes for the keyboard, monitor, and printer. Plugging in any of those items while the computer's power is on can "fry" something you've paid a lot of money for. It's best to turn off the computer, plug in your goodies, and then turn everything back on again.

Don't Force a Disk into the Drive

If it doesn't go in, the disk is probably pointed in the wrong direction. Or worse, what you're sticking the disk into is probably not a disk drive, or there's a disk already *in* the drive. Refer to "Changing Disks" in Chapter 2 for the details.

Never Format a High-Capacity Disk to Low Capacity

First, it's a waste of money. Second, many low-capacity drives can't read high-capacity disks formatted to low capacity. Third, it's hard to force the machine into reformatting the disk back to high capacity later.

Never Format a Low-Capacity Disk to High Capacity

Oh, you can try. The results are usually a disk that's riddled with errors, or a disk that fails miserably over time and loses lots of data. Don't be fooled by some huckster into thinking that a $19.95 hole-punching device can do the trick for you; don't be cheap with your disks and your prized data.

Never Load Software from an Alien Disk

Only buy software *shrink-wrapped* from a reputable computer dealer. Any other program you get, especially those on cheaply labeled disks, is suspect. Don't trust it! This is how computer viruses are spread, so it's best not to load anything from an alien disk. And, for God's sake, never boot from such a disk.

Never Use These Dangerous DOS Commands

The following commands serve special purposes way beyond the reach of most beginning computer users. It's OK to let someone who knows what they're doing use these commands, but you should never try them yourself. The consequences are just too horrible to think of.

CTTY
: This command unhooks DOS from the keyboard and screen. Don't try it.

debug
: This is a programmer's tool used to create programs, modify memory, and — if you're careless — mess up a disk drive. Don't run this program. (If you do, type **Q** to quit.)

FASTOPEN
: Sounds nifty, after all the FASTOPEN command must do something faster, right? Wrong! This was an honest but primitive attempt to speed up disk access. Windows handles this job now.

fdisk
: This command could destroy all information on your hard drive if used improperly. Why it's still around, I haven't a clue.

FORMAT C:
: The FORMAT command should only be used with drives A and B to format floppy disks. Never format drive C, or any drive letter higher than C.

recover
: This command sounds healthy, but RECOVER is dumb and deadly. If you type this command it will destroy all files on your disk and remove all your subdirectories, replacing them with garbage — all without a Y/N warning. This command was probably deleted when you upgraded to Windows 95. If not, don't bother with it.

Chapter 20

Ten Things You Can Do Better or Faster in DOS than in Windows

. . . .

In This Chapter

▶ General reasons DOS is better

▶ Renaming a group of files

▶ Copying a group of files

▶ Displaying a select group of files

▶ Renaming a file extension

▶ DOS games (Yippee!)

▶ Bob. Bob. No Bob. Bob.

. . . .

I'll admit that this List of Ten is only designed to make you feel better, and most of it is debatable. Since I wrote a similar list (a list of arguments, actually) in *MORE DOS For Dummies* (IDG Books Worldwide), I'm always getting letters from readers who tend to agree with me that DOS is better or faster. So the next time some Windows geek puts you down for using a "dead" operating system, just hit him in the noggin with one of the following. Stand by your DOS!

General Reasons DOS is Better

Windows may have multitasking. It may "manage" memory better. You can see fonts and graphics on the screen. And, of course, it looks pretty. Even so, here are some valid points DOS scores against it:

✔ DOS is smaller than Windows. MS-DOS 6.22 took up maybe 3MB on a hard drive — that's including the DOS Shell (which you had to order extra, but who's counting), Editor, QBasic, and a host of utilities. Even Windows 3.11 took up more space at 12MB. Windows 95? They *say* 40MB, but it eats up at least 100MB on my PC.

✔ DOS doesn't require extra memory. DOS needs only 256K of RAM to work. That's 256 kilobytes, not 256 megabytes. (Older versions of DOS required even less memory.) Windows is pitifully slow on anything less than an 8MB screaming monster.

✔ DOS is faster than Windows. DOS loads in no time flat. Blammo! There's the DOS prompt. There is no graphical overhead, and since the PC is naturally a text machine, everything flies up on the screen.

✔ DOS programs load faster. Want to start WordPerfect? Type **WP** and press the Enter key. In Windows? At the keyboard, forget it. But with a mouse, you have to trudge through the Start thing's menu and blah-blah-blah. (Of course, starting it as an icon is easier, but that requires extra setup.)

✔ When you goof up in DOS and get an error message, you can type the CLS command to clean the screen and avoid eye-catching embarrassment. Windows? No way to clear the screen. Error messages stay there and await ridicule by family and co-workers.

✔ DOS is cheaper. The MS-DOS 6.22 upgrade was only $9 if you owned MS-DOS 6.2, otherwise it was maybe $38. Windows? Try $89 — and the costs go up since you have to upgrade all your software to take advantage of Windows' new features. *Ka-ching!*

✔ DOS is cheaper still when you consider PC hardware. You don't need lots of memory, a larger hard drive, or fancy graphics to run DOS programs.

✔ Some will say DOS can't multitask and Windows can. Wrong! Go check out Quarterdeck's Deskview/386. It will multitask DOS better than Windows, hands down. Try this: Using Deskview/386 you can format a disk while working on your word processor *and* downloading a program with your modem. Windows won't let you do *anything* else while it formats a disk. ("A minor quibble," they may scoff, but Windows cannot do it — so tough!)

✔ DOS has a batch file programming language, Windows doesn't. A big part of that is the AUTOEXEC.BAT file, which runs startup programs. While Windows does have a Startup folder, it doesn't have any smarts like an AUTOEXEC.BAT file could.

✔ DOS comes with its own programming languages: a BASIC interpreter in QBasic and a mini-assembler in DEBUG.

✔ DOS programs are more efficient than Windows since they don't have to carry the graphical overhead, nor do they have to "share" the computer with other programs. Trust me, WordPerfect *smokes* on a Pentium.

✔ DOS don't crash.

✔ Sure, DOS programs may crash the computer, but DOS itself is rather stable.

There are, however, two overpowering reasons that DOS is not better than Windows. I shudder to think of them, but they're both undeniably true:

- ✔ Bill Gates says DOS is dead, and he means it. There will never be another DOS version. (Granted, this is stupid financially since he still makes a great deal of money from DOS. But don't expect the Computer Boy Wonder to hit home runs forever.)
- ✔ Software developers believe Bill Gates and, therefore, will stop developing their DOS software. This will truly end DOS's reign, but maybe not for a few years or so.

Things DOS Can Do with Files (of Which Windows Only Dreams)

Windows pales when it comes to file management. While a graphical interface does make it easier to understand files, and it can be fun, it's wholly impractical for those of us who truly get their hands dirty with them.

Renaming a group of files

Windows flat out won't let you rename a group of files. When you select the group and choose File⇨Rename, only the last selected file is renamed. After renaming it, the others you put in the group are no longer in a group. That stinks.

In DOS, you can rename all .TXT files to .DOC with one command:

```
C> REN *.TXT *.DOC
```

Nothing to it.

Copying a group of files from drive A

Say you want to copy a group of graphical files from drive A to your C:\GRAPHICS directory. In Windows, that would involve several steps:

1. **Open My Computer or the Explorer.**
2. **Open the Drive A icon.**

3. **Select the graphics files you want to copy.**

   This can be made easier by sorting the files by their type; choose View⇨ Arrange Icons⇨by Type. Then the files must be selected by Ctrl-clicking the mouse or by some other file selection technique in Windows. All told, it's several mouse clicks.

4. **Copy the files.**

   You either choose the Edit⇨Copy command or click on the toolbar's shortcut button (if available) or press Ctrl+C.

5. **Open the drive C icon.**

   Click-click.

6. **Open the GRAPHICS folder.**

   Click-click.

7. **Paste the files.**

   Choose Edit⇨Paste or use the toolbar button or press Ctrl+V.

Using DOS, it takes only one command line to do all that:

```
C> COPY A:*.BMP C:\GRAPHICS
```

Granted, that's a bit of typing. And some key combinations *might* strain your fingers. And you may get it wrong and have to type it over again. But it's only one step, versus at least seven for Windows.

DIR for a select group of files

Here's one Windows can't do at all. Say you want to see a list of only a certain type of files, say program files. Using the DIR command, you'd type:

```
C> DIR *.COM
```

Then DOS displays all the files with the .COM extension. Simple. Painless.

Can't be done in Windows.

Renaming a file extension

Suppose you have a .TXT file that's too big for Windows' Notepad to edit. If so, Windows will constantly urge you to use WordPad instead. Big time waster. A simple solution is to change the file's "type" from .TXT to .DOC, which doesn't change the file's contents but changes how Windows opens the file. Alas, this cannot be done in Windows.

Only in DOS can you rename a file's extension:

```
C> REN README.TXT README.DOC
```

Again, this only changes the file's name (or type) and not the file's contents. After the above command, Windows will use WordPad to open the README.DOC file.

In Windows, if you try to rename the files the end result is README.DOC.TXT. That's because Windows hides the file extensions; you end up only renaming the first part of the file.

✔ Any Windowphiles reading this: Yes, it can be done in Windows. But it's a bother. The idea here is that it's just easier in DOS to rename a file extension.

Playing DOS Games

There's a reason they write those games for DOS and not Windows. DOS gives your programs free reign over the entire PC. It lets anything rule the roost. Windows isn't so nice and won't share all that it has. Therefore, the game developers choose DOS since they want full control.

Now Bill Gates has promised that Windows will be more friendly to DOS game developers. He even dressed like the DOOM guy when he announced DOS was dead. (Nothing a *Hell Knight* couldn't fix.) Only time will tell if the game people believe him. Personally I think they're rather happy knowing the PC is the best, fastest, and most powerful game machine around — provided DOS and not some wimpy, whiney, cute operating system is in charge.

Perhaps the Best Reason DOS is Better

There isn't a DOS-based version of Bob.

✔ Bob was Microsoft's "friendly" interface they put on Windows, thinking some people were apparently too "dumb" for Windows. Boy, were they wrong! One thing Microsoft just doesn't get: There are no dumb users, only dumb operating systems.

Chapter 21

Ten Utterly Worthless DOS Terms and Acronyms

· ·

In This Chapter

▶ ASCII

▶ AUTOEXEC.BAT

▶ CONFIG.SYS

▶ DOS

▶ EMS (expanded memory)

▶ Extended memory

▶ HMA

▶ TSR

▶ UMB

▶ WYSIWYG

· ·

*N*ow that Windows 95 is here, you can conveniently chuck your assortment of DOS acronyms you formerly used to impress your friends and co-workers at cocktail parties. No more will you be able to talk about shuffling an ASCII DBF[1] into EMS thanks to a nifty TSR.[2] Nope, these babies are all gone, gone, gone. But that really isn't any excuse for one last look at what are perhaps the most horrid ten acronyms ever dreamt up — all marching to the sunset at Olympus to join the departed gods of pantheons past, et cetera and so on.

[1] Data Base File — not relevant enough to include in this prestigious list.

[2] There was actually a program that did this, by the way.

ASCII

What it stands for: American Standard Code for Information Interchange.

Pronunciation: ASK-ee.

Meaning: Usually used to identify a type of file that contains only readable text, one that can be displayed with the TYPE command and read by a human.

As used in a sentence: Here is the ASCII version of that file because I know you're too lame to buy a real word processor.

D.O.A. because: Thanks to IBM and Bill Gates there *are* no other computers to share information with!

Please don't read this

ASCII is a coding scheme used to identify characters in a computer. Each character, letter, number, or symbol is assigned a code number from 0 through 127. All personal computers use the same coding scheme to represent these characters, which means that basic (text-only) files can be transferred between two computers without the need for translation and blah, blah, blah.

AUTOEXEC.BAT

What it stands for: An AUTOmatically EXECuting BATch file.

Pronunciation: Otto-Ecks-Eck-Bat.

Meaning: An optional, though highly useful program, that ran every time the computer started. AUTOEXEC.BAT was used to hold a whole stack of DOS commands you'd normally type at the prompt every time the PC started. By putting them into the AUTOEXEC.BAT file, the computer would type them all automatically for you, presto!

As used in a sentence: Milton's a PC genius. He wrote his own AUTOEXEC.BAT file that does everything, so all he does is turn on the computer and watch.

D.O.A. because: Windows ignores it. But you can have a startup batch file for your DOS windows. See Chapter 7, "Creating an AUTOEXEC.BAT-like file for each of your DOS windows."

CONFIG.SYS

What it stands for: CONFIGuration file for the SYStem.

Pronunciation: Kon-Fig-Sis.

Meaning: A file that both configured the PC's file system as well as loaded programs called *device drivers*. The device drivers were required to operate parts of the PC's hardware unknown to DOS or to enhance certain features.

As used in a sentence: Only a bold human messes with a CONFIG.SYS file.

D.O.A. because: Windows uses its own configuration files *that you can't touch!*

DOS

What it stands for: Disk Operating System.

Pronunciation: It rhymes with *boss*. (Don't pronounce it *dose*.)

Meaning: The main program that controls your computer, though most computerati have dropped the "D" since all computers come with disks now. It's really just an OS, operating system. So Windows 95 is called an OS (operating system), even though it loads DOS secretly before it loads itself. (Shhh! Don't tell.)

As used in a sentence: The Microsoft Legal Department would be oh so pleased if we all called it MS-DOS instead of just DOS.

D.O.A. because: Windows ate its progenitor!

EMS (Expanded Memory)

What it stands for: Expanded Memory Specification.

Pronunciation: Letters only, E-M-S.

Meaning: A memory scheme for early PCs to provide more memory for those DOS programs that needed it. This scheme was eclipsed by extended memory, which is better and also automatically comes with all of today's computers. Only older DOS programs may need expanded memory, which makes this turkey one acronym worth forgetting.

As used in a sentence: Having a program that requires EMS is like driving a car that must have regular (leaded) gasoline.

D.O.A. because: Windows programs no longer use this type of memory. In fact, it's merely "simulated" on your PC for any DOS program that thirsts for it.

Extended Memory

What it stands for: Any memory beyond 1MB of memory in today's computers.

Pronunciation: Ecks-Tend-Ed-Mem-O-Ree.

Meaning: A term for extra memory in a PC besides EMS. Actually, this type of memory is simply memory that DOS couldn't use on a 286 or later PC.

As used in a sentence: You think with all the IQ floating around Microsoft they could have come up with two terms more different than expanded and extended memory.

D.O.A. because: Since Windows eats only this type of memory, this and all other memory terms have fallen by the wayside.

HMA

What it stands for: High Memory Area.

Pronunciation: Letters only, H-M-A.

Meaning: The first 64K of extended memory, which could actually be used by DOS. This trick allowed a lot of memory to be freed up for ancient DOS applications.

As used in a sentence: By stuffing DOS up into the HMA, I'm guilty of illegal imprisonment of the computer program and must spend time in the PC pen.

D.O.A. because: Windows may or may not use the HMA so it's no longer an issue, and weird HMA messages never appear on the screen to bug people anymore.

TSR

What it stands for: Terminate and Stay Resident.

Pronunciation: Letters only, T-S-R.

Meaning: A special type of program that stays in memory after it quits. The *real* term is *memory-resident program,* though the marketing droids use the programmer's acronym instead (because they're in marketing and don't know much about real life). A TSR is a program that does something special: helps you use a mouse, gives you more control over your keyboard, or in some way augments what DOS does.

As used in a sentence: Bob spent six years incommunicado writing that TSR for DOS. Anyone have the heart to tell him?

D.O.A. because: It was probably the TSR craze of the mid-'80s that led to the need of a program like Windows. Like TSRs, Windows lets you control various parts of a computer (like a mouse) and run several programs at a time. Also like TSRs, Windows can really crash your computer, locking it up tighter than gum under a cold school desk.

UMB

What it stands for: Upper Memory Block.

Pronunciation: Letters only, U-M-B.

Meaning: A secret cubbyhole of memory in the super secret "reserved" part of the PC. When memory was tight under DOS, special programs could relocate themselves to a UMB, thereby making more memory available to DOS programs.

As used in a sentence: Should not be used in a sentence.

D.O.A. because: Under Windows, all memory management issues are dead.

WYSIWYG

What it stands for: What You See Is What You Get.

Pronunciation: WIZZY-wig (yup, it's true).

Meaning: The stuff you see on the screen looks identical to the way it will appear when printed. Sort of. This was a selling point of early DOS programs but became the defacto standard under Windows. In fact, if it doesn't look the same on the screen as it does when it's printed, you probably didn't spend enough money for your printer.

As used in a sentence: WYSIWYG looks a lot better when I take my glasses off.

D.O.A. because: It's now the standard and no longer such a big deal. It would be like Chrysler coming out with a new ad touting their *windshields* to keep the bugs out of your teeth while you drive.

Part VI

Windows 95 DOS Command Reference for Real People

The 5th Wave

In this part...

*1*s there really a need for a DOS reference anymore? Yes. Don't think this is your standard DOS reference, such as those endless pages with cryptic notations that used to muddy up the DOS manual. There is no DOS manual any more! (Nor is there a Windows manual.) This reference contains two chapters: Chapter 22 has ten common DOS commands you may be using every day, with information on how they work. Chapter 23 contains commands beyond the everyday. This information is simply an explanation of what the command does; formatting and command examples have been cheerfully omitted.

Chapter 22

DOS Commands You Can Use (the Top Ten)

*T*here are a few DOS commands mentioned more than once in this book. I've added a few more to round the number out to ten.

You'll probably use other DOS commands with as much frequency as some of these. They're listed in the following chapter, along with every other stupid DOS command whether you'll use them or not. But here are the ones most people find the most useful.

The CD Command

Purpose: To display the pathname of the current directory.

Sample: CD

Comments: Type **CD**, and you'll see the name of the current drive and directory — the pathname — displayed. That name tells you where you are in the maze of your hard drive structure.

Other purpose: To change to another directory.

Sample: CD \WP51\DATA

Comments: The CD command is followed by a space and the full name of the directory to which you're changing. The directory's pathname usually *starts* with a backslash but doesn't *end* with a backslash.

Where to look: Almost all of Chapter 11; "Finding a Lost Subdirectory" in Chapter 12.

A longer version of this command is CHDIR. Both CD and CHDIR do the same thing; CHDIR was just designed for large bureaucracies, where typing must take longer to occupy time that would otherwise be spent being efficient.

The CLS Command

Purpose: To clear the screen.

Sample: CLS

Comments: CLS clears the screen, or the DOS window if you're being graphical. It erases the display and any embarrassing error messages that may be glowing therein. Simple enough.

The COPY Command

Purpose: To make a copy or duplicate of a file.

Sample: COPY C:FILE1 A:FILE2

Where to look: "Duplicating a File," "Copying a Single File," "Copying a File to You," "Copying a Group of Files," and "Moving a File," all in Chapter 9; you may also want to check "What Is a Pathname?" in Chapter 11 and "Wildcards (or Poker Was Never This Much Fun)" in Chapter 12.

The general rule here: First comes the location and name of the file you're copying, and then the location and name of the copy you're making. If you're already logged to the source or the destination, you can leave that location off, but if that's confusing, just give the entire location (the "pathname") for both halves of the command.

Give the entire pathname; for example:

```
C> COPY C:\WP51\DATA\FILE1\ A:\FILE1
```

This command copies FILE1 from drive C to drive A. You *can* change the name of the copy — and if you're making a copy to the same place as the original, you *have to* change the name.

The DEL Command

Purpose: To delete one or more files, eliminating them from a disk and freeing up the space they used.

Sample: DEL USELESS.TXT

Or: DEL *.BAK

Comments: The DEL command totally zaps a single file (or a group of files if you use a wildcard). This practice is necessary to eliminate older files and to give yourself more disk space.

A handy trick to use with the DEL command is to tack on the /P (slash-P) switch. For example:

```
DEL *.* /P
```

This command directs DOS to prompt you, yes-or-no, for each file deleted:

```
C:\COMMAND.COM Delete (Y/N)?
```

Type **Y** to delete the file or **N** to save it from certain peril.

Where to look: "Deleting a File," "Deleting a Group of Files," and "Moving a File" in Chapter 9. Check out "What Is a Pathname?" in Chapter 11 and "Wildcards (or Poker Was Never This Much Fun)" in Chapter 12; also see "The Perils of DEL *.*" in Chapter 14.

DEL has a twin brother, ERASE. Both DEL and ERASE do the same thing: ruthlessly kill files. The ERASE command was implemented for certain southpaw extremist groups because you don't need the right hand to type it.

The DIR Command

Purpose: To display a list of files on disk.

Sample: DIR

Or: DIR C:

Or: DIR C:\WP60

Comments: DIR is probably the most common DOS command, being the only way DOS has to look at the files on disk. You can see a list of files on any drive or in any subdirectory by following the DIR command with the drive letter or subdirectory pathname.

Where to look: "The DIR Command" in Chapter 2; "That Funny <DIR> Thing" in Chapter 11; "Using the DIR Command," "The wide DIR command," and "Displaying a sorted directory," all in Chapter 12.

The EXIT Command

Purpose: To quit DOS, closing a DOS prompt window.

Sample: EXIT

Comments: This command used to be a special nerd command. But now that DOS is treated like a mere application in Windows, the EXIT command is used to close the DOS window.

Where to look: "Quitting Your DOS Prompt" in Chapter 1.

As a nerdy aside, you can type anything you want after the EXIT command, making your DOS departure more dramatic. Such as:

```
C> EXIT THIS USELESS OPERATING SYSTEM!
```

This trick has no redeeming value.

The FORMAT Command

Purpose: To prepare floppy disks for use.

Sample: FORMAT A:

Comments: All disks must be formatted before you can use them. The FORMAT command must be followed by the drive letter (and a colon) of the floppy drive containing the disk to be formatted. *Never* use the FORMAT command with any drive letter higher than B.

Where to look: "Formatting a Disk" and "Formatting a Low-Capacity Disk in a High-Capacity Drive" in Chapter 10. Also look up "Reformatting Disks" in Chapter 10.

The MORE Command

Purpose: To view text files one screen at a time.

Sample: MORE < FILENAME

Comments: The MORE command is followed by a space, a less-than symbol (<), another space, and then the name of a text file you want to view. At the end of each screen you'll see the *more* prompt; press the spacebar to see the next screen. Press Ctrl+C to cancel.

Where to look: Refer to "Looking at Files" in Chapter 2; "The Tree Structure" in Chapter 11 discusses another interesting use for the MORE command; also look at the TYPE command in this chapter.

The REN Command

Purpose: To rename a file, giving it a new name without changing its contents.

Sample: REN OLDNAME NEWNAME

Or: REN "OLD LONG NAME" "NEW LONG NAME"

Comments: What's to comment? Just follow the DOS naming rules. DOS will object if you try to give the file the same name as another file in the same directory.

Where to look: "Renaming a File" in Chapter 9; also "Name That File!" in Chapter 12.

If you think REN is really the name of a cartoon character, you can use the longer version of this command, RENAME. Both REN and STIMP, er, RENAME do the same thing.

The TYPE Command

Purpose: To display a file on the screen, enabling you to read its contents.

Sample: TYPE BYEDOS.DOC

Comments: The TYPE command displays any file you name, though only files that contain readable text can be understood by humans. If the file displays as *garbage,* press Ctrl+C to cancel the TYPE command.

Where to look: "Looking at Files" in Chapter 2.

Chapter 23

Beyond DOS Commands You Can Use (the Other 50 or So)

. . . .

. . . .

*H*ere is a list of some more DOS commands. You may want to use some of these from time to time (but they didn't make the top-ten list in the previous chapter). The rest of these commands others can use. They're useful, but they won't be covered here as they are beyond the scope of the book.

Each command is briefly described. If necessary, a reference is made to the command elsewhere in this text. Otherwise, I just poke fun at it and leave it at that.

Full details on all MS-DOS 6 commands are found in the online help included with MS-DOS — the HELP command. Refer to Chapter 15 for more information.

Each of these commands is specific to DOS as it lives in Windows. If you didn't upgrade from a previous version of DOS, you'll have fewer commands available in most cases. Those commands flagged by the Windows 95 icon are new for this DOS version.

Commands You May Occasionally Use

CHKDSK	This command reports the status of a disk, how many files are on it, and how much of the disk is used by what. See Chapter 10.
COMP	The COMP command compares the contents of two files line by line and tells you if they're identical. If you upgraded from a later version of MS-DOS, the FC command is used instead.
DATE	This command displays the current date (according to the computer, at least) and gives you the opportunity to enter a new date.
EDIT	The EDIT "command" runs the DOS Editor program, which you can use to create and edit text files on disk. Refer to Chapter 8 for your editing pleasure.
FC	FC stands for *file compare.* Unlike the old COMP command, FC offers more detailed descriptions of the differences between two files, and it's not as chicken about looking at files as the COMP command was.
MD	The MD (also MKDir) command is used to make a subdirectory. Refer to "How to Name a Directory (the MKDIR Command)" in Chapter 12.
MOVE	The MOVE command moves a file or group of files from one place to another. It works like a combined COPY-DEL command; you first COPY files to another place, and then you thoughtlessly slaughter the originals. See "Moving a File" in Chapter 9.
MSAV	The Microsoft Anti-Virus command, MSAV, as well as information on fighting the viral plague, is divvied up in Chapter 15.
MSD	The Microsoft Diagnostic, MSD, program — a true PC privacy peeker — is discussed covertly in Chapter 15.
PROMPT	This command changes the appearance of the DOS prompt. Refer to "Prompt Styles of the Rich and Famous" in Chapter 3.
SCANDISK	Window's ultra-keen disk check-up tool, ScanDisk will find and repair any disk maladies you may have, hard or floppy disks no problem. Refer to Chapter 11 for the full details.
START	The START command is used to start another program in another window. See the sidebar, "Trivial asides on the START command you don't need to read," in Chapter 2.
TIME	This command displays what DOS thinks is the current time and gives you the chance to enter a new time whenever you want.
TREE	The TREE command displays a "visual" representation of your hard drive's tree structure — a map of your subdirectories. Refer to Chapter 11 for an example.

UNFORMAT	Another lifesaver, the UNFORMAT command undoes whatever it is the FORMAT command does to a disk. (Of course, being careful with the FORMAT command in the first place always helps.) See Chapter 14.
VER	The VER command displays DOS's name and the version number. Refer to "Names and Versions" in Chapter 3.
VOL	This command displays a disk's volume label. Refer to "Changing the Volume Label" in Chapter 10.
XCOPY	This is like a super copy command; much faster and smarter than the plain old copy command — a super COPY! You can use XCOPY as a straight-across substitute for the COPY command if you like. It even copies subdirectories! Wow, this modern age.
XCOPY32	The super-duper COPY command. XCOPY32 has a few extra options and settings that make it even more obnoxious — and difficult to type — than XCOPY. Sheesh.

Commands You May See Others Use

APPEND	Weird command. Like the PATH command (listed later), this command enables DOS to look in other subdirectories to find data files. It's not really as keen as it sounds and generally causes more trouble than it's worth. A command best avoided.
ATTRIB	This command changes a file's attributes, which describe how DOS can treat a file. Refer to "The File! I Cannot Kill It!" in Chapter 9.
BREAK	The BREAK command turns special Ctrl+C and Ctrl+Break testing on or off. With it on, Ctrl+C may be a little more responsive; with it off, your computer runs faster.
CALL	This is a batch file command used in batch file programming. The CALL command runs a second batch file from within another batch file.
CHOICE	This batch file command waits for a certain key to be pressed. It's really quite cool if you're into batch files. Ignore it otherwise.
COMMAND	The COMMAND command is actually DOS, the program that runs in every DOS window (it's COMMAND.COM). You'd type in this command to start another DOS window.
DISKCOPY	This command duplicates an entire floppy disk. See Chapter 10 for a how-to.

(continued)

DOSKEY	The DOSKEY command runs a special keyboard enhancer that gives you more editing power and control over the command line. This can be a fun and useful tool, but it's a little too advanced for this book.
ECHO	This is a special batch file command that displays information on the screen, usually the line of text following ECHO.
FIND	This command is used to find text in a file, or it can be connived into searching for text in a DOS command. A sample of this feat is offered in "Finding a Lost Subdirectory" in Chapter 12.
FOR	This is a special batch file programming command. Even in books I've written on batch file programming, it's been hard to explain what this command does. Best leave it alone.
GOTO	Yet another batch file programming command, which is only useful inside a batch file; there's really nothing to *go to* at the DOS prompt.
IF	IF is a special batch file command used in making decisions. For example: IF THE COMPUTER EXPLODES, I SHOULD WEAR AN APRON. That's computer logic for you.
LABEL	The LABEL command is used to add or change a disk's volume label. See Chapter 10 for more information.
LFNFOR	This command permits the FOR batch file command to understand, use, and swallow long filenames or not. LFN means Long File Name. OK.
LOCK	The LOCK command allows older DOS utilities to directly access the hard drive. Normally this would be prevented by Windows.
MEM	The MEM command tells you about memory in your computer and how it's used. Trivial, really.
PATH	The PATH command creates the DOS *search path*, which is a list of one or more subdirectories in which DOS will look for programs to run. It's maintained by Windows, though some DOS installation programs may modify it for you.
PAUSE	This is a special batch file command that displays a press any key message and (surprise) waits for you to press a key before going on.
QBASIC	More than a command, QBasic is MS-DOS's free-of-charge Basic programming language interpreter. If you want to get into the Basic programming language, consider picking up a book on QBasic and teaching yourself to program. It's much more fun than playing with the DOS prompt.
REM	This is a batch file command that enables you to put comments or remarks into a batch file program.

RMDIR	The RMDIR command (also RD) is used to delete a subdirectory. The subdirectory has to be empty first.
SET	The SET command is used in two ways: First, by itself SET displays the contents of DOS's *environment*. Second, SET can be used to place items into the environment or to remove them. Yawn.
SHIFT	Another batch file command. This one does something so complex I'd have to tell it *twice* to Mr. Spock.
SORT	This command is used to sort the output of some other DOS command or text file.
SYS	The SYS command is used to make a disk bootable. It transfers the DOS system files to a disk so that disk can be used to start any computer using DOS as its operating system. Sneaky that they left this one hanging around.
UNLOCK	This command does the opposite of the LOCK command; it prevents a DOS utility from accessing and modifying the drive. Normally your drives are UNLOCKed.
VERIFY	This command turns on double verification of all the information DOS writes to disk. With the command on, you'll be certain that the information is properly stored. On the downside, it slows down your computer. Normally, VERIFY is off.

Commands No One Uses More Than Once

CHCP	This is the *change code page* command, which enables you to switch in an alternate character set for the screen. (Sounds like fun, but setting up a PC to do that is complex and confusing.)
GRAPHICS	The GRAPHICS command works with IBM and Hewlett-Packard printers, enabling them to accurately print graphics.
KEYB	The KEYB command loads a foreign language keyboard driver into memory, enabling you to type using special foreign language characters. (Ooo, la, la! C'est très intéressant!)
NLSFUNC	Yet another *code page* program. This adds *natural language support* to DOS, enabling foreigners to type in their own native lingo.
SETVER	This command is used to fool some old DOS programs into thinking they're running under their favorite DOS versions. It's best that you leave this command alone.
SUBST	The SUBST command is used to fake DOS into thinking a subdirectory is actually a disk drive. And dangerous, too.

Commands Not Worth Bothering With

	CTTY	The CTTY command is interesting, but typing it can disconnect your keyboard and monitor, forcing you to reset the computer in order to regain control. It's more of a curiosity than a command you can get any mileage out of.
	DEBUG	This is really a secret snooper type of program, intended for use by programmers and not mere mortals such as you or I.
	DELTREE	The DELTREE command is a powerful and merciless version of the tamer DEL command. Don't tempt fate by messing with this command. Even the experts don't use it without a garlic wreath, silver bullet, or recent backup handy.
	EXPAND	This program is covertly used by the Setup program when it installs MS-DOS or Windows. There's no need for you to bother with it here.
	FASTOPEN	This is a program used to speed up access to files on disk. I've heard nothing but problems with it, especially with switching floppy disks. Don't use this command.
	FDISK	The FDISK command is used when you first set up a hard disk. It prepares the disk for formatting. Using this command after the disk has been prepared could damage your hard drive. Do not use this command; only let an expert play with FDISK.
	LOADFIX	If you ever see the message `Packed file corrupt` when you try to run a program, don't panic. At the next DOS prompt, type **LOADFIX,** a space, and then type the name of the program again (plus any options or other doodads). That should fix the problem, and that's about all this command is good for.
	LOADHIGH	This is a memory management command, along with its shorter version, the LH command. Probably not needed anymore, but kept around because it's easy to pronounce.
	PRINT	Although a logical person such as yourself would assume that the PRINT command prints files — and it does — the illogical truth is that it does a lot more, additional unnecessary stuff. Refer to Chapter 9 for information on printing files and avoid the ugly PRINT command.
	REPLACE	Interesting command: It will search out and replace all files on the hard disk with newer versions on a floppy disk. Because most programs come with their own INSTALL or SETUP program, you rarely need to use the REPLACE command.
	SHARE	The "something to do with networks" command. Windows handles all these duties now, though some DOS program may install SHARE for you, thinking it's not in Windows. Silly.

	UNINSTAL	This gem uninstalls Windows 95, removing it from your computer and restoring your old version of DOS and Windows. It's nice that they included such a one-time command, and interesting that you can do such a thing from the DOS prompt. Obviously, keep this one out of the hands of small children.
	VSAFE	The lesser-half of MS-DOS 6's anti-virus brigade, VSafe is actually more of a pain than it's worth.

Appendix

Songs to Sing to Lament the Demise of DOS

. . . .

*O*n October 31, 1995, Bill Gates threw a big party at Microsoft and officially declared RIP DOS. After 15-odd years, the operating system used by 80 percent of the computers in the world — an operating system that made Bill Gates a multi-billionaire and still generates substantial revenue for Microsoft — was dead.

Computer pundits had predicted this ever since 1987, when Microsoft and IBM both came out with OS/2. That was the first time DOS was supposed to die. So on Halloween 1995, DOS died its second death, this one more substantial because Bill Gates was singing and dancing on the coffin. And, after all, he *owns* DOS, so I guess he can kill it off any time he wants to.

Of course, millions and millions of people still use DOS. Windows users afraid to upgrade to Windows 95 are still using DOS. DOS is still a valuable, reliable, stable operating system and friend. Sure, I chide DOS a lot and, for all the supposed IQ points Bill Gates hires, it's amazing they never did more with it. This doesn't mean DOS vanishes overnight, however. It means DOS, like many dead operating systems before it, slowly fades away. And this is a good thing, since the alternative would be Bill Gates publicly praising DOS's virtue while Microsoft privately kills it off. I'm glad that's not the case.

So instead of dragging your feet, weeping and droning on with the DOS dirge, here are some peppy songs I've written praising the demise of DOS. Feel free to sing these any time, whenever Windows 95 really bugs the bejeezus out of you and you long for a simpler day, a day when DOS ruled the earth and windows were for staring out of on a boring afternoon.

Stand by Your DOS

(Sung to the tune of *Stand By Your Man*)
Sometimes it's hard not being trendy,
Hangin' on to things long dead and gone.
But DOS is still real trusty
Even though it may be rusty
Living in a window from now on.

Chorus:
Stand by your DOS.
It's been a friend you turned to
Ever since that you first learned to
Type F3
And use Control+C
Stand by your DOS
And boot up at the C prompt
Those who want Windows are truly lost!
Stand by your DOS!

My Poor DOS

(Sung to the tune of *My Bonnie Lies Over the Ocean*)
Now I'll admit DOS was quite stupid.
It's cryptic and ugly to see.
But it was small and un-ob-trusive.
So why did they take it from me? Oh . . .

Chorus:
Bring back, bring back,
Bring back my DOS to full screen, full screen!
Bring back, bring back,
Bring back my DOS to full screen!

I've come a long way with my PC.
I've gotten to know AUTO'XEC.
And now I am forced to use Windows.
They just sent my OS to heck! Oh . . .

Chorus:
Now they've put DOS in a window.
It's graphically stuck in a box.
Microsoft must really hate us.
Upon their compilers a pox! Oh . . .

The DOS Error Message Song

(Sung to the tune of *Jingle Bells*)
It's been a lovely day.
No error message in sight.
I have some time to play
A cool DOS game to-night.
But on the screen I see
A message blaring bright.
It's `Insufficient memory`
When will this thing work right?

Chorus:
Oh!
`Syntax error`
`ECHO OFF`
`Allocated / Free`
`Bad command or filename`
Bring it back to me!
`DIR` and `REN`
`HMA`
`924 bytes free`
`Abort, Retry, Ignore, Ignore`
My DOS just for me!

Win-dows gets in my way
Though it can be a pest.
And DOS games it does play
Bill says he knows best.
Of course it isn't true.
It's just paradox.
I see the same err' mess-ag-es
But graphic'lly in a box.

The DOS Fighting Song

(Sung to the tune of *The Marine Corps Hymn* [*From the Halls of Montezuma*])
From the malls of Redmond, Wash-ing-ton
To the shores of Boca Raton.
We will all start using Win-dows
It's the OS of the land.
We will click on tiny i-cons
We will drag and we will drop.
If I only could use DOS again
All this madness, it would stop.

RIP DOS

(Sung to the tune of *On Top of Old Smoky*)
On top of Old Smoky,
The champion sits.
It looks like it's Windows,
DOS was blown to bits.
But it isn't buried,
It's not in the grave.
DOS must live in Windows
Chained up like a slave.

DOS's Lament

(Sung to the tune of *Oh, My Darlin' Clementine*)
On the desktop,
In a window,
Multitasking all the time.
MS-DOS sits quite un-happy
Life is over, it's a crime.

With no power,
With no purpose
With no software or control.
Might as well have
Bought a Mac 'cause
Without DOS it's rather droll.

I hate Windows
It's confusing
And it really isn't fun.
There's no C prompt
Or COMMAND.COM — Oh!
Take me back to '81.

DOS Was the Perfect Old System for Me

(Sung to the tune of *My Favorite Things*)
XTree and *Quattro*
and *PC Tools 7*
Quicken, WordPerfect.
It was just like heaven.
Mul-ti-plan, Q-EMM
and *dBASE III.*
DOS was the perfect old system for me!

VisiCalc, WordStar,
and programs from Norton
Sidekick and *SuperKey*
and *DesqVIEW* was such fun.
FDISK and EDLIN
and using DOSKEY
DOS was the perfect old system for me!

Chorus:
Now there's Windows.
Who cares! Windows
'Cause it's slow and it's bad.
But then I just think of my fav'rite DOS things
And then I don't feel so sad.

ProComm, Magellan
'n' *LapLink* and *Q&A*
GrandView and *DOS Word*
Ven-tu-ra and *MultiMate.*
Turbo Pascal, BASIC,
and *1-2-3.*
DOS was the perfect old system for me!

DOOM and *Descent*
and Cyberlords killing.
Playing good DOS games
Can be only thrilling.
Windows can't cut it;
It's lame as can be.
DOS was the perfect old system for me!

Chorus

Glossary

● ●

386

Number that refers to all computers that have an 80386 microprocessor or brain.

80286

This is the number of a microprocessor or brain in an AT or 286 computer. It's one notch less than an 80386 and one notch greater than an 8086.

80386

This number refers to the microprocessor or brain in all 80386 computers. There are two types: the 80386DX and the 80386SX. The SX is simply a cheaper version of the DX model, with all the caffeine but only half the calories.

80486

This number refers to the brains found in an 80486 computer. It's a notch better than an 80386 system and will put a bigger dent into your wallet.

8086/8088

These two numbers refer to the first processors in the first line of PCs out the chute. Although a lot of these models were sold, and many are still up and running, few are sold today.

Alt+key

A key combination involving the Alt key plus some other key on the keyboard, a letter, number, or function key. When you see Alt+S, it means to press and hold the Alt key, type an S, and then release both keys. Note that Alt+S doesn't imply Alt+Shift+S; the S key by itself is fine.

applications

This is a term applying to computer programs, generally programs of a similar type. For example, you can have word processing applications, spreadsheet applications, and so on. There are several computer programs that fit into each application category. And everything is generally referred to as *software*, which makes the computer do its thing.

arrow keys

These are keys on the keyboard that have directional arrows on them. Note that some keys, such as Shift, Tab, Backspace, and Enter, also have arrows on them. But the traditional arrow keys are used to move the cursor. See *cursor keys*.

ASCII

An acronym for American Standard Code for Information Interchange. ASCII (ASK-ee) uses code values from 0 to 127 to represent letters, numbers, and symbols used by a computer. In DOS, you'll often see ASCII used to refer to a plain text file, one that can be viewed by the TYPE command and read by a human.

back up

A method of copying a whole gang of files from a hard drive to a series of floppy disks (though other devices, such as tape systems, can also be used). It could also refer to a duplicate of a single file — an unchanged original — used in case anything happens to the copy you're working on.

backslash

The \ character, a backward-slanting slash. Under DOS, the backslash character is used as a symbol for the root directory, as well as a separator between several items in a pathname.

baud

Part of the old computer cliché, *byte my baud*, it actually refers to a technical description of a signal change. With computers, people often use the term baud to refer to bits per second or bps, the speed of a modem. Baud comes from the 19th-century French telegrapher, J.M.E. Baudot. See *BPS*.

binary

A counting system involving only two numbers, which in a computer are one and zero. Humans, which includes most of you, use the decimal counting system, which consists of ten numbers, zero through nine.

BIOS

An acronym for Basic Input/Output System. The BIOS is actually some low-level instructions for the computer, providing basic control over the keyboard, monitor, disk drives, and other parts of the computer. When the computer is on and running, DOS is actually in charge. But to use the computer, DOS will itself use the BIOS to *talk* with other parts of the PC.

bit

A contraction of *binary digit*, a bit refers to a single tiny switch inside the computer, which contains the values one or zero. There are millions of such switches — bits — inside the typical PC. They form the basis of all the memory and disk storage.

block command

Blocks are chunks of text in a word processor: a word, sentence, paragraph, page, or several words that the word processor treats as a group or block. Block commands manipulate a block of text somehow. Typical block commands copy, cut, delete, or perform a variety of functions on a whole group of words at once.

boot

The process of turning on a computer that, surprisingly enough, doesn't involve kicking it with any Western-style footwear. When you turn on a computer, you are *booting* it. When you reset a computer, you are *rebooting* it or giving it a *warm boot* (which sounds kind of cozy, you must admit).

BPS

An acronym for bits per second. It refers to the number of bits a modem can send over the phone line in one second. Typical values are 300, 1200, 2400, and 9600 bits per second. The higher the value, the faster information is sent. Note that this is the accurate term used to describe how fast a modem sends information; the term baud is often, though incorrectly, used interchangeably with bps.

byte

A group of eight bits, all clustered together to form one unit of information inside a computer. Conceptually speaking, a byte is one single character stored inside a computer. The word *byte* would require four bytes of storage inside your PC. Bytes are also used as a measure of capacity; see *kilobyte* and *megabyte*.

capacity

The amount of stuff you can store, the total number of bytes that can be stored in memory or, more likely, on a disk. Some hard disks have a capacity of 100 megabytes. Floppy disks have storage capacities ranging from 360K on up through 2.8MB. Some closets have a capacity for 24 pairs of shoes, though many women find miraculous ways to put more shoes into that tiny space.

CD-ROM

An acronym for Compact Disc-Read Only Memory. It's a special optical storage device that contains millions of bytes of information. Like the musical CDs, you can use the appropriate CD-ROM hardware to have access to the volumes of information stored on a CD disc. And just like a musical CD, you cannot record any new information on the disc; it's read only.

Centronics port

See *printer port*.

CGA

An acronym for Color GraphicFolio Adapter. The CGA was the first video system for the PC that offered both color text and graphics. The text was lousy and the graphics were only good for the chintziest of games. CGA was soon replaced by the *EGA* graphics standard.

circuit breaker

This is a safety device installed between a power source and delicate electronic equipment, such as a computer. If the power going through the line is too strong, the circuit breaker *blows*. This shuts off the power, but in the process it stops nasty electrical things from invading your computer.

clock speed

The measure of how fast a computer's microprocessor, or brain, can think. It's measured in millions of cycles per second or megahertz (see *MHz*). The faster the clock speed, the faster the computer (and the more it costs).

clone

Oh give me a clone, yes a clone of my own, with the Y chromosome changed to the X. And when I'm along, 'cause this clone is my own, she'll be thinking of nothing but ___. Actually, *clone* is a term used to describe an imitation of an original. It doesn't appear much these days, but nearly all PCs are clones of the first IBM microcomputers, the original PC and PC/AT systems.

CMOS

This acronym refers to special memory inside the computer. The CMOS memory stores information about your PC's configuration, its hard drive, and it keeps track of the date and time. This is all maintained by a battery, so when the battery goes, the computer becomes terribly absentminded. CMOS. See MOS run. Run, MOS, run.

compatible

A term used to refer to a computer that can run DOS software. This used to be an issue a few years ago. But today, nearly all PCs are completely compatible with DOS and all its software.

console device

This is nerd talk for your screen and keyboard.

conventional memory

This is memory DOS uses to run programs. Most PCs have the full 640K of conventional memory, also called *DOS memory* or *low DOS memory*.

conventional memory

This is a common term, so I've listed it twice.

CPU

An acronym for Central Processing Unit, CPU is another term for a computer's microprocessor or brain. CPU. Don't step in the PU. See *microprocessor*.

Ctrl

The name of the Ctrl key as it appears on the keyboard. See *Ctrl+key*.

Ctrl+key

A key combination involving the Control (or Ctrl) key plus another key on the keyboard, typically a letter, number, or function key. When you see Ctrl+S, it means to press and hold the Control (Ctrl) key and type an S, after which you release both keys. Note that Ctrl+S shows a capital S, but you don't have to press Ctrl+Shift+S.

cursor

The blinking underline on the screen. The cursor marks your position on the screen, showing you where any new text you type will appear. Cursor comes from the Latin word for runner.

cursor keys

These are special keys on the keyboard used to control the cursor on the screen. The four primary keys are the up-, down-, left-, and right-arrow keys. Also included in the cursor key tableau are the PgUp (page up) and PgDn (page down) keys, and the Home, and End keys.

data

Information or stuff. Data is what you create and manipulate using a computer. It can really be anything: a word processing document, a spreadsheet, a database of bugs your daughter has collected, and so on.

default

This is a nasty term computer jockeys use to mean the *standard choice*, the option or selection automatically taken when you don't choose something else. They should really use the term standard choice instead. Default is a negative term, usually associated with mortgages and loans.

DIP switch

A tiny switch inside a computer, on the back of a computer, or on a printer. DIP switches are used to control the way a computer or printer automatically behaves, to tell the system about more memory, or to configure some doohickey to work properly. This only needs to be set once, twice if you weren't paying attention the first time.

directory

A collection of files on disk. Every disk has one main directory, the *root directory*. It can also have other directories or *subdirectories*. Files are saved to disk in the various directories. You view the files using the DIR, or directory, command.

disk

A storage device for computer information. Disks are of two types, hard disks and floppy disks. The floppy disks are removable and come in two sizes, 3 $\frac{1}{2}$ inch and 5 $\frac{1}{4}$-inch.

diskette

This is a term applied to a floppy disk, usually to distinguish between it and a hard disk (which isn't removable). Diskettes are often referred to as disks. See *disk*.

display

The computer screen or monitor. The term display is rather specific, usually referring to what is displayed on the screen as opposed to the monitor (which is hardware).

document

A file created by a word processor. The term *document* means something you've saved with your word processor, usually a file that contains formatting information, various text styles, and so forth. This marks the line between a file created by a word processor (the document) and a plain text file, which lacks the formatting information (and can be viewed by the TYPE command).

DOS

An acronym for Disk Operating System. DOS is the main program that controls all of your PC, all the programs that run, and anything that saves information to or loads it from disk.

DOS memory

This is another term for *conventional memory*, the basic 640K of memory in a PC. See *conventional memory*.

dot matrix

A type of printer that uses a series of pins to create an image on paper. Dot-matrix printers are a cheap, quick, and noisy way to print computer information, not as slow as the old daisy-wheel printer, and not as fast, expensive, or as cool as a laser printer.

dump

A place where you take the computer after you're fed up with it. Actually, *dump* is an old computer term that means to wash out one thing and dump it into another. For example, a screen dump takes the information displayed on the screen and literally dumps it out to the printer. See *screen dump*.

eek! eek!

This is the noise a computer mouse makes. See mouse.

EGA

An acronym for Enhanced Graphics Adapter. The EGA was the second graphics standard for the PC, after CGA. It offered many more colors than CGA, plus it has the benefit of easy-to-read text. EGA has since been superseded by the VGA standard. See VGA.

EMS

An acronym for Expanded Memory Specification. The EMS, or more precisely, the LIM EMS (LIM for Lotus/Intel/Microsoft) is a standard for accessing extra memory on all types of PCs. This memory, expanded memory, is directly of use to DOS and most DOS applications. See *expanded memory*.

Escape

The name of a key on the keyboard, usually labeled *Esc*. The Escape key is used by many programs as a cancel key.

expanded memory

This is extra memory in a PC, useful to DOS and lots of DOS applications. To get expanded memory you must add expanded memory hardware and software to your PC. (For a 386 system, you need only the software.) But, once installed, your computer will have access to lots of extra memory, which can be put to immediate use by many applications.

expansion card

This is a piece of hardware that attaches to your computer's innards. An expansion card expands the capabilities of your PC, enabling you to add new devices and goodies that your computer doesn't come with by itself. Expansion cards can add memory (such as *expanded memory*), a mouse, graphics, a hard disk, or external devices like CD-ROM drives, scanners, plotters, and so on.

expansion slot

This is a special connector inside most PCs that enables you to plug in an expansion card (see preceding entry). The typical PC has room for five to eight expansion cards, allowing you to add up to that many goodies.

extended memory

This is extra memory in an 80286 or 386 computer; it's not expanded memory. Extended memory is primarily of use to operating systems other than DOS. On an 80286, it's better to have expanded memory. On a 386 system, you can add extended memory — as much as you like — and then convert it to the more usable expanded memory using special software.

field

A field is an area on the screen where you enter information. It's part of database-speak: A file is a collection of records; records contain fields; fields contain elements. For example, a folder full of employment applications is like a file; each application is a record; and the fill-in-the-blanks items on each application are fields.

file

A collection of stuff on disk. DOS stores information on disk in a file. The contents of a file could be anything: A program for DOS, a word processing document, a database, a spreadsheet, a graphics image of Claudia . . . , you name it.

fixed disk

An old, IBM word for a hard disk. The word fixed refers to the fact that a hard disk cannot be removed, unlike the floppy disk. See *hard disk*.

floppy disk

A removable disk in a PC, usually fitting into a 3 $\frac{1}{2}$-inch or 5 $\frac{1}{4}$-inch disk drive. Refer to *disk* or *diskette*.

font

A typesetting term used in computer desktop publishing or word processing. The term really should be typeface, or a specific style of text. For example, many books use the Cheltenham typeface or font. Other fonts are usually available, depending on your printer or the software you're using. (The term *font* actually refers to a style of typeface: bold, italic, and so on.)

form factor

This is a heavy-duty term that really means the size of something. Typically, you'll see form factor used to describe a disk drive. Essentially it means what size the disk drive is, what kind of disks it eats, and how much information you can store on the disks. When you see form factor, just replace it mentally with the word dimensions.

format

The process of preparing a disk for use by DOS. All disks come naked out of the box. For DOS to use them, they must be formatted and prepared for storing files or information. That's done under DOS by the FORMAT command.

free

Nothing is free.

function keys

These are special keys on the keyboard, labeled F1 through F10 or F12. Function keys perform special commands and functions, depending on which program you're using. Sometimes they're used in combination with other keys, such as Shift, Ctrl, or Alt. (WordPerfect takes this to the max, with up to 42 combinations of function keys to carry out various actions in the program.)

geek

A nerd with yellow Chee-tos between his teeth.

gigabyte

A perilously huge number, typically one billion of something. (And that's billion with a "b.") A gigabyte is one billion bytes or 1000MB (megabytes).

graphics adapter

A piece of hardware that controls your monitor. Three common types of graphics adapters are found on the PC: monochrome, EGA, and SVGA. The graphics adapter plugs into an expansion slot inside your PC.

hard disk

A high-speed, long-term storage device for a computer. Hard disks are much faster and store lots more information than floppy disks.

hardware

The physical side of computing, the nuts and bolts. In a computer, hardware is controlled by the software, much in the same way an orchestra plays music; the orchestra is the hardware and the music is the software.

Hayes-compatible

A type of modem that works like the original Hayes Micromodem, or at least that shares similar commands. Getting a Hayes-compatible modem guarantees that your communications software will work with it.

Hewlett-Packard

HP makes calculators and special scientific devices, but it's their computer printers that make them popular with the PC crowd. A Hewlett-Packard laser printer will be compatible with just about every piece of software out there. I say this for two reasons: I personally don't have an HP printer and it's a real pain. And I want to be nice to them so they'll send me a freebie.

hexadecimal

This is a totally nerdy way to count: in base 16, where you have the numbers 0 through 9 and then the letters A through F to represent values 11 through 15. The number 10 in hexadecimal is 16. Why bother? No reason, unless you're a programmer or know someone who speaks programmer lingo.

IBM

International Business Money or something like that. They made the first original IBM PC, which formed the platform on which the modern PC industry was launched. Some 6 million PCs later, IBM no longer plays a leading role in the industry, but it still makes quality computers (mostly for the Mercedes crowd).

I/O

An abbreviation for Input/Output, the way a computer works. Computers gobble up input and then spit out output. This is also what the Seven Dwarfs were singing when they went down into the mines.

icon

A religious symbol or painting. However, when you run Microsoft Windows, an icon is a teensy, tiny picture that represents a program. For example, Word for Windows has a pretty icon that looks like a big blue *W* stamped over a newspaper. That's how Windows presents programs to you: pretty pictures or icons. (DOS uses ugly text and — heck — the Phoenicians were doing that 7,000 years ago!)

i486

This is a common way of describing the Intel 80486 microprocessor. They write *i486* on the top of the chips, so many folks write i486 when they refer to that microprocessor. See *80486*.

K, KB

Abbreviations for kilobyte. See *kilobyte*.

keyboard

The thing you type on when you're using a computer. The keyboard has a standard typewriter-like part, plus function keys, cursor keys, a numeric keypad, and special computer keys.

kilobyte

One thousand bytes or, more accurately, 1024 bytes. This is equal to about half a page of text. Note that kilobytes is abbreviated as K or KB. So 24K is about 24 thousand bytes (more or less).

laptop

A special, compact type of computer, usually running off of batteries, that you can take with you. Laptops are popular additions to a desktop system, allowing you to compute on the road. They are, however, considerably more expensive than regular computers.

laser printer

A special type of printer that uses a laser beam to create the image on paper. Most laser printers work like a copying machine, except that they use a laser beam to help form the image instead of smoke and mirrors. Laser printers are fast and quiet, and they produce excellent graphics.

LCD

An acronym for liquid crystal display, a type of computer screen particular to laptop computers. Most LCDs are compatible with a desktop system's VGA display, though they're limited to displaying black and white or shades of gray.

load

To move information (a file) from disk into the computer's memory. Only after you've loaded something, say a worksheet or document, into memory can you work on it. See *save*.

M, MB

An abbreviation for megabyte. See *megabyte*.

macro

A program within a program, usually designed to carry out some complex function, automate a series of commands, or make life easier for anyone who doesn't want to hassle with a program's complexities. Macros exist in just about every application — even DOS — to make routine things easier. (Under DOS, the macros are called *batch files*.)

math coprocessor

This is a special companion chip to a computer's microprocessor, specifically designed to perform complex arithmetic and to do it faster than the microprocessor can by itself. The math coprocessor chip is numbered similarly to the microprocessor, except that the last digit is a 7 instead of a 6. Note that the 80486 microprocessor has its math coprocessor built in.

megabyte

One million bytes, or 1024K. A megabyte is a massive amount of storage. For example, *War and Peace* could fit into a megabyte with room to spare. Typically, hard drive storage capacity is measured in megabytes, with about 40MB being a popular size.

memory

Where the computer stores information as it's worked on. Memory is temporary storage, usually in the form of RAM chips. The microprocessor can only manipulate data in memory. Once that's done, it can be saved on disk for long-term storage.

memory-resident program

This is a special type of program that stays in memory when it's done. Memory-resident programs do one of two things. First, a memory-resident program will add to or modify some function of DOS. A mouse driver, a printing program, a program allowing you access to more memory, and so on are examples. Second, memory-resident programs can be pop-up utilities, that is, programs activated by pressing special key combinations that then appear on the screen — as if by magic. These include pop-up editors, calculators, printing-control programs, and so on. Borland's SideKick was probably the best example of a pop-up memory-resident program.

menu

A list of commands or options in a program. Some menus are displayed across the top or bottom of the screen, giving you one-word commands or choices. Some fill the screen, asking you *what next?* Some menus are graphical pull-down menus that display a hidden list of items or commands. Fun, fun, fun.

MHz

An abbreviation for megahertz. This refers to how fast a computer's microprocessor can compute. The typical PC zips along at 20MHz. The typical human brain, scientists have discovered, works at about 35MHz — or 40MHz after six cups of coffee.

microprocessor

The computer's main brain, where all the calculations take place and the control center for the entire computer. Microprocessors are also called processors or CPUs. They're given numbers such as 80286, 80386, and so on. (Refer to the numbers at the start of this glossary.)

modem

A contraction of *modulator-demodulator*, a modem is a device that takes electronic information from your computer and converts it into sounds that can be transmitted over the phone lines. Those sounds can be converted back into electronic information by the other computer's modem.

monitor

The computer's display or video system. The monitor is like a TV set, showing you information. It's actually only half of your computer's video system. The other half is the graphics adapter, plugged into an expansin slot inside your PC.

Pentium

The official name Intel gave to the 586 microprocessor. This is to keep all the knock-off goofs from calling their chips the 586 (but they'll do it anyway), since Intel can't copyright numbers.

peripheral

Any item attached to the outside of the computer, such as a printer, a modem, or even a monitor or keyboard.

pixel

An individual dot on the computer's display, used to show graphics. A graphic image on a computer is made up of hundreds of dots or pixels. Each pixel can be a different color or in a different position, which creates the image you see on the screen. The number of pixels horizontally and vertically on the display give you the graphics *resolution*.

pixel dust

That thin layer of dust that coats your monitor. It's deposited there nightly by the pixel fairy.

port

Essentially this is a connection on the back of the computer to which you attach various external items (*peripherals*). There are two primary ports on each PC, a *serial port* and a *printer port*, though what the keyboard and monitor plug into could also be considered ports.

printer

This is a device that attaches to your computer and prints information. A printer is necessary to give you hard copy, which is printed output of the information inside your computer.

printer port

This is the connection on the back of the PC into which you plug a printer cable, thereby attaching a printer to your computer. Most PCs have the cability to handle several printers, though you need to add special hardware to give your system the extra ports. The printer port is also known as the *parallel port*, or sometimes you'll hear some dweeb call it a *Centronics port*.

program

This is a special file on disk that contains instructions for the computer. Under DOS, all programs are stored in files with their second part named either .COM, .EXE, or .BAT. To run a program, you need to type in only the first part of the filename.

prompt

This is the ugly C> thing you see when you use DOS, telling you to "type that ridiculous command line here." The DOS prompt is the most familiar of all the prompts. Other programs may use their own prompts, each of which is designed to show you where information is to be entered on the screen. Handy.

RAM

An acronym for random access memory, this is the primary type of memory storage in a PC. RAM = memory.

redundant

See *redundant*.

resolution

This refers to the number of dots (*pixels*) on the screen. The higher the resolution, the greater the number of dots vertically and horizontally, the finer the graphics image your computer can display.

RGB

This is an acronym for red-green-blue, or the three primary colors. These colors are used in all computer displays to show you all colors of the rainbow and from which graphics are created. In the old CGA days of computing, RGB also referred to a type of monitor for use with a PC.

ROM

An acronym for read-only memory. These are special chips on the computer that contain instructions or information. For example, the computer's BIOS is stored on a ROM chip. ROM chips are accessed just like regular RAM memory, but unlike RAM they can't be changed; they're read-only.

root directory

The primary directory on every DOS disk. Other directories, or subdirectories, branch off of the root directory. The symbol for the root directory is the single backslash (\).

RS-232

This is a technical term used to describe a serial port. See *serial port.*

save

The process of transferring information from memory to a file on disk for permanent, long-term storage.

screen dump

An ugly term for taking the information on the screen and sending a copy of it to your printer. A screen dump is performed on a PC by pressing the Print Screen key, which may be labeled Print Scrn, PrtSc, or something along those lines. Note that the screen dump does not include graphics screens, and if your printer can't handle the special IBM characters, then God-knows-what will happen.

SCSI

An acronym for Small Computer System Interface, it's like a very fast and versatile serial port. I only mention it here because it's pronounced *scuzzy,* and I think that's cool.

serial port

A special type of port into which a variety of interesting devices can be plugged. The most common item plugged into a serial port is a modem (which leads some to call it a modem port). You can also plug a computer mouse, a printer, a scanner, or a number of interesting devices into the serial port. Most PCs have one or two serial ports.

shareware

This describes a category of software that's not free, yet it's stuff you don't have to buy before you try it. Generally, shareware consists of programs written by individuals and distributed hand to hand through user groups, national software clearing houses, or via modem. You try the software and, if you like it, you send the author the required donation.

slide rule

Whoever is on top of the ladder gets to go down the slide first.

software

This is what makes a computer worth having. It's the vast collection of programs that control the hardware and enable you to get your work done. Software controls computer hardware.

source

The original from which a copy is made. When you copy a file or duplicate a disk, the original is called the source. The source drive is the drive from which you're copying. The destination, or the location to which you're copying, is referred to as the target.

string

In computer lingo, this term applies to any group of characters. A string of text is a line of text, a command you type, or any other non-numeric information. Don't let the term throw you, or force you to insert twine or yarn into the disk drive.

subdirectory

A term for a directory in relation to another directory. All directories on a disk are subdirectories of the root.

SVGA

An acronym for Super Video Graphics Array; the next generation VGA. Turn the computer off and you get mild-mannered Clark Kent VGA.

syntax

The format of a DOS command, the things you must type, the options, what order they go in, and what they do. When you goof up and specify something out of order, DOS tosses you back a `Syntax Error`. Not fatal, it just means you need to find the proper syntax and retype the command.

tab shooter

Someone you employ to make a tab stop real fast, or a whimpy drink made with tequila and a popular diet drink.

tab stop

Just like on a typewriter, a tab stop on a computer is the location where characters will appear after you press the Tab key. Sometimes, the Tab key simply produces eight spaces. In most word processors, you can set tab stops at specific positions on a line of text.

target

The location of a copy or duplicate of an original file. A target can be a filename, a sub-directory, or a disk drive — the final destination of the file. Copying things on a computer is a lot like archery.

text editor

A special type of word processor that creates or edits only text files, often called ASCII, unformatted, or nondocument files. A text editor lacks most of the fancy formatting features of a word processor. Oh, you might want to look up *ASCII* since I mentioned it here. (Not that it helps much.)

toggle

Something that can be on or off; a single switch that's pressed once to turn something on and again to turn it off. This term appears when describing something you can do in a program that turns a function on and then doing it again turns it off.

TSR

An acronym for terminate but stay resident. Believe it or not, that's an MS-DOS programmer's function, not anything any human being will use. Yet it's a quick-and-dirty term that can be used to describe *memory-resident programs.*

user

The person who operates a computer or runs a program. The computer is then the usee.

V20

A special, faster type of 8088 chip, usually found in some of the cheaper laptop computers. See 8086/8088.

V30

A special, faster type of 8086 chip, found in some lightweight laptop computers. See 8086/8088.

VGA

An acronym for Video Graphics Array, the current top-of-the-line in PC graphic systems. VGA offers you stunning color graphics, great resolution, a crisp text, much better than its predecessor, *EGA.* A SuperVGA (also known as *SVGA*) is available that extends the powers and capabilities of VGA.

window

An area on the screen where special information appears. It can be a graphic window, à la Microsoft's Windows program, or it can be a text window, outlined with special graphic text characters.

word wrap

The capability of a word processor to move a word from the end of one line to the beginning of the next while you're typing. Word wrap enables you to type an entire paragraph of text without having to press Enter at the end of each line.

write protect

A method of protecting information on disk from being accidentally changed or erased. This is done by putting a write protect tab on a $5\frac{1}{4}$-inch disk, or by sliding the little tile off of the hole of a $3\frac{1}{2}$-inch disk. Once that's done, the disk is write protected and you cannot change, rename, delete, or reformat it.

WYSIWYG

An acronym for what-you-see-is-what-you-get. It refers to a program's capability to display information on the screen in exactly the same format in which it will be printed. Sometimes this works, sometimes it doesn't. Generally speaking, if a program is WYSIWYG, what you see on the screen will be close enough to what you get when it's printed.

Index

(continued)

(continued)

(continued)

Notes

A:/ RESETC

A:/ AUTOEXEC   —> RE-BOOT

IDG BOOKS WORLDWIDE REGISTRATION CARD

RETURN THIS REGISTRATION CARD FOR FREE CATALOG

Title of this book: DOS For Dummies, Windows 95 Edition

My overall rating of this book: ❑ Very good [1] ❑ Good [2] ❑ Satisfactory [3] ❑ Fair [4] ❑ Poor [5]

How I first heard about this book:

❑ Found in bookstore; name: [6]   ❑ Book review: [7]

❑ Advertisement: [8]   ❑ Catalog: [9]

❑ Word of mouth; heard about book from friend, co-worker, etc.: [10]   ❑ Other: [11]

What I liked most about this book:

What I would change, add, delete, etc., in future editions of this book:

Other comments:

Number of computer books I purchase in a year: ❑ 1 [12] ❑ 2-5 [13] ❑ 6-10 [14] ❑ More than 10 [15]

I would characterize my computer skills as: ❑ Beginner [16] ❑ Intermediate [17] ❑ Advanced [18] ❑ Professional [19]

I use ❑ DOS [20] ❑ Windows [21] ❑ OS/2 [22] ❑ Unix [23] ❑ Macintosh [24] ❑ Other: [25]_____
(please specify)

I would be interested in new books on the following subjects:
(please check all that apply, and use the spaces provided to identify specific software)

❑ Word processing: [26]   ❑ Spreadsheets: [27]

❑ Data bases: [28]   ❑ Desktop publishing: [29]

❑ File Utilities: [30]   ❑ Money management: [31]

❑ Networking: [32]   ❑ Programming languages: [33]

❑ Other: [34]

I use a PC at (please check all that apply): ❑ home [35] ❑ work [36] ❑ school [37] ❑ other: [38] _____

The disks I prefer to use are ❑ 5.25 [39] ❑ 3.5 [40] ❑ other: [41]_____

I have a CD ROM: ❑ yes [42] ❑ no [43]

I plan to buy or upgrade computer hardware this year: ❑ yes [44] ❑ no [45]

I plan to buy or upgrade computer software this year: ❑ yes [46] ❑ no [47]

Name: _____ Business title: [48] _____ Type of Business: [49]

Address (❑ home [50] ❑ work [51]/Company name: _____)

Street/Suite# _____

City [52]/State [53]/Zipcode [54]: _____ Country [55] _____

❑ **I liked this book!** You may quote me by name in future
IDG Books Worldwide promotional materials.

My daytime phone number is _____

IDG BOOKS
THE WORLD OF COMPUTER KNOWLEDGE

❑ YES!
Please keep me informed about IDG's World of Computer Knowledge.
Send me the latest IDG Books catalog.